Vandalism

Pruitt-Igoe Housing Project, St. Louis, Missouri
Photograph: NEW YORK TIMES/LEE ROMERO

VANDALISM

Edited by Colin Ward

VNR VAN NOSTRAND REINHOLD COMPANY
New York   Cincinnati

Van Nostrand Reinhold Company Regional Offices:
New York   Cincinnati   Chicago   Millbrae   Dallas

Copyright © 1973 by Colin Ward
Library of Congress Catalog Card Number 74-4112
ISBN 0-442-29195-7

Printed in the United States of America

Published by Van Nostrand Reinhold Company
450 West 33rd Street, New York, N.Y. 10001

Originally published in Great Britain by Architectural Press, Ltd., London

15   14   13   12   11   10 9 8 7 6 5 4 3 2 1

364.1
Wa

Contents

Acknowledgements 6
Contributors 9
Introduction 13

PART I: THE SOCIAL BACKGROUND
1 **Property destruction: motives and meanings** 23
   Stanley Cohen
2 **The meaning of the environment** 54
   Laurie Taylor
3 **Delinquency and some aspects of housing** 64
   Gail Armstrong and Mary Wilson
4 **A field experiment in auto shaping** 85
   Philip G. Zimbardo
5 **Hey, mister, this is what we really do . . .** 91
   Ian Taylor and Paul Walton

PART II: THE DESIGNER'S RESPONSIBILITY
6 **Vandalism and the architect** 96
   Alexander Miller
7 **The architect's dilemma: one firm's working notes** 112
   Farmer and Dark
8 **What the architect can do: a series of design guides** 117
   Alan Leather and Antony Matthews

PART III: VANDALS WITH POWER
9 **Planners as vandals** 173
   Colin Ward
10 **Developers as vandals** 184
   Dan Cruickshank

PART IV: COPING WITH VANDALISM
11 **Campaigning against vandalism** 215
   Stanley Cohen
12 **Community involvement** 259
   David Pullen
13 **Notes on the future of vandalism** 276
   Colin Ward

Notes and references 312
Bibliography 319
Index 321

512407

Acknowledgements

Chapter One is a somewhat expanded version of two articles by Stanley Cohen, 'The Politics of Vandalism' and 'The Nature of Vandalism' which appeared in *New Society* 12 December 1968. Some of the material is also adapted from a forthcoming article "Breaking Out, Smashing Up and the Social Context of Aspiration" in B. Biven (ed.): *Youth at the Beginning of the Seventies.*

Chapter Four is part of Philip G. Zimbardo's paper 'The Human Choice: Individuation, Reason and Order, vs. Deindividuation, Impulse and Chaos' given at the Nebraska Symposium on Motivation, March 1969, and is reproduced with acknowledgements to the University of Nebraska.

Chapter Five is a slightly extended version of an article by Ian Taylor and Paul Walton which originally appeared in *Social Work Today* 12 August 1971 and is used by kind permission of the editor of that journal.

In Chapter Six, Alexander Miller draws on material collected during his research work at the Building Research Station. This material and the photographs are published by kind permission of the Director of the Building Research Establishment.

Chapter Eight is based on the work produced by Alan Leather and Antony Matthews as fifth year students at the Liverpool Polytechnic School of Architecture as part of the requirements of the course, and the editor is grateful to the authors and the Polytechnic for making it available. The authors' acknowledgements are due to:

County Architect's Departments for Derbyshire, Lancashire, Lincolnshire, East Riding, North Riding, West Riding.

City and Borough Architects' Departments for Birmingham, Edinburgh, Kirkby, Leeds, Manchester, Sheffield, Skelmersdale, York.

City and Borough Engineers' Departments for Blackpool, Brighton, Bristol, Coventry, Nottingham, Peterborough, St. Helens.

Direct Works Departments, Leeds and Manchester.

Housing Department, Bristol.

Parks, Allotments and Cemeteries Departments, Leeds.

Newspapers: *Birmingham Evening Mail, Lancashire Evening Post.*

Building Research Station.

Royal Insurance Company.

Crime Prevention Department, Liverpool and Bootle Constabulary.

Liverpool Polytechnic, Faculty of Construction; Members of Staff of the School of Architecture.

Miss A. McGrath.

The editor is obviously indebted to the contributors to this book, and especially to Stanley Cohen. He is also obliged, for information, discussion and argument, to John Barton, Michael Brown, Kenneth Browne, Paul Clark, Marshall Coleman, Alan Cunningham, David Downes, Gabriel Epstein, Tony Gibson, Simon Nicholson, John O'Connor, Keith Paton, Peter Shepheard, Peter Smith, Tony Southard, Harriet Ward, George West, students at Wandsworth Technical College, and all those whose opinions are quoted.

None of these is responsible for conclusions drawn editorially: all are thanked for their time and thought.

Picture Acknowledgements

Page 1: Gwyn Richards;
2, 3: Alan Leather and Anthony J. Mathews;
4: Russell Firth;
12 top: Courtesy of Abacus Municipal Ltd.;
12 bottom: Tony Ray-Jones/*The Architectural Review;*
15 top left: Hans Joachim Schmidt in *Nature in Focus;*
15 top right: Alan Leather and Antony J. Matthews;
16: Camera Press Ltd.;
17: Marilyn Stafford in *The Architectural Review;*
20: Reproduced by permission of the Controller, Her Majesty's Stationery Office from *Council House Communities: A Policy for Progress* Edinburgh: 1970 HMSO
21: William Slack;
26: Charles Haines;
28 top: Geoffrey Drury;
28 bottom: Alan Olley/ *The Basingstoke Gazette;*
37 top left, top right and centre: Eddie Harris/*The Hackney Gazette and North London Advertiser;*
37 bottom: Courtesy of Abacus Municipal Ltd.;
38: Topix (Accompanying poem reproduced by kind permission of Tim Daly);
39: George Oliver in "Reflections on 'Strategy: Get Arts" by Richard Demarco, *Pages—International Magazine of the Arts;*
42: *Time Out;*
43: Tony Nicholls in *Time Out;*
47: *The Times*
49: Camera Press Ltd.;
51: Christopher Ridley;
57 top left: Eugène T. Brooks in 'The Urban Design Workshop, Los Angeles,' *L'Architecture d'aujourd'hui;*

57 top right: Peter Boyce;
57 lower: Adam Ritchie;
65: Syndication International;
75: Reproduced by permission of the Controller, Her Majesty's Stationery Office from *Council House Communities: A Policy for Progress* Edinburgh: 1970 HMSO
77: Courtesy of J. & C. Coughtrie Ltd., manufacturers of polycarbonate light fittings;
85-89: Philip G. Zimbardo;
93, 94: Michael Barber;
95: Alan Denman;
98-111: Courtesy of the Building Research Station;
113 top: Courtesy of *The Architectural Review;*
113 bottom: Courtesy of Airscrew-Weyroc Ltd.;
122-169: Alan Leather and Antony J. Matthews (Diagrams re-drawn by Andrew Morris);
174: Topix (Accompanying text reproduced by kind permission of *New Society*);
177 top and bottom: Martin Stevens in 'The Fall of Rodmersham Mill' by Griselda Jay and Derek Abbott, *Defend Kent* 1971;
179: Gwyn Richards;
183: Courtesy of *The Architects' Journal;*
186, 187 bottom: Dan Cruickshank;
187 top: National Monuments Record;
188 top: From J. C. Bourne *Drawings of the London and Birmingham Railway* London: 1838;
188 bottom: National Monuments Record;
189 top: Kenneth Browne/*The Architectural Review;*
192, 193: National Monuments Record;
194, 195: Dan Cruickshank;
196 top inset and bottom left: National

Monuments Record;
196 top: Dan Cruickshank;
196 bottom right: Henk Snoek
Photography & Associates/ *The
Architects' Journal;*
198, 201, 202, 204: Dan Cruickshank;
205, 207, 208, 209 bottom, 210 top: Dan
Cruickshank/*The Architects' Journal;*
209 top, 210 bottom, 211: Dan
Cruickshank;
213: Press Association;
216: Reproduced by permission of the
Controller, Her Majesty's Stationery
Office;
228: Courtesy of the City of Birmingham
Parks Committee;
234: West Ham United programme;
236: *The Times;*
237: Ralph Steadman;
239: Jane J. Miller in *The Teacher;*
240: Courtesy of *The Orpington and
Kentish Times;*
243 top: Heath/*Private Eye;*
243 lower left and lower right: Gwyn
Richards;
246, 247: Courtesy of the Local
Government Information office;
248: Picture Coverage Ltd., Sale;
251 top: Peter Boyce
251 bottom: *The Daily Telegraph;*

258, 260, 263, 264, 266, 267, 268, 270,
272, 273: Gwyn Richards;
277: *The Daily Mail*
280: Martin Chaffer Photography;
282: Michael St. Maur Sheil—Transworld;
286: Peter Boyce;
291: Bill Toomey;
293 top: *The Times*
293 bottom: Reproduced by permission of
the Controller, Her Majesty's Stationery
Office;
296 top: *The Guardian;*
296 bottom: *Children's Rights* No. 1, 1971
297 top: Mircea Campeanu;
297 bottom: Courtesy of the Great
Georges Project;
298 bottom: *Guardian: independent radical
newsweekly* (New York);
298-9 top: William Milson/*The Evening
Standard;*
301: R. L. Palmer (Northern Press
Photo Service);
305: Vernon Richards;
306-7: J. Edward Bailey in *Newsweek;*
308 top: *Bridge on the River Kwai*, a
Sam Speigal Production. Still Copyright
Columbia Pictures;
308 top inset: *The Times* (private
copyright);
308 bottom: Lewis Woudhuysen

Contributors

GAIL ARMSTRONG graduated in sociology from Strathclyde University in 1966. After spending some time in social work she returned to Strathclyde as a research assistant to undertake an investigation of the violent gang. She teaches at the Mackintosh School of Architecture and will shortly publish, with Mary Wilson, a book which will combine their researches in Easterhouse, as well as a paper on 'City Politics and Deviancy Amplification' in *Politics and Deviancy*, ed. Taylor and Taylor (Penguin Books Ltd.).

STANLEY COHEN took a degree in sociology and psychology at Witwatersrand University, South Africa, and worked in London as a psychiatric social worker before completing his Ph.D. research on societal reactions to juvenile delinquency. In 1967, after lecturing at Enfield College for two years, he moved to Durham and more recently to the University of Essex. He is the author of a book on the Mods and Rockers and editor of *Images of Deviance* (Penguin Books Ltd.). Together with Laurie Taylor he recently published *Psychological Survival* (Penguin Books Ltd, 1972).

DAN CRUICKSHANK, born 1949, lived as a child in Gower Street, and went with his family at the age of 8 to live in the Old Town of Warsaw for three years. On their return to England, after numerous schools and colleges, he took a 4-year Diploma in Art and Design at the London College of Printing, working especially on architectural projects. He now works for the Architectural Press, and is at present preparing a book on the lesser known Georgian architecture of London.

FARMER AND DARK are a firm of architects in private practice in London.

ALAN LEATHER, born 1948, was educated at Prescot Grammar School, 1959-66 and Liverpool Polytechnic School of Architecture 1966-72. He now works on City Centre Redevelopment in the North-West.

ANTONY MATTHEWS, born 1946, was educated at Wellingborough Technical Grammar School, 1958-65 and Liverpool Polytechnic School of Architecture 1965-72. He works for a firm of architects in private practice in Shrewsbury.

ALEXANDER MILLER trained at the Glasgow School of Architecture, worked in architects' offices in Glasgow, and joined the Building Research Station in 1934, becoming Chief Technical Officer at the Scottish Building Centre in 1938 and working at the Ministry of Works before returning to the BRS in 1946. (There he worked on studies of non-traditional housing, refuse disposal in high blocks of flats, access to flats, housing layouts, maintenance technology and wilful damage on housing estates). He retired from BRS in 1970 and is now Technical Officer for the British Standards Institution.

DAVID PULLEN was invited, on the strength of his community work experience in London to help promote and monitor voluntary projects financed by Liverpool's Vandalism Steering Group. In November 1971 an end-of-year report was submitted in which it was recommended that finance should be made available to employ nine workers, each to operate in neighbourhoods at present deteriorating through extensive vandalism. It was accepted that such workers, most of whom will live in the area in which they work, should be employed and given complete freedom to promote the improvement of their neighbourhoods in whatever way seemed most appropriate.

IAN TAYLOR graduated in history at the University of Durham and after completing a Diploma in Criminology at the University of Cambridge, he returned to Durham, where he carried out participant-observation research in an approved school. He then lectured in sociology for a year each at Glasgow University and at Queens University, Kingston, Ontario. He has published articles on approved schools and on soccer hooliganism, and was project officer on a study of problems of immigration at the University of Bradford. He is now lecturer in criminology at the University of Sheffield.

LAURIE TAYLOR spent several years working in industry before graduating in psychology at Birkbeck College, London University. He then obtained a higher degree in sociology at the University of Leicester, and he has been a lecturer in sociology at the University of York for the past five years. His research has been concerned with deviancy, in particular the areas of industrial sabotage, sexual offences and the effects of long-term imprisonment. He is a regular contributor to *New Society* and his book *Deviance and Society* was published in 1971 by Michael Joseph. A book on long term imprisonment, written jointly with Stanley Cohen has recently been published under the title *Psychological Survival* (Penguin Books Ltd. 1972).

PAUL WALTON graduated in sociology from the University of York and then went as a research student to the University of Durham where he worked for a year in a study of deviancy and rationality in industry. He is now a lecturer in sociology at the University of Bradford.

COLIN WARD is Education Officer for the Town and Country Planning Association and edits its Bulletin of Environmental Education, BEE. He worked for many years on the design of housing and schools in the offices of several well-known architects, before becoming lecturer in charge of liberal studies at Wandsworth Technical College. He edited *Anarchy* from 1961 to 1970 and is the author of *Violence* and *Work* in the Penguin Connexions series.

MARY WILSON graduated in sociology from Strathclyde University in 1968. As a post-graduate student there she made a study of societal reactions to delinquency. She teaches at the Mackintosh School of Architecture and will shortly publish, with Gail Armstrong, a book which will combine their researches in Easterhouse, as well as a paper on 'City Politics and Deviancy Amplification' in *Politics and Deviancy*, edited by Taylor and Taylor (Penguin Books Ltd.).

PHILIP G. ZIMBARDO is Professor of social psychology at Stanford University. He is the author of *Cognitive Control of Motivation* (Scott-Foresman), *Influencing Attitudes and Changing Behaviour* (Addison Wesley), *Peace Manual* (Society for the Psychological Study of Social Issues), *Psychology and Life* (Scott-Foresman). His research and theoretical efforts are now being directed towards understanding the process by which normal men become mad, and other men label them as such.

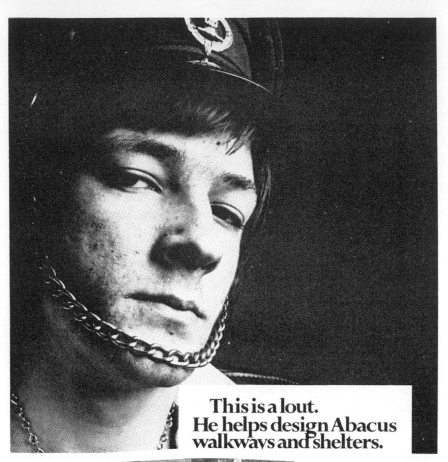

**This is a lout.
He helps design Abacus
walkways and shelters.**

*Stereotype
of the vandal*

*Penal enough
already?*

12

Introduction

The human environment is subject to every kind of wear, decay, attrition, erosion, change, renewal and destruction, some of which we label vandalism. Those who earn a living by modifying the environment have an interest in the durability of their handiwork, those charged with its maintenance are usually concerned with its survival, those who inhabit it are expected to show some degree of care for it. Consequently we all have opinions on vandalism.

We all know the vandal. He is somebody else. In general terms he is someone whose activities in the environment we deplore, but we usually give the word a much more specific meaning. The stereotype of the vandal—as you can see from the advertisements for 'vandal-proof' building components—is that of a working-class male adolescent, and his act is the 'wanton', 'senseless', or 'motiveless' destruction of property, usually public property of some kind. He and his behaviour constitute a 'social problem'. Architects, municipal engineers and housing managers have every reason to be aware of this problem, and one function of this book is to serve as a manual to help the designer avoid the selection of materials and components which experience has shown to be most vulnerable to attack.

There is undoubtedly a need for a guide of this kind. "He should have known that it wouldn't survive," is the phrase we use after the event, looking at someone else's failure of judgment, when we see what happens to materials or components where for cheapness, or through careless choice, or for lack of adequate detailing or appropriate design, they have been selected without regard to the degree of use and abuse which could have been predicted. "No one," remarked Nan Fairbrother, "would furnish a coffee-bar with fragile antiques, or upholster bus-seats in damask and expect them to survive—or even to look attractive . . ."

But it soon becomes evident that this approach alone is inadequate, and could even be self-defeating. Firstly because, carried to its logical conclusion, it implies that the ultimate solution would be to design all buildings considered to be at risk with the impregnability of prisons. Many a block of municipal flats is penal enough already, and it doesn't seem to have helped. In any case prisons themselves despite constant surveillance and specially designed fittings, certainly suffer from what some people would call vandalism. Secondly, this approach is open to the obvious criticism that it attempts to minimise symptoms rather than deal with causes. (I do not subscribe to this view: architects, like teachers, are victims of 'role-inflation' and we cannot expect more of them than that they do their job competently, though in the course of doing so they may very well become 'anti-architects' in the same way as some very competent and thoughtful teachers become 'de-schoolers'.) Thirdly, architects themselves look beyond mere indestructibility as a solution, and evolve their own social and behavioural theories which influence their approach to design.

Systematic observers, like the architectural contributors to this volume, note that certain aspects of design can facilitate or discourage the activities of the vandal. They find, for example, that public spaces are less prone to wanton destruction if they appear to be private places, related to the adjoining buildings: that this will discourage abuse by outsiders and will give the occupants a protective and surveillant attitude to them. But we all adhere in one way or another to wider and vaguer theories about human behaviour. The theory that people respond differently to different attributes of the environment is one to which we all subscribe. An atmosphere of dereliction and neglect evokes misuse and careless, if not wilful, destruction by some users, while good maintenance and surfaces of good quality, are respected and sometimes cherished. The environment, in other words, transmits signals to which users respond. Following this theory, one architect who was conscious of the usual drab, cold, litter-strewn appearance of staircase landings in blocks of flats, persuaded his client that it was useful to carpet the landing and provide a radiator. Over the radiator he installed a shelf, and was later gratified to see that a tenant had put a bowl of flowers on the shelf. The signal read CIVILIZED.

Landscape architects, whose work is even more vulnerable than buildings, have also evolved behavioural theories of vandalism— theories which, if acted upon, have a profound effect on maintenance and management policies. One is the application to the site as a whole of the notion of environmental signals. Frequently, because of urgent need, or because they know from experience that completed but un-occupied flats are a magnet to vandals, housing managers will install tenants before site works and landscape treatment are complete. Quite apart from the invitation to acts of mischievous destruction which the presence of suitable missiles constitutes, and quite apart from the psychological effect of living in a morass of mud and rubble, the unfinished character of the site works will make them the subject of a more rigorous testing-out by the local children than would a fully-finished scheme which they entered as a going concern. But suppose that the task of completing the estate was the responsibility of the ten-ants and not that of the landscape contractor?

Another behavioural theory is Peter Shepheard's well-known Law of Diminishing Vandalism, which suggests that "persistence in re-planting and replacing destroyed plants until the children get tired of

14

. . rigorous testing out by local children

. . . until the children get tired of destruction

destruction or learn better" is rapidly repaid. Allan Blenkarn, recreational services manager for the British Waterways Board applies this theory: "Vandals smash a place up at the weekend. Repair it first thing on Monday morning. They come again next weekend. Repair it again. The third weekend they probably won't come back."[1]

But there are pitfalls in the environmental signalling system. Do the designer and the user read them in the same way? The story is told of the Dockland tenants who were outraged by the piece of abstract sculpture bestowed on their estate by the Council, which had sent out the signal ART FOR THE PEOPLE (the Moscow Metro Message). Most unusually a meeting was convened, attended by the architect and the sculptor, prepared to do battle, or at least educate in a missionary spirit, in the cause of non-representational art. But it emerged from the meeting that the tenants' objection was not to do with content but with materials. They felt they had been fobbed off with a load of old driftwood and *objets trouves* while other estates had fully-certificated

15

Art among the vandals: municipal sculpture (protected from vandalism) amid the systematic destruction by demolition of the environment

minerals like stone and bronze. The signal sent out as ART was received as SECOND-CLASS CITIZEN.

The architectural signal known as the New Brutalism has been received in this way everywhere from Newcastle to Bethnal Green. Here is an example from South London:

"The surfaces of the buildings are in the fashionable blue brick and exposed rough-shuttered concrete, which visually create an impression of romantic toughness—perhaps on the principle that in tough Cockney areas only tough Cockney architecture will do, as anything softer will be destroyed by vandals. In fact the Canada Estate is the most obviously vandalised of any housing estate in London of the last decade: armour glass smashed, paintwork defaced, the drying cabinets wrecked (and removed by the council). Yet those few families on the ground floor maisonettes of the lower blocks, who have been given the privilege of private gardens, have turned them into sanctuaries of ornamental softness with expertly tended flowers and trellises, which do their best to absorb the harshness of the architecture."[2]

If both architects and the ultimate beneficiaries of their professional activities have each evolved a theory of vandalism, it is appropriate for

16

Canada Estate, Southwark

us to invite the contribution of sociology to the discussion, and it is fortunate that a group of sociologists should have emerged who not only use plain English, but who have also asked fundamental questions about 'deviance' in society. They have adopted what Stanley Cohen calls the *sceptical* approach to deviance. In his words,

"a sociological truism has been re-asserted: namely that deviance is not a quality inherent in any behaviour or person but rests on society's reaction to certain types of rule-breaking . . . One must understand deviance as the product of some sort of transaction that takes place between the rule breaker and the rest of society. Similarly, a 'social problem' consists not only of a fixed and given condition but the perception and definition by certain people that this condition poses a threat which is against their interests and that something must be done about it."[3]

But of course, once we adopt this standpoint we lose our stereotype of 'the vandal' and we may also become aware that his activities are far less devastating, lethal and expensive, than the destruction and attrition of the urban environment by other forces in society. No reader will disagree that the motor vehicle has been the greatest destructive factor by far in our environment: in its terrifying casualty rate, in the way that provision for it has for years been tearing out the heart of our cities and towns, in the way addiction to it for leisure purposes has destroyed the human habitat at the point of departure, at the destination and all along the route. Tourism, as Guy Debord notes, is "a by-product of the circulation of commodities: human circulation considered as consumption is basically reduced to the leisure of going to see what has become banal . . . The same modernisation which has removed time from travel has also removed from it the reality of space."[4] To eliminate not only time and space, but even *difference* is surely the ultimate vandalism. You can experience it any day in the impeccably unvandalised Heathrows of every capital in every continent.

Ralph Nader, addressing the annual conference of the American Institute of Planners put the matter in perspective:

"The problem of environmental violence is one which should be a major subject of focus because even to this day, I think we will have to admit, pollution is still considered by most people as something that is foul smelling or evil or ugly looking, but is not considered as perhaps one of the two most domestically virulent forms of violence in our society, the other being traffic crashes. Street crimes, burglaries, campus disruptions, don't amount to a fingernail's proportion of the destruction of human beings and their health and their property from traffic crashes and environmental contamination."[5]

Considering pollution as a criminal activity, Peter Hoefnagels, Professor of Criminology at the Netherlands Economic University, defines environmental crime as "that behaviour which brings about, or threatens to bring about, physical, psychological or social damage to persons, groups or societies by the disturbance of the physical environment." He notes among the characteristics of environmental crime the following:

1. A small number of criminals.
2. A large number of victims.
3. Relative invisibility of the criminal and difficulty in defining the crime.

4. Inequality of power between the criminal and the victims.
5. Relative invulnerability of the criminal.
6. Localisation of the problem to the victims most immediately concerned.
7. It is an aspect of "white collar" crime.
8. At the moment it is more the concern of law-making than of law-enforcement.[6]

But to suggest that motormania and pollution, the environmental spin-offs of an industrialised mass society are in the same category as our subject is to invite the rejoinder that at least they are the regrettable by-products of rational, utilitarian activities, while vandalism, as we all know, is senseless, irrational and non-utilitarian. Here again, the sociologists of deviance can enhance our perception of the activities we dismiss as vandalism, through what Dr Cohen called their *defence of meaning*, their "concern to defend both a conception of deviance as meaningful action and the status of the meaning which the deviant gives to his own activities."

"People cannot allow deviation to threaten their picture of what their society is about. Part of this picture involves recognising and accrediting certain motives as legitimate; if these motives cannot be found, then the behaviour cannot be tolerated, it must be neutralised or annihilated. Thus vandalism, unlike theft, cannot be explained, in terms of the accredited motives of acquiring material gain, so it is described as motiveless. The only way of making sense of some actions is to assume that they do not make sense. Any other assumption would be threatening . . ."[7]

These are valuable insights for anyone who wants to get beyond baffled denunciation and to struggle with the meaning of "meaningless" acts, as Part One of this book makes clear. In the first chapter an attempt is made to sort out the different reactions which society employs when faced with the different forms of deliberate destruction of property, and to categorise the various and varying motives which lie behind the act itself. In Chapter Two the various theories of environmental determinism are examined for the light they throw on the explanations of vandalism. The authors of Chapter Three pursue this theme further. Several propositions emerge from their study of the Easterhouse district of Glasgow:

1. That behaviour is not determined by built form as such.
2. That much of what we call deviant behaviour is a convenient label for what is really social protest.
3. That when an area acquires a bad reputation its actual performance tends to reinforce that reputation.
4. That architects should, above all, study how people actually live —the social fabric of an area.

19

. . . surveyed many scenes of desolation

In Chapter Four, Professor Zimbardo describes what happens to un-attended cars in two areas of the United States, relating his findings to social and physical anonymity. Chapter Five discusses the function of vandalism in children's play.

The three Chapters of Part Two discuss the professional responsibi-ties of the designer, and will at the very least alert him to the ways in which the consequences of vandalism can be minimised, or the oppor-tunities reduced. The first of these is by a distinguished building researcher, the second consists of the working notes of a firm of practis-ing architects, representing their accumulated experience, and the third is a systematic series of design guides whose authors have consulted many local authorities and surveyed many scenes of desolation.

Part Three examines some aspects of legitimised vandalism. It would be tempting to include a section on the motorist as vandal, industry as vandal, the Ministry of Defence as vandal, and of course the Great British Public as vandal. (For it is certain that the annual cost of our habit of treating this country as one vast rubbish dump is far greater than that of making good malicious damage). This wider discussion would, however, fill a book in itself, and instead this section confines

One vast rubbish dump

itself to the vandalism we can witness in the professional activities of architects, planners and developers.

The final part of the book considers solutions. In a long and detailed chapter Dr Cohen examines the effectiveness of campaigns against vandalism, and the various methods of control and prevention which have been recommended and applied. The approach by way of community involvement is described by the Liverpool project officer. No attempt has been made to impose a common point of view on the contributors to this book nor to iron out any contradictions in their different approaches to the theme. This would have been both impertinent to the authors and misleading for the reader. But it has made it necessary to exercise an editorial privilege in the final chapter on the future of vandalism by making it a rag-bag of speculations about, quotations upon, and interpretations of aspects of the themes which have not been emphasised elsewhere in the book.

The architectural reader will not be getting his money's worth if he confines himself to the technical chapters. The sociological reader will be sold short if he ignores the architectural contributions. Administrators, revolutionaries and citizens should read them all too. The book is an incitement to informed and rational action by the community.

1 Property destruction: motives and meanings

Stanley Cohen

I want to start by considering some of the problems involved in defining vandalism. At first sight, this might sound like an arcane theoretical exercise with no reference to a real world in which 'everyone knows' what vandalism is and clearly recognises it as a problem, threat or menace. Let us imagine, though, having to explain to a foreigner what vandalism is; at some point we would find ourselves using a definition something like this: 'the illegal destruction or defacement of property belonging to someone else.' In other words, we would have to explain to him that vandalism is a form of rule-breaking. Now this immediately creates problems and complications: it is evident that not *all* the rules that forbid deliberate property destruction are enforced and that by no means *all* such breaking of rules is regarded as deviant, problematic, or is even called 'vandalism'. We end up with the uncomfortable recognition that vandalism is neither a precise behavioural description, nor a recognisable legal category, but a label attached to certain types of behaviour under certain conditions.

Something like a continuum exists from—at one end—deliberate forms of property destruction to which society somehow accommodates itself or which it absorbs, without invariably regarding them as vandalism or processing them as criminal offences, to—at the other—behaviour invariably labelled as vandalism, processed as criminal offences and widely regarded as socially problematic. This continuum refers less to categories of behaviour than to conditions under which illegal property destruction becomes tolerated, acceptable, institutionalised or, as some sociologists have expressed it, *normalised*. Let me give a few examples of such conditions.

VANDALISM AS INSTITUTIONALISED RULE-BREAKING
I will concentrate on the conditions of *ritualism; protection; play; writing-off; walling-in;* and *licensing*.

(*i*) *Ritualism:* Although no contemporary industrialised society has the exact equivalent of the tribal potlatch ceremony in which certain types of property were ritually destroyed, there are certain fixed occasions on which property destruction is expected, condoned or even encouraged.

Examples in our society would be November 5th (Guy Fawkes Night) or ritual joy occasions such as Armistice Day. Certain rules are also relaxed on New Year's Eve during which ceremonies such as those taking place in Trafalgar Square, London, might result in a considerable amount of property destruction. A clearer example in America is Hallowe'en, during which various forms of property destruction, usually referred to as 'pranks' are formalised and ritualised to a considerable degree.

Despite indications of increasing public impatience and intolerance about this sort of behaviour, much of it is still not regarded as deviant or as being the same as 'ordinary' crime and delinquency. The police and courts seem to regard the processing of such offences as a tiresome chore and the offenders view such proceedings with mild amusement.

These are only extreme types of ritualisation. There are other occasions and settings—for example, certain sporting fixtures, festivals and fetes, private parties, such as weddings, farewell parties and bachelor parties, sporting club dinners and so on—where property destruction is to some degree normalised.

(*ii*) *Protection:* Closely allied to the first condition is the behaviour by certain groups who are given something like a collective licence by the community to engage in vandalism. Notable among these groups have been students of various types, especially when the behaviour takes place during ritual occasions such as rags, initiation ceremonies and sporting fixtures like Boat Race night and the Hospitals Cup Final. Routine destruction might also take place at parties—especially end of term parties—and in the course of such practices as 'climbing in.' Such behaviour has been regarded as 'fun' or 'letting off steam' and the offenders have been either not punished at all or punished only by unofficial bodies like college disciplinary committees. Even if the offence is processed formally, the punishments are seldom as severe as those that would have been given to members of an unprotected group. A sociologist makes this point in connection with public school boys:

". . . the party of public schoolboys who damage property during the course of a 'rag' are behaving very differently from a street corner gang who smash street lamps or shop windows just for the fun of it or to work off their aggression. The mores of the public school community allow and even encourage such explosively expressive behaviour in its restricted setting whereas the casual destructiveness of promiscuous gangs has no such approval to sustain it."[1]

It is fairly obvious in this sort of case, that protection is awarded on a social class basis. It is probable that the breaking down of the traditional insulation which students have enjoyed is decreasing this direct sort of protection. The increase of militant student politics and the association of students with new horrors like drug-taking, has created a new hostility which has carried over to traditionally licensed types of rule-breaking.

This type of carry-over, however, has not been complete and despite the gradual withdrawal in the degree of license given to students, the notion of 'protected-group vandalism' still seems viable and the existence of such behaviour undeniable. Society is still more tolerant of the old style of rule-breaking than of rule-breaking in the course of political demonstrations. As the following legal comment on 'violence by union pickets and hooligan youths' indicates, some people at least, are prepared to carry on tolerating property destruction by protected groups as long as it is done for the 'right' reasons:

". . . while we disapprove strongly of such incidents as stealing an eagle from the London Zoo as an incident of what is called a student rag, it is at least to be said that this and similar incidents, while ill-judged, have a genuine purpose somewhere behind them and we have been spared in this country the violent scenes promoted in other less civilised countries by students or so-called students who so far as their mental capacities permit, disapprove of the way in which they are governed."[2]

The decision in cases like these to label some types of rule-breaking as merely 'ill-judged' and others as hooliganism, clearly involves political criteria.

Students are by no means the only possible protected group, although they occupy a special position in the mythology about hooliganism. Another group which is given less publicity is the armed forces.* Reminiscences of most servicemen will contain stories of 'orgies of destruction' in barracks, officers' messes and similar settings. This behaviour is invariably handled within the organisation: incidents of ritual window smashing during parties in RAF officers' messes, for example, are usually dealt with by token fines and no mark is made against the record of the officer concerned. Other more interesting examples occur in ordinary public settings, such as small towns near air force or army bases and ports where naval forces land for short periods. In these instances it is less a question of civil authorities turning a blind eye to any damage (usually done in the course of drunken sprees) than of the existence of a clear demarcation between civil and military authorities. Such behaviour would be dealt with by naval patrols, military police or their equivalents, often resulting in harsher penalties than would be imposed by the civil authorities. Naval officers in training have impressed upon them the cardinal principle of never letting their men fall into the hands of the civil authorities: this of course applies to drunkenness, violence, theft and a whole range of rule-breaking other than hooliganism. In this respect at least, members of the forces constitute more of a protected group than students.

(iii) *Play:* There are many settings in which rule-breaking never gets labelled as vandalism because it forms part of play activity. In certain areas window breaking by small children during the course of a game (usually a competition to see who can break the most windows) is a

---

*Needless to say, I am not referring here to the vandalism which is the day to day work of such groups.

25

'Fair game'

highly institutionalised form of rule breaking. Derelict houses or houses under construction are usually chosen and other frequent targets are empty milk bottles and beer bottles. Such activity is usually not regarded as deviant simply because it is part of local tradition, or because the targets are regarded as 'fair game.' In the case of very young children, the damage might be accidental or the actors not thought to be old enough to understand the value of property. In any event the behaviour is seen as adventure, play or exuberance by both the actor and the audience, although neither, of course, need be totally unaware that what is being done might be looked upon as wrong or illegal.

Such destructive play is highly susceptible to being re-defined from institutionalised rule-breaking to 'real' vandalism. This might occur if the damage exceeds some level of tolerance by becoming too visible or excessive. Referring to such behaviour, Clinard and Wade remark:

". . . most of this vandalism seems to grow out of random play activity. In the beginning stages this activity is inherently neither recreational nor delinquent. Later it may be defined as one or the other, depending on whether the culmination of the activity is acceptable or unacceptable to the community."[3]

The factors determining such acceptability are obviously extremely complex and in some cases can be virtually fortuitous: for example an empty house is bought by a private owner, taken over by the local council or made subject to a preservation order. The nature of the destruction then somehow changes, the rule breaking cannot be tolerated, the play becomes vandalism.

The labelling of the act as play or vandalism is also affected by the

26

two dimensions of rule breaking I have already listed; if the act takes place on a ritual occasion or is carried out by a protected group, it is more easily definable as play. The type of environment in which the act takes place is also of importance: in rural areas, for example, certain types of property destruction are more likely to be tolerated and institutionalised. Again such play is subject to changing definitions: damage to hay ricks before the war was thought to be unimportant, but during the war it was brought to court under the Defence Regulations.

(iv) *Writing-off:* There are certain types of rule breaking, which although they are often referred to as vandalism, differ from conventional vandalism offences in that they are so rarely formally reported and processed that they contribute virtually nothing to the public image of vandalism or its reflection in the official statistics. These are types of rule-breaking which 'victim organisations' I interviewed were aware of, but for all practical purposes ignored or wrote off. Examples include the vast amount of minor property defacement: graffiti on lavatory walls, hoardings or posters; names scratched on the walls of ancient monuments, buildings or statues; chewing gum stuck under cinema seats, etc. Such damage or defacement is institutionalised in the sense that it is expected (one would be surprised if one did not see scribblings on the walls of the lavatories in a public house) and is regarded by those who own the property in much the same way as, say, a large supermarket will write off a certain amount of loss from shoplifting and theft by employees. Firms often have a name for such a loss: "stock shrinkage". The damage becomes normalised and routinised: lavatory attendants and caretakers of public buildings regard the cleaning of walls as part of their daily routine. Many advertising agencies, as a matter of routine, supply large contractors—such as London Transport—with a number of extra copies of posters to paste over any copies which have been defaced. The damage is not usually reported and no attempt is made to trace the offender.

The central reason for non-enforcement is that which applies to vandalism as a whole: the fact that this is one of the most safe and anonymous of offences. There is no personal complainant, nor any property to carry or dispose of. Consequently detection rates are low and most damage is not thought worth bothering about. Although the total cost might be considerable, each individual act is too trivial to respond to in any other way than to ignore it.

The form of written-off vandalism known as graffiti—drawings or writings on walls and other surfaces—is a particularly interesting one.[4] While the rule breaker himself might be looked upon as deviant or pathological, this is because of the sort of person he is thought to be or the sort of views he is thought to hold, rather than because of his act of writing about himself or his views on a public wall. Thus the person who indicates on the wall of a public toilet his desire for an obscure sexual fetish, is regarded as a 'pervert' and not as a vandal. The person

Written-off vandalism known as graffiti

Symbolically sacred property . . .

who daubs racialist slogans on walls is condemned for being a racialist (i.e. for the content of the message, and not for writing the message). It is even thought legitimate to reply to such slogans or to change them. Thus "NO BLACKS HERE" becomes "MORE BLACKS HERE", etc.

Society's ambiguity towards this type of rule-breaking is shown by the fact that although there are detailed legal proscriptions against it, it is widely regarded with tolerance and even amusement. Graffiti are hailed as legitimate and amusing forms of self-expression. An article in one students' magazine gave helpful advice on scrawling in underground trains: the best writing instruments to use, which stations are dangerous and which are the best for a beginner to "gain confidence". A recent article in a literary journal produced by students at the University of Keele describes graffiti as "the last urban folk art"; the author goes on: "The artists are completely anonymous. I've never seen one and never been seen".[5] The writing of graffiti—the term originally applied to the wall scrawlings of Pompeii—is a form of behaviour with a long history of institutionalisation. The slogans on the Pompeii walls, such as "VIBIUS RESTITUS SLEPT HERE . . ." are echoed in the more contemporary versions such as "KILROY WAS HERE" which are virtually part of the national heritage. Few national monuments are free of the names of visitors, scratched on the walls for immortality.

An interesting category of written-off vandalism is the type of damage that gets done in the course of some other activity which does not involve rule-breaking. An example of this is the damage done to the countryside—breaking of fences, plants, fields—in the course of various hunts. Such damage is regarded as an unfortunate but unavoidable part of the sport and is seldom branded as vandalism. (Groups, however, who have tried to disrupt hunts by throwing meat and aniseed to the dogs, are invariably referred to as 'hooligans' or 'vandals'.)

Another setting in which such incidental vandalism occurs is that of large commercial exhibitions. At the Motor Show in Earls Court, for example, damage estimated at several thousand pounds regularly occurs. Although some firms take security measures, such as roping off the area around the car, it is generally thought that damage to the cars cannot be prevented. As one newspaper described it: "Dents, scratches, cigarette burns to the upholstery and carpets, and bent doors are all part of the accepted risk of putting the latest models on show to the public."[6] Some firms, indeed, regard the show as a test of strength: if various handles, switches and accessories have not been ripped off the car by the end of the show, the car is regarded as a durable model.

Such property destruction can easily become converted into conventional vandalism. The same amount of incidental trivial damage is magnified if the target is of a particular kind: defacement of religious property and other symbolically sacred property such as war memorials is more likely to be processed as vandalism. Also the damage might accumulate to such an extent that it becomes impossible to write it off: it gets defined as 'going too far' or 'getting beyond control'. More important, if the defacement involves some disapproved-of ideological message, it will be defined as unacceptable. Thus, while routine defacement of posters and hoardings—for example, by painting moustaches on female faces—is written off, definitions change if the message threatens any powerful group's interests.

(v) *Walling-in:* This condition refers to property destruction which occurs within the confines of a fairly closed setting such as a factory or a school. The act of rule-breaking is rarely processed as a conventional vandalism offence for much the same reasons that apply to written-off vandalism: the damage is too trivial or occurs too routinely to be taken much notice of. When attention is paid to the rule-breaking—and this is the chief characteristic of this condition—it is sanctioned *within* the framework of the organisation. The more 'total' the organisation or institution, the less likely it is that the rule-breaking will ever be legally processed. The vandalism is thus invisible: it is rarely defined as deviant by the wider society, because it is unknown to all but the rule-breaker and other members of the organisation. Both the rule-breaker and the informal (although at times highly intricate and ritualistic) sanctions it sometimes evokes, are institutionalised. They form part of the unwritten folklore of the organisation.

Factories and other work places provide a major setting for this sort of vandalism. The deliberate destruction of plant or machinery, the use of ingenious techniques to restrict output or ensure extra rest periods are all part of the unwritten history of work. Given the prevalence of such behaviour—industrial sabotage as it is labelled in some contexts—it is surprising that only recently have sociologists begun to analyse its complex meanings and motivations.[7]

For the most part, industrial sabotage is accepted by management and workers as something which 'happens'. Little is done unless things are seen as having gone too far, the damage is associated with overt political or industrial conflict, or is too disruptive to be contained within the walls of the institution. Industrial sabotage can be observed in extreme forms in more total institutions such as ships, where other avenues of protest for the worker are limited, and he does not always have the escape route of walking out of the job, or even temporarily absenting himself from work. Ramsay, an observer with many years of experience at sea, considers that "the most blatant private expressions of hostility at sea took the form of outright acts of sabotage such as fouling up the tanks while tank-cleaning. This type of act was by no means uncommon."[8] Other examples he cites include: buckets being thrown over the side of a ship which had no running water for washing; members of the catering staff heaving a pile of dirty dishes through the port-hole instead of washing them; stewards doing personal laundry making a 'mistake' by burning a hole through a shirt with the iron. Other routine examples cited by Peter Fricke include throwing tools overboard, and painting slogans and signs on the hulls of ships belonging to rival lines.* Sanctions against such activity are difficult to enforce, and might only take place when it goes 'too far', and becomes problematic, although even then, it is rarely processed as a conventional vandalism offence. The following extract from a Master's report to his shipping company, illustrates the point:

". . . The conduct of the crew at this port has just about reached its lowest ever standard, and the Deck ratings can no longer be considered an efficient working force . . . the Deck ratings under the insidious influence of X are doing everything possible to prevent the efficient working of the ship by such actions as dropping their working tools, chipping hammers, paint brushes, over the side. All of which is very difficult to prove . . . unless firmer disciplinary actions are taken we just cannot hope to run our vessels efficiently."

Moving away from work situations, a number of other examples of walled-in vandalism may be cited, each case again involving complex motivational patterns. Much school vandalism is of this kind: only the more spectacular incidents (such as mass breaking of windows, full scale destruction of classrooms or—more usually—the headmaster's study) are processed as offences. The personal reminiscences of virtually anybody who has been to school testify that such destruction of property is routinely carried out within the confines of the school and is never formally reported. Examples are legion and part of the unwritten folklore of the school: graffiti on the lavatory walls: scratching names and slogans on desks; flooding the changing rooms or cloakrooms by plugging the sinks and turning the taps on; defacing textbooks; breaking various items of sports equipment; tearing off coat hooks from cloakroom walls, etc. Such rule-breaking may be institutionalised because of some of the other conditions I have distinguished: it is usually rationalised as play activity, it is incidental in the sense that it is just put up with and accepted as normal, and the damage often occurs on ritual occasions, especially the end of term when there are school leavers.

A final example of rule-breaking within the confines of an organisation is the type of destruction carried out by inmates of institutions such as mental hospitals and prisons. As in the case of industrial sabotage, such damage—which usually takes the form of breaking windows, furniture, equipment and eating utensils—is often motivated by impotent rage and hostility against authority. It might also be a way to relieve boredom or a conscious tactic to draw attention to a particular grievance. One psychiatrist[9] has interpreted the damage and destruction in children's residential institutions as related to the need to vent one's

---

*A more unusual incident he recollects took place after deck hands, who had already thrown their rubber gloves overboard because they were fed up with the job, refused the mate's order to paint the deck with creosote (Deckol), a painful job which burns the hands unless one uses gloves or grease. The men proceeded to paint the creosote on the testicles of fifteen bulls in the hold. The bulls had to be destroyed when the ship docked.

feelings on the immediate surroundings: this might serve as a safety valve in that the institution is able to wait and allow for the damage and the child can search for a means of restitution.

In some therapeutic establishments, such damage is not only normalised, but welcomed as a sign that an inhibited person is learning to express himself. Although there are often institutional rules against such behaviour, the staff are trained to tolerate the rule-breaking under certain conditions, and to blandly sit back, for example, while the patient (usually a child) smashes various items of furniture and equipment. In one of the classic accounts of the treatment of disturbed delinquents, Aichhorn wrote:

"As a direct result of our attitude, their aggressive acts become more frequent and more violent until practically all the furniture in the building was destroyed, the window panes broken, the doors nearly kicked to pieces . . . The building looked as though it harboured a crowd of madmen. In spite of this, I continued to insist that the boys should be allowed to work out their aggression, that there should be no intervention except where necessary to prevent physical injury . . ."

In more conventional therapeutic and penal establishments, such tolerance of vandalism rarely exists. Nevertheless, as with most other forms of rule-breaking the behaviour is contained, and sanctioned if necessary, within the walls of the institution. Most students of prison life[10] have noted the frequency of 'smashing up': the periodic frenzied but systematic destruction of all furniture and equipment.

One way in which walled-in vandalism becomes re-defined is when it is associated with other forms of rule-breaking in the same setting. If there is a spectacular incident of window-breaking in a school, the school authorities or mass media might draw attention to the incidence of the more routine types of vandalism. Similarly, if there is a scandal about say, drug-taking, sexual promiscuity, or general indiscipline in a school (or in an approved school) then the ordinary walled-in vandalism might become more visible in the ensuing 'exposure'.

(vi) *Licensing:* This condition overlaps with most of the other categories I have distinguished and extracts certain features common to them. It refers again to situations in which vandalism is benevolently tolerated or allowed for. It might be regarded as a nuisance and somewhat troublesome, but seldom more than that. Despite the fact that —unlike walled-in vandalism—it may occur in a highly public setting and—unlike written-off vandalism—its manifestations might be spectacular, the damage is rarely officially reported, processed or regarded as socially problematic. The reason for this might be that a protected group is involved, or that the damage takes place on a ritual occasion or in the context of play or that the actors are under the influence of alcohol—or a combination of all these factors. The end result is that vandalism is chartered or insured against in the sense that even before the damage takes place, some informal arrangement is made whereby

32

the rule-breakers can be ritualistically sanctioned. The sanction often takes the form of financial reparation and in some cases an insurance fee will be paid before the event to cover any possible costs.

An example of licensed vandalism is the type of damage done to hotels by resident sporting teams, especially during sports festivals. Rugby and men's hockey teams are particularly notorious for this type of behaviour. Some hotels extract 'danger money' from the team before it arrives to cover the cost of such damage as smashing glasses and bottles, emptying sand buckets or turning on fire extinguishers in the corridors and breaking furniture. Other hotel managements will unobtrusively add the cost of damage to the team's bill; in the case of professional teams, such costs will usually be subtracted from wages or fees. When this behaviour takes place in small towns—as, for example, in coastal resorts in the south of England—it is well-known to virtually the whole population and even reported in the local press: yet nothing is done about it. The charter for this type of rule-breaking is easily lifted. Hotels discover, for example, that the profits from the stay of a few rugby teams do not compensate for the cost of the damage, and decide to ban a particularly offensive team. Such a sequence, however, very rarely occurs: on the whole it is commercially sound to allow for this type of rule-breaking.

Vandalism by various protected groups might also be chartered in certain settings. Colleges or halls of residence of some universities in this country have, for example, evolved schemes where by students have to pay danger money (usually about £25) when they enrol. This money would be to cover any damage or petty pilfering. Public schoolboys coming home on trains at the end of term used to be made to pay for any damage themselves; this would not be reported to the police. Some degree of licence or charter is also given to armed forces, particularly on occasions such as the first night in port after a voyage or the last night prior to embarkation.

VANDALISM AS A LABEL

The somewhat peculiar typology I have presented so far has little to do with the question of why people commit vandalism: each type and subgroup within it (for example industrial sabotage or school vandalism) covers a wide range of motives and meanings. The list merely illustrates the variable conditions under which illegal property destruction might not be labelled and processed as vandalism. Before discussing the patterns and meanings behind more 'conventional' vandalism I want to consider the conditions under which the label *is* used and the senses in which such labelling can be seen as political.

The historical and etymological meanings of the term 'vandalism' derive from the Vandals, an East German tribe who invaded Western Europe in the fourth and fifth centuries and eventually sacked Rome in 455. They were traditionally regarded as the great destroyers of Roman art, civilisation and literature and their actions were associated

33

with a general barbaric ignorance, lack of taste and sensibility. According to the Oxford English Dictionary, the term 'vandal' was used in 1663 to refer to a "wilful or ignorant destroyer of anything beautiful, venerable or worthy of preservation" and was broadened to include any reckless, uncultured or ruthlessly destructive behaviour—particularly in connection with works of art. One source suggests that the noun 'vandalism' was coined in 1794 by an apologist for the French Revolution who, attempting to cast blame for the destruction of works of art during the Revolution on its enemies, likened this destruction to the behaviour of the original Vandals. The connection between 'vandalism' and aesthetic destruction was retained in the nineteenth century when the term was used, for example, to refer to the pulling down of medieval buildings to make room for new ones of Churchwarden Gothic. The contemporary meaning of vandalism is still given in the dictionary as "ruthless destruction or spoiling of anything beautiful or venerable," or, in the weakened sense: "Barbarous, ignorant or inartistic treatment."

It is not clear when the term 'vandalism' became used to describe destruction of property in general. Its etymological connection with the destruction of aesthetic objects is obviously too restrictive to cover the range of behaviour conventionally described as vandalism. Nevertheless, the original connotations of the term should not be lost sight of. Dryden's image of the Vandals encapsulates this historical legacy:

> Till Goths and Vandals, a rude Northern Race
> Did all the matchless monuments deface

The adjectives connected with aesthetic vandalism—barbarous, wilful, ignorant, reckless, ruthless—remain as part of the contemporary stereotype of vandalism and are used—particularly in political contexts —to justify certain forms of social control.

The term vandalism can be used as a general mode of abuse but more particularly, because of the images it conjures up, it is employed to discount and discredit the meaning of certain actions. In the case of conventional juvenile vandalism offences, this tendency is less obvious because the stereotypes of senselessness and pointlessness are so pervasive. In a society dominated by utilitarianism and property motives, few can find any rationality in behaviour which does not appear to be directed to economic ends. A few more people, though, will understand that in the case of property destruction connected with explicit ideological conflict (racial, religious, class) descriptions such as 'reckless, ignorant vandals' or 'sheer vandalism' are political in that they tend to deny the legitimacy of the motives behind the behaviour. Any study of the image of the Northern Ireland conflict as presented in the mass media and the rhetoric of politics will show this tendency.

IDEOLOGICAL VANDALISM

There is clearly a category of property destruction which has either or both of the following characteristics:

(i) the rule is broken as a means towards some explicit and conscious ideological end.

(ii) there is no consensus over the content of the rule which is being broken and, more particularly, the content of the rule is being explicitly and consciously challenged.

Now, to the extent that many acts which I discussed under the heading of 'institutionalised rule-breaking' and others I will discuss as 'conventional vandalism' may themselves be motivated by ideological reasons, it is dangerous—as well as ideological in itself—to designate some forms of vandalism as ideological and others as not. Nevertheless, there is a recognisable type of property destruction, which, although it may be simply dismissed as 'sheer' hooliganism or vandalism, involves a clear ideological component if only in the sense that it allows itself moral justifications and appeals to an explicit and articulated set of beliefs. In such circumstances, the actor is regarded not as an outsider or deviant to be punished, nor even excused because he was 'only having fun', but is seen as a hero or martyr, fighting a just cause. Whether he is called a hero or a hooligan, a visionary or a vandal depends on the same political processes which determine whether a member of a Rhodesian African Party who sabotages a power station is called a 'terrorist' or a 'freedom fighter'.

It would be tendentious and repetitive to give too many illustrations of such ideologically justified property destruction, some of which are given more attention elsewhere in this book. Recent manifestations of this phenomenon (for example, stoning embassy windows, destruction by students and workers during demonstrations) have been regarded as somehow innovatory. It is probable, however, that there was a greater amount of such ideological property destruction in pre-industrial times. The main reason for this was the absence for the vast bulk of the population of legitimate means of expressing grievances: particularly through political parties and trade unions. Rudé's discussion of crowd disturbances in France and England between 1730 and 1848 contains many illustrations of ideological vandalism. These acts were, of course, not reducible to a single motive. There was, for example, the traditional riot by the 'labouring poor' in the eighteenth century as a means of redressing a particular grievance:

"On such occasions, market towns, miner's villages and country lanes echoed to the sound of marching feet, crashing timber, or broken glass as working men and women settled accounts with corn factors, religious dissenters, mill owners, farmers, or enclosing landlords."[11]

There was in addition the type of damage during episodes such as the English Food Riots of 1766, sparked off by a sudden increase in the price of grain. On these occasions mills were destroyed, flour thrown into rivers and records destroyed. Probably the best known historical example of ideological vandalism is the Luddite episode. The term

eological vandalism
emolition of the Vendome Column in 1871. In 1852 Karl
arx had prophesied "when the imperial mantle finally falls on
e shoulders of Louis Bonaparte, the bronze statue of Napoleon
ll crash from the top of the Vendome Column"

The fascination of destruction

If Nelson's was one of ours, there'd be no cleaning problem.

Column, we mean.

Abacus can make raising and lowering columns up to a hundred feet high which one man can bring down to ground level and raise again.

All in minutes. Simplifying maintenance and reducing labour commitments to a new low.

May we send all the facts you need on these and other lighting columns?

The coupon will bring details of the particular Abacus products which are of interest to you.

The new ideological vandalism: on 22 Jan. 1969 when anti-Vietnam-war militancy was at its height, Timothy John Daly, a 20-year-old poet, was sentenced to four years imprisonment for setting fire to the Imperial War Museum, London.

The ballad of an anti-war criminal by Tim Daly
Those two fanatic demons of honesty and love
Held me against emotion as the sky grew mad above
I myself determined to see this mission through
As the will to free all children from the sins of parents grew

Memories of soldiers dead for causes true and just
Their killing long forgotten as was the soldiers' lust
Then on the night's horizon my frantic eyes did find
A building almost beautiful but there the war enshrined

So I made myself two molotovs as result of what I planned
For this travesty of beauty I could no longer stand
On a Sunday night at half past eight up to its dome I made
There I threw down my freedom where were documents displayed

Now in my cell my freedom gone I yearn for friends I knew
My strength is getting smaller where before it only grew
And yet I know with all my heart atonement for my act
For my heart believed in what I did and can man say more than

'Luddism' is often used in connection with the type of industrial sabotage which involves ideological undertones. Recent analyses of Luddism by economic historians such as Rudé, Hobsbawm and Thompson are more relevant than first appears to the contemporary study of vandalism in that they challenge the stereotype of such destruction as being 'pointless and frenzied' or as being a mere 'overflow of high spirits'. Of particular interest also is Hobsbawm's distinction between the two types of machine breaking: the first was 'collective bargaining by riot' in which the wrecking implied no special hostility to machines as such but was, under certain conditions, a normal way of putting pressure on

38

employers, particularly to concede wage increases. The second type of wrecking was directed against machinery as such, particularly labour-saving machinery, and is explained in terms of working class hostility to the new machines of the Industrial Revolution. A point that both Hobsbawm and Rudé make about this type of machine-breaking is again of contemporary interest, namely that the destruction was not altogether indiscriminate: selected targets were chosen and there was often talk of 'lists' of persons whose frames should be destroyed.

Contemporary ideological vandalism has moved to many more areas than the industrial. Property is destroyed in mass situations, such as demonstrations and riots (throwing stones at embassy windows, breaking cars, uprooting trees, paving stones and street signs) or by individuals—often referred to as 'saboteurs': blowing up embassies, destroying communications or power installations.

In all these types of vandalism—although certain individuals taking part are motivated by different reasons—property destruction is used as a conscious tactic: to revenge, or draw attention to a specific grievance, to gain publicity for a general cause, to challenge symbolically, or insult a particular individual or group, etc. There is another type of ideological vandalism, however, where the very content of the rules is being challenged. In the same way as the slogan "Property is Theft" has sometimes been interpreted literally to mean that the rules governing the theft of property are not to be thought of as binding, so certain movements have advocated property destruction as a legitimate end in itself. This view can be seen, for example, in the current of anarchist thought which has literally interpreted slogans such as Bakunin's "Let us put our trust in the eternal spirit which destroys and annihilates only because it is the unsearchable and eternally creative source of all

Destruction as art

life. The urge to destroy is also a creative urge." Contemporary variations on this theme can be found in ideologies urging 'urban guerillas' to destroy the artefacts of Western civilisation, in movements such as the International Situationists, the Constructive Nihilists, the Black Hand Gang, the Weathermen, and in a diluted form in other political groupings whose ideologies are beyond my scope to analyse here.

Other variations may be found in aesthetic movements such as Dada and Surrealism. Contemporary examples might include 'vandalisable sculpture' devised by such sculptors as William Turnbull; Auto-Destructive Art and the breaking up of musical instruments on stage by pop groups (such as The Who and Move).

But what have 18th-century food riots, anarchist bombers and auto-destructive art got to do with 'the vandalism problem'? The point is that we cannot take for granted the exclusion of such behaviour from the subject matter of what someone like a criminologist conventionally studies under such headings as 'vandalism'. Does he exclude ideological vandalism because he doesn't have enough space? Or because he doesn't think this is 'really' vandalism? The criminologist—as well as the ordinary member of the public interested in the vandalism problem—must be alert to the following:

(i) Much ordinary, conventional vandalism might in fact be ideologically inspired.

(ii) Much conventional vandalism is *thought* to be ideologically inspired: for example, the term 'sabotage' with its ideological connotations, is often used to describe acts of play vandalism by small children. A pacifist, writing about the formation of "non-violent elites", welcomed signs of Luddism in small communities which he hoped could be canalised into peaceful forms of action:

"In recent months I have observed the genesis of a number of acts which I would place in this category—obstruction and incendiarism on railway lines, carried out mostly but not solely by children. Without reading too much into these activities, the involved spectator sees growing here an articulate group-consciousness directed not merely against British Rail itself, but against the alien standards it buttresses." [12]

It is not important that this appears to be a strange position for a pacifist to take, nor is it important whether Moody's interpretation of railway vandalism is correct or not. What is important is the lack of consensus over rules and the way in which ideologies can be imputed.

(iii) The perception of an act of vandalism as being ideologically motivated, rather than 'motiveless', affects society's attitude to the act and the way in which it is dealt with. This is a complex relationship; on the one hand, acts which are seen to have a motive, to 'make sense', might be less subject to the violent reactions usually directed to acts perceived as motiveless. But on the other hand, motives can be approved or disapproved of and if the vandalism is associated (correctly or not) with an ideology one disapproves of, then the reaction will be more punitive.

The very selection of certain types of rule-breaking for public attention, and for being defined as problems, is affected by ideological factors. In the interests of the dominant ideology, or consensus, or what is described as 'the public good', both 'institutionalised rule-breaking' and 'conventional vandalism offences' are responded to selectively. So, for example, certain types of written-off vandalism are more likely to be defined as problematic than others. Racialist slogans abound on posters on the London Underground but very little is done about them. At the beginning of 1968 the posters of a large department store advertising "Buy American Week" were changed so that the slogan WE CLOTHE VERY LATE became WE CLOTHE EVERY CHILD IN NAPALM. This received a large amount of attention and all the posters that were written on were immediately replaced.

(iv) A final reason for wanting to study ideological vandalism lies in the simple fact that its overt behavioural characteristic—the wilful and illegal destruction of property—is identical with that of conventional vandalism. This is not, of course, to say that the behaviour means anything like the same to the actor or to society. It does justice to neither phenomenon to try to make them fit the same explanatory framework. One cannot, for example, explain a group of Negroes smashing hundreds of shop windows in Los Angeles in the same way as one might two boys kicking in the glass panes of a telephone kiosk in South London. Nevertheless, we should be alerted to the fact that these very different phenomena might have common features of interest other than the fact that property was destroyed. In this case there might be significant parallels in the role of the mass media in spreading the behaviour. This is a possibility that one should not ignore in the name of 'narrowing one's field of interest'.

CONVENTIONAL VANDALISM—MOTIVES AND MEANINGS

I will now return to what 'everyone knows' is the vandalism problem: those acts which not only violate the rules forbidding the destruction of property, but which are usually recognised and labelled as vandalism and processed as delinquent or criminal offences. To the extent that there is a mythology or set of beliefs about vandalism, these acts are the basis on which the mythology is formed. To the extent that there is a societal control culture directed towards controlling vandalism (by prevention, deterrence, punishment or therapy) these are the acts which the theories are designed to explain. In any context in which society's reaction to vandalism is conventionally discussed, these are the acts which are being reacted to.

The two central stereotypes about vandalism which I have been concerned to dispel, are of the behaviour as *homogeneous* and as *meaningless*. Most people will probably not find much difficulty in distinguishing between a ten year old boy throwing an old tyre on to a

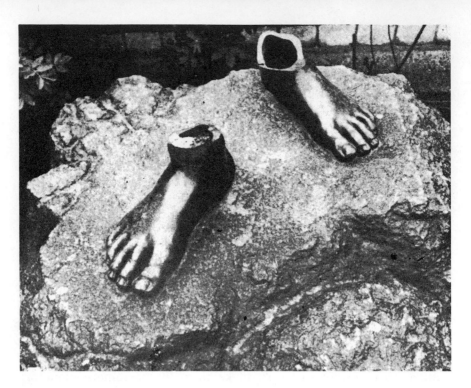

Acquisitive vandalism

railway line, a group of football fans smashing shop windows on a Saturday afternoon, and someone deliberately wrenching off the coin box of a public telephone. People tend to react, however, *as if* they cannot make these distinctions, as if there is a homogeneous vandal type responsible for the whole range of behaviour. No such category exists, though, even within the range of officially labelled and apprehended vandals. Thus, nearly two-thirds of telephone vandals are adults, while most railway vandalism (such as putting objects on the railway line) is carried out by young children between ten and twelve years old.

The most pervasive stereotype is of vandalism as meaningless, senseless or wanton. One can counter this image by finding patterns either in the nature of the property that is damaged or in the clusters of different meanings and motives attributed to the action by the offender. I have distinguished the following five types of conventional vandalism (to which should be added the important but problematic category of ideological vandalism which I have already discussed): *acquisitive; tactical; vindictive; play* and *malicious.*

(i) **Acquisitive Vandalism:** the damage is done in the course of or in order to acquire money or property. This includes what used to be called *junking* (stripping lead, copper or brass from buildings to sell to junk dealers); *collecting* (removing objects such as street signs, car insignias, name plates—this is often done by students) and *looting:* of parking meters, automatic vending machines, telephone coin boxes,

42

*Kensington and Chelsea council attempted to cover Powis Square
playground with tarmac against the wishes of the residents
who tore up the surface as fast as it was laid*

gas and electricity meters, slot machines, pin tables and juke boxes.
Contrary to the public stereotype, the larger proportion of telephone
kiosk vandalism is of this type.

(ii) **Tactical Vandalism:** the damage done is a conscious tactic used to
advance some end other than acquiring money or property. The damage
does not necessarily involve the expression of hostility and while the
target itself may be chosen somewhat arbitrarily, the choice of property-
destruction as a form of action is deliberate and planned.

Much ideological vandalism is tactical, with the end in mind of drawing attention or gaining publicity for a particular cause. Thus slogan-
painting and other property defacement is of this type: the author is
putting across a particular message which, perhaps because of the
absence of, or lack of faith in, other channels, he has decided to do in
this illegal way. The choice of method and target is deliberately made
and the consequences of the act are deliberately assessed.

Tactical vandalism directed towards attracting attention might result
from personal troubles rather than ideological convictions. Psychiatric
committals are sometimes precipitated by an incident of property
destruction: these actions are less often the result of manic excitement,
than an attempt by a depressed or suicidal person to draw attention to
his plight.

Another form of tactical vandalism is the use of window-breaking

43

to be arrested and provided with food and a bed. Although such behaviour seems a somewhat esoteric and insignificant form of vandalism, it contributes a fair proportion to the numbers of adults committed to prison for vandalism. In one sample of 98 window smashers in a London prison,[13] 19 said that their motive was to "get under care". Whether the object was short term care (police station) or long term care (prison) the situation in each case was of a homeless, destitute man looking for a warm bed and food. These men often preferred prison to a hostel or reception centre, and some were regular window breakers, coming in particularly at the beginning of winter. Their tactics included throwing a brick at a police car or through the window of a police station, or conspicuously breaking a window in front of a policeman.

Another context in which tactical vandalism occurs is in the industrial setting. Industrial sabotage might be carried out to ensure regular rest periods and relieve the monotony of work, for example, by jamming a machine. Such vandalism, as noted, rarely becomes visible and is often institutionalised. An allied type of tactical vandalism is illustrated in the following case:

"Two naval airmen wanted to get out of the Navy for domestic reasons. Several applications on compassionate grounds had failed and as a last resort they went into a hangar on board a commando carrier and damaged a helicopter, smashing the windows, the exhaust pipe, etc."*

(iii) **Vindictive Vandalism:** the use of property destruction as a form of revenge is an extremely important sub-type of vandalism. It looms much larger in the total vandalism picture than is apparent and it accounts for many more cases which, on the surface, look wanton or meaningless. There is a range of problems for which vandalism offers itself as a solution, for example, where one feels one has been unfairly treated, as a form of spite, in order to get one's own back or to settle a long term grudge. The grievance might be imagined rather than real and the eventual target of destruction only indirectly or symbolically related to the original source of hostility—but the end result is the same.

Vandalism of this sort is not only—in the short run at least—emotionally satisfying, but also a very safe outlet: detection is unlikely, and one is far less likely to be hurt than if personal violence was resorted to. Personal violence is, in any event, often an impossible alternative because the object of one's grievance is inaccessible.

Prewer nicely sums up the meaning of a personal act of vindictive vandalism:

". . . to break a man's window is a much safer way of paying him out than to punch him on the nose, for example. The victim is left with a cold draught, to be followed later by a glazier's bill; and he may remain

---

*The result was not simply dismissal from the service, but also 18 months' detention. The story has an ironic twist in that one of the men's application for a discharge had been recommended on the morning of the episode.

in complete ignorance as to who has done the deed. The smash itself may be pleasurable, so that this form of revenge is often safe, usually certain and always sweet."[14]

Twenty men in his sample of adult window smashers claimed that their motive was to get revenge. A further 11 used window-breaking to draw attention to a grievance (the act was therefore also 'tactical') although bearing no grudge against the actual owner of the window (in this sense the act was 'wanton').

Reported examples of vindictive vandalism of this sort—mainly carried out by adults—include:

breaking his employer's office equipment by a man who felt he was wrongfully dismissed;
breaking the windows of an Employment Exchange by a man who alleged that an official had discriminated against him;
breaking the windows of a National Assistance Board office by a man who had been refused money.

Of more importance in contributing to the general stereotype of vandalism are acts committed by juveniles. The most obvious situation in which this type of vindictive vandalism occurs, is when a group or individual feels victimised by a particular adult; for example, a school teacher, shopkeeper or youth leader. A shop-keeper may have his windows broken after reporting someone to the police, or—more commonly —a group might break a window of a club or coffee bar from which it feels it has been unfairly excluded, sometimes returning to completely wreck furniture and equipment.

Much school vandalism is motivated by a sense of revenge. More often than is apparent, evidence indicates that the culprits are not outsiders, but pupils of the school. In these cases the vandalism is preceded by punishments, deprivation of privileges, expulsions or other potential sources of grievance. The following episode, although typical of such vandalism, occurred in a type of school in which vandalism is not usually reported:

"More than 40 pupils at a £400-a-year school for sons of Colonial civil servants and foreign businessmen have been withdrawn by their parents after disturbances to which the police were called . . . The pupils . . . ran through the buildings . . . smashing windows and overturning furniture. Then they threw a bust of the Headmaster . . . into the river. . . . The school has been the scene of open conflict between pupils and Mr M. (the Headmaster) for a year. Trouble broke out when the boys' privileges, for which their parents paid extra fees, were withdrawn. They claim their clubs were shut down and that they were barred from using the swimming pool and common room. The following day the boys broke down the common room door, overturned furniture and smashed windows."[15]

It is probable that vindictive vandalism is a large proportion of the total amount of vandalism committed by gangs. Juvenile gang activity is very much a part of the image of senseless violence and vandalism, but one recent American study of 150 gangs[16] shows that not only is property damage a relatively minor part of the gang's activity, but that the damage was not entirely random and wanton. The objects and facilities damaged were those used and frequented in the course of everyday life and most damage was to public or semi-public (e.g. gyms, social agencies) rather than to private property. Moreover, the damage was directed to specific targets; both examples that Miller gives are of vindictive vandalism: defacing the automobile of a mother responsible for having a gang member committed to a correctional institution, and breaking a window of a settlement house after being rejected. Miller's comments are important:

"Little of the deliberately inflicted property damage represented a diffuse outpouring of accumulated hostility against arbitrary objects; in most cases the gang members injured the possessions or properties of particular persons who angered them as a concrete expression of that anger . . . There was little evidence of senseless destruction: most property damage was directed and responsive."[17]

It is, of course, true that most vindictive vandalism is rational and utilitarian only in the sense of providing for the actor the satisfaction of knowing that he has obtained his revenge and that his victim has been discomforted. It is non-rational and non-utilitarian in the sense that only in rare cases will the victim be moved to change his position because of the vandalism: the club leader is unlikely to be intimidated into admitting a gang because it has broken the club windows, neither will security agencies change their minds about giving assistance. In fact, the consequences for the actor if he is apprehended, might be to leave him in a worse position and increase his grievance. Much vindictive vandalism is only carried out with the thought of expressing immediate indignation and anger, as the following incident indicates:

"West Ham fans, angered by their team's defeat by 3rd Division Swindon in an FA Cup replay, were believed to have smashed the windows of a sports shop (opposite the Club's ground) owned by West Ham's captain, Bobby Moore.
    The symbolic nature of vindictive vandalism is illustrated clearly in the following archetypical case:

"A thirteen year old boy, disappointed at the Christmas gifts received after praying, decided to 'get his own back on God' and damaged and then set fire to a church, resulting in £50,000 loss."

Although such behaviour might be characterised as irrational, it is by no means wanton in the sense of being arbitrary.

Children playing in a deprived area of Portsmouth

(iv) **Play Vandalism:** enough property is destroyed in the course of play activity to have justified my discussing it earlier as a form of rule-breaking which is virtually institutionalised: in many contexts, of course, the action is not seen as breaking any rules at all. In much play vandalism, there is also little of a malicious element: motivations such as curiosity and the spirit of competition and skill are more important.

The quantity of the damage will be stressed—for example, how many windows or street lamps can be broken—or particular skills tested, for example, in aiming at moving targets or standing various distances from the target. Wade cites a good example of the casual atmosphere in which such vandalism occurs:

"The first time we did vandalism, me and my brother and another boy down at the garage, we were smoking and playing cards. They had some old cars in the back; we played around there. We cleaned them out one day . . . This one guy threw a whiskey bottle up on the roof; I threw another. It hit the side of the window. When we were through, we had broken twentyseven of them. We saw who could break the most. There wasn't anything else to do. We finally got tired and just left . . ."[18]

In play vandalism, the fact that property is destroyed might be a minor or even incidental part of the game. The participants might be surprised that their behaviour is disapproved of, although in some cases this knowledge gives an additional edge of enjoyment to the game. There is also an imperceptible point at which 'fun' becomes malice; to quote one boy from a classic study of Chicago gangs in the twenties:

"We did all kinds of dirty tricks for fun. We'd see a sign, 'Please keep the street clean,' but we'd tear it down and say, 'We don't feel like keeping it clean'. One day we put a can of glue in the engine of a man's car. We would always tear things down. That would make us laugh and feel good, to have so many jokes."

(v) **Malicious Vandalism:** my final category is the one which reveals most clearly the vicious and apparently senseless facade which society finds so difficult to understand. But such vandalism not only expresses malice, aggression and anger—this is true of most forms of vandalism. The action is neither, on the one hand, as specific as in vindictive, tactical or acquisitive vandalism, nor on the other, as differentiated, diffuse or arbitrary as terms like 'wanton' imply. The action, to use Miller's terms, is both 'directed' (in the sense that the identity and ownership of the target is not entirely irrelevant) and 'responsive' (in the sense that it is a response to particular situations or needs).

The term 'malicious' often carries the implication not just of hatred but of action enjoyed for its own sake and even action that is found amusing. Thus the practical joker obtains *malicious* satisfaction at the expense of his victim. This combination of hostility and fun is present in many cases of vandalism. If the Chicago example I quoted was on the fun side, the edge of impotent rage is more obvious in the following:

"Using the hatchet from the emergency tool kit, four youths smashed or tore off the following objects in fourteen parked train coaches: 228 windows, 128 compartment mirrors and picture glasses, 86 window blinds, 38 window straps, 180 electric light bulbs and 8 fire extinguishers."

Examples of this sort could be multiplied: pouring acid on car roofs; pulling out all the flowers of floral clocks; strangling swans in ornamental lakes; slashing the tyres of all the cars in a car park; stripping the insulation round water mains; dumping the manhole covers in a sewage farm; putting matches in the tyre valves of police cars (which

48

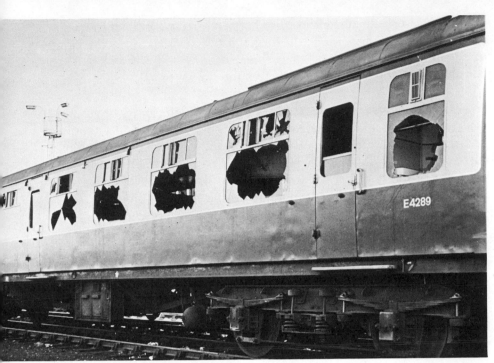

The edge of impotent rage . . .

causes the tyre to leak, and when it gets hot, the match ignites); throwing life belts into the sea; placing sleepers on railway lines; throwing stones at the drivers of passing trains; urinating in public telephone receivers; defecating in the lifts of council flats; pouring dye or acid into swimming baths; sabotaging the engines of children's miniature trains; ripping out lavatory chains in public conveniences; placing bicycle chains on railway overhead wires to cause short circuits . . .

It is beyond my scope to discuss all the possible subjective feelings which might precede such vandalism; these include boredom, despair, exasperation, resentment, failure and frustration. It is significant that in everyday language the escape from such states is often expressed in metaphors such as *breaking* out, *breaking* away and *breaking* clear. Perhaps another illustration from life in the merchant navy will convey some of these subjective meanings:

". . . we brushed bucketloads of rust under the bends in L-shaped girders, and in the furthermost corners we brushed nothing at all. It would all come out when the next cargo of petrol was delivered, and we sincerely hoped that it would give engine trouble to every motorist who used it in his car; if it ruined their engines altogether, that would be all the better.

When sailors are loading stores and accidentally let a sling load crash on to the wharf below, their action is usually one of suppressed glee rather than sorrow. Deck crews who are driven too hard can quite calmly paint over oil and water and take a malicious delight in doing so. All these private acts of hostility happen directly, without premeditation, without going through the formal process of making a complaint and getting no satisfaction: the seamen know the futility of making formal complaints and save themselves the time."

This is, of course, a very specific situation, which cannot be generalised to other types of vandalism. But I believe that an understanding of the context in which these other types occur, will render the behaviour just as intelligible. Among the more general patterns which emerge are:

(i) the property destroyed is much more likely to be publicly than privately owned. This is due not just to the greater opportunities to attack public property, but also to its anonymous nature and symbolic value. The target is de-personalised and not easily identified with; it belongs to 'them'.

(ii) some patterning in the physical characteristics of the targets is also apparent: the property tends to be derelict, incomplete or badly kept. Again, such property might be seen as fair game and not really belonging to anybody. Incomplete buildings—such as housing estates under construction—also offer very attractive targets, an important factor in play vandalism.

(iii) areas of high vandalism can also be distinguished by their social characteristics. Thus, in regard to council housing vandalism, more takes place on flatted, rather than cottage estates, and in large, rather than small estates. In the case of school vandalism, one American study some years ago[19] found that high-damage schools were located in lower socio-economic areas, with low occupational status of the fathers and high transiency and instability (although not necessarily areas of high delinquency arrest rates). The schools themselves showed the following characteristics: rapid staff turnover; low staff morale; little identification among parents, teachers and pupils with the school; a record of adverse publicity and a bad reputation; dissatisfaction with the administration; obsolete school apparatus; failure to repair broken equipment and over-crowding—all of which were interpreted as a lack of interest in the students' welfare. Overall, there was a general atmosphere of insecurity and dissatisfaction and a perception by staff and students that the authorities were not interested.

(iv) studies of the social characteristics of the offenders are important, if only to counteract the image of homogeneity which assumes the existence of something like a 'vandal type', responsible for all sorts of vandalism. Clearly no such personality type exists. Juvenile vandalism has one of the lowest reconviction rates of all offences and (in one study) was the only 'symptom' in child guidance clinic referrals not predictive of later personality disturbances or related to any specific psychiatric diagnosis. The more important patterns that exist are of *age:* a peak in late adolescence, but another peak for such types as railway vandalism of the play type at a much earlier age (10-12), and *company:* vandalism is almost always a group rather than an individual offence.

Building site vandalism

So any answer to the question, "Why do they do it?" can only be expressed at a most abstract level and cannot really do justice to the wide range of behaviour that the term vandalism covers. Within this range, some types—the group of 10 year olds smashing windows as part of a game, the merchant seaman trapped in the galley, the old tramp breaking windows outside a police station—may be more easily intelligible than others. But—with patience—at least a plausible story can be told about the other types. Let me conclude this introductory chapter by briefly summarising one perspective on the type most difficult to understand: malicious, apparently senseless vandalism occurring in late adolescence, in large groups, often in public settings and by almost exclusively working class offenders.

VANDALISM AS MANUFACTURED MALICE AND EXCITEMENT

What are the routes to malicious vandalism in late adolescence? One is suggested by David Downes's account of the working class adolescent's dissociation from school and work and his subsequent adoption of manufactured excitement as a solution to the problems society has created for him.[20] The argument is that a stream of working class boys goes through the school system without showing any allegiance to its values or absorbing the aspirations it tries to inculcate. "The school", to quote from an essay written by an East End boy, "was always trying to turn you into something you were not. It was a waste of time." For a few, this perception is tied up with some sort of conscious revolt against the school, but most realise the pointlessness of lashing out there and retreat into a sullen resentment of the rules of the game.

As Hargreaves makes clear in his study of a Northern secondary modern school, while the boy is still at school he is powerless. The teachers make and apply the rules and little open rebellion against them can be sustained. The odd rule is broken, you are invariably detected and punished. The occasional arena for more active flouting of the rules is provided, for example, by a weak teacher. The low stream boy rejects the 'good pupil' role—not just, as Hargreaves suggests, because it is one he cannot succeed in or (later) is antithetical to delinquent values—but because it seems so absurd (getting one's hair cut, not wearing jeans to school).

As soon as possible the boys leave school. They fairly accurately perceive the implications for their future lives of the education they've received. They are being realistic. The scope is small for non-apprentices, and their aspirations reflect this low-ceilinged job market. As Downes says, they are not inherently disillusioned about jobs any more than they are about education; the jobs are also dull and tedious. Money is therefore, and quite rightly, just about the most important occupational criterion. There's no point in ambition if you're driving a van, working on a building site or doing an unskilled factory job. Downes quotes the memorable words of Christine Keeler's girl friend, Mandy Rice-Davis: "Nobody made a bomb by plodding along in a dull job." Theoretically, they might want the job to be interesting, but they know it really won't be. As Goodman says, nobody asks whether jobs are useful, worthy, dignified, honourable. People don't think that way, they grow up realising that "during my productive years I will spend eight hours a day doing what is no good."[21]

Such feelings are, of course, not confined to one social group: students, for example, also feel useless and redundant. But they have more distractions, more culturally approved modes of solution, and the ultimate consolation of prestige and monetary success.

For working class kids in this country over the last fifteen years or so, not many options have been open and one significant element—the mass teenage leisure culture—has pointed to new aspirations, but aspirations which are difficult to fulfil. Although the more traditional leisure pre-occupations such as football are still strong, they cannot compete very well with the glossy commercial image. The conventional youth service is equally unappealing and with few honourable and well-known (and mostly short-lived) exceptions, it has never freed itself from its patronising image or has simply not been what the kids want. Involvement in political or community work (VSO, Task Force and so on) has never been the option that it has to their middle class peers —even in a transitory or uncommitted way. Direct satisfaction through education or occupation is precluded, and anyway not aspired to.

So only the town is left, and here the group that asks the most gets the least. Opportunities for excitement, autonomy or, less ambitiously, a simple sense of *action*, are blocked. Either there is nothing there—in some housing estates, in towns round about the 50,000 population mark, in the less glamorous outer suburbs of large cities—or what is there is drab and mediocre. What the young person wants—or what the Message tells him he should want to want—cannot be reached. He doesn't have enough money to participate fully, even vicariously, and he doesn't have the talent, luck or contacts to really make it directly.

Faced by leisure goals he cannot reach, with little commitment or attachment to others, and lacking any sense of control over his future, his situation contains an edge of desperation. This is the feeling identified by some sociologists as preceding the drift into delinquency.

There are elements in working class culture itself, in the insulated forms it still maintains in some parts of this country, which facilitate this drift: the stress on toughness and excitement, the need to prove one's masculinity. Such elements are both reflected and strengthened by the teenage entertainment culture and the whole leisure ethic of society, with its high valuation of excitement for its own sake, disdain for routine work, and the acceptance of physical prowess as a proof of masculinity.

Vandalism is just right. It is the ideal form of rule-breaking both in *expressive* (expressing certain values) and *instrumental* terms (solving certain structural problems). It is satisfying and provides just the right amount of risk. If one is looking for toughness, excitement, action and a sense of control (however self-defeating and illusory in the long run) then school and work do not provide the right arenas. One deliberately enters into situations which provide real testing grounds, where the action is, where risks have to be taken. Here one plays what Goffman has called "character contests". These are ways of seeing who will have the honour and character to rise above the situation. Action gets restructured around the familiar settings of streets, sports ground, the weekend by the sea, railway stations. The settings are given new meanings by being made stages for these games. Vandalism is ideally suited for this: it is a perfect activity to raise the stakes, to make things more contrived. Thus one sprays acid on a whole street of parked cars, one waits for the last possible minute to do what could have been done easily. If the stakes are raised in public, so much the better. This is a way not just of increasing risk of being observed and detected, but of deliberately provoking, of making a gesture. For the moment it might feel as if it works, but it defeats itself: it proves that, after all, you are just a hooligan, a vandal and good for nothing else.

If this analysis of the routes to such vandalism has even the slightest validity, it follows also that this 'solution' will increase in frequency and intensity. For as the contradictions of our educational system become more apparent, the demands for occupational qualifications upgraded, the pool of unemployed juveniles widened and viable political solutions seem more remote, so will the potential for such delinquency increase.

The truism that society creates its own vandalism, then, must be understood at a number of levels, and is a necessary introduction to the subject.

2 The meaning of the environment

Laurie Taylor

It is tempting to think at times that there may be such a psychological trait as *environmental sensitivity*. There appear to be individuals who are maximally sensitive to their physical environment, who cringe at the sight of roadside billboards, who are struck dumb by Gothic cathedrals and cast down by soaring tenements. Others, however, move through the world apparently unaffected by the arrangements of bricks and steel and concrete through which they pass. They can become exuberantly inebriated in a cavernous estate pub and drive without comment or apparent awareness through a mediaeval town.

Of course there are differences in the extent to which individuals have been taught to appreciate the environment, and there are certain reactions to the environment which are not so much signs of sensitivity to physical surroundings as indications that the individual knows how to assert his membership of a particular status group. To know a good housing development when one sees one can be as important in certain groups as keeping your skirt at the right length. But despite such considerations differences remain.

Must we then talk of some people enjoying more environmental sensitivity than others? Are there some who smash and destroy aspects of the environment because they are especially affected by its ugliness or its monotony?

Fortunately there is another way to explain individual differences in reactivity to the physical environment. We can begin somewhat paradoxically by looking at a series of psychological experiments which appeared to provide evidence of differential environmental sensitivity between individuals.

These experiments, which are variously referred to as the 'coffin' or 'blackbox' or 'sensory deprivation' studies, are too well known to need detailed description here. [1] The experimenters simply set out to deprive individuals of differentiated light and sound by the use of goggles and earphones. In addition the subject was placed alone in a small room and give a 'panic-button' to press when he found the specially constructed environment had become too unbearable. The experimenters were greatly surprised to find out how disturbed their subjects became. Not only did they report hallucinations and delusions but few of the subjects could apparently stay within the room for any length of time despite being paid good money to do so. Later work in this area established that extroverts were less able to stand such sensory deprivation. At this stage of the game psychologists felt themselves to be well on the way to an account of differential environmental sensitivity, even suggesting that there might be a neuro-physiological basis for such observed individual differences. [2]

It was Martin Orne, another experimental psychologist, who put an end to some of these grander illusions and at the same time provided an important clue to the way in which man's varied relationships with his environment may be characterised. [3] Orne's experiment included all the 'accoutrements' of the usual sensory deprivation studies such as the screening of the subjects and the presence of a 'panic-button', but the actual environment was far from deprived. The subjects merely had to sit in a small well-lighted room with comfortable chairs, ice water and a sandwich. A control group received identical treatment except that they were told that they were control subjects for a sensory deprivation experiment and they had no panic-button. The results showed that the experimental subjects (those with the panic-button in the room) produced reactions to their situation which matched up to results obtained in other studies of sensory deprivation. Without the same experience, they were nevertheless still able to show the effects. They had in other words decided upon the *meaning* of their environment and responded in what they assumed to be an appropriate way.

This little experiment illustrates how even the most indefinite and undifferentiated environments are conceptualised by individuals, it shows that even the most temporary and artificial surroundings produce a distinctive reaction—a reaction based not on their intrinsic qualities, their abundance or their lack of stimulation, their size, shape or colour, but upon the characteristics with which they are imbued by the subjects who spend time within them. The subjects in the Orne experiment showed that they 'understood' their environment. They knew—or thought they knew—exactly what it meant and responded accordingly in terms of that meaning. The subjects were acting as they thought sophisticated psychology students should react to experimentally constructed environments. In the early experiments the experimenters had mistakenly assumed themselves to be the only beings who conceptualised the environment in distinctive ways.

The Chicago ecologists were far more sensitive than the experimental psychologists to problems about the meaning of the environment. This eminent group of sociologists who provided such a comprehensive picture of the development of urban life in America during the 1930s and 40s, did, for all their sensitivity to the environment, hold certain preconceptions about the way in which it would be conceptualised by those who occupied it. [4]

They observed certain characteristics of inner urban life—the deteriorating old houses, the high density of population, the lack of social facilities, the diversity of nationalities, and the high rate of mobility amongst the population. They did not simply say that such conditions determined particular psychological reactions but suggested that they led to a degree of social disorganisation which in its turn did produce some forms of psychic disturbance which was manifested as mental illness or deviance.

The ecologists looked at the characteristics of the urban environment, at the physical dereliction of the buildings, at the broken-down houses, the lack of community centres, and from this environmental conglomeration—this physical shambles—they generalized to a psychic disorganisation. The mix-up of buildings and people and nationalities— the whole general confusion—was said to have implications for the individual's attitudes:

"Everything is in a state of agitation—everything seems to be undergoing a change . . . *Habits can only be formed in a relatively stable environment* . . . Any form of change that brings any measurable alteration in the routine of social life tends to break up habits; and in breaking up the habits upon which the existing social organisation rests, destroys that organisation itself. Every new device that affects social life and social routine is to that extent a disorganising influence. Every new discovery, every new invention, every new idea, is disturbing."[5] (my italics).

But agitation and confusion as much as panic, depend upon the way in which the subject defines his situation. Did the subjects in the Orne experiment *really* panic and were the children of Chicago as confused and agitated as their interpreters thought them to be? The danger is that the ecologists create, through their impositions of a particular meaning upon the environment, a certain sort of delinquent. The one who smashes or breaks or fights will, according to this interpretation, be acting in this way because he lacks routines, norms, patterns. We know he lacks these because of our interpretation of his environment. It is surprising how readily we can slip from an environmental characterisation into a prediction of deviant behaviour. Consider the following description:

"Though the lines of the flats were clear and straight—the main asset— these blocks which were half a dozen years old already seemed to reflect a certain weariness of the spirit. Perhaps it was that skimpy detail spoke of the accountancy of remote public bodies: the entrance and stairways had already the neglected air of a place not loved; the whole impression was of too much public anonymity, of a space-saving set of buildings for those lucky enough to get in, but which produced no satisfying new way of community life."[6]

The writer generalises from the neat, weary, neglected, anonymous buildings to those who live in them—amongst whom are the Teddy Boys, a group of deviants whose behaviour is then interpreted as an

56

. . . the ghetto became recognised as a place constituted by compulsion not election . . .

attempt to find some alternative to this weary anonymity. Again this has a plausible ring. But the actual behaviour of the Teddy Boys may not have been very different from that of the Chicago delinquents—the behavioural descriptions which are available certainly do not make the distinction clear—but in one case the deviance is said to be produced by a disorganised environment and in the other by a highly organised one. In both cases we do not know enough about how the world looked to the boys themselves. Did they feel their world was physically disorganised or anonymous until they were told it was? Once told they could, of course, act up to the explanation just as well as those subjects in the Orne experiment who thought that they were on to the real

57

meaning of their situation. But before the interpreters got to work did the youth of the transitional zones of Chicago and of the council estates of England see their environments as 'deteriorated' or 'anonymous'?

This question is important because it may be that delinquents and deviants change more readily in response to cultural interpretations of their environment than they do in response to changing objective characteristics of that environment. The largest change which may have occurred in black urban ghettoes in the United States in recent years may be the wide-spread use of the term 'ghetto'. The environment becomes transformed by its description in these terms. Shop windows and lights and gas mains and street signs became 'theirs' and are therefore rendered expendable. The ghetto became recognised as a place constituted by compulsion, not by election. Once the environment is thus changed, the behaviour which takes place within it has a new meaning: 'Burn Baby Burn' is the cry of the political radical, not the individual arsonist.

We should take care therefore not to attribute some primitive aesthetic sense to working class children who smash up their council flats or the public flower displays. They may aesthetically prefer the flats and the flowers to the town slums and open bombed sites which they knew before, but they do know now that the flats and the flowers are not theirs. It is their meaning and not their intrinsic quality which is being reacted to. No amount of objective environmental manipulation will dissipate the destructive behaviour in this situation. It would be palpably absurd to back a scheme to brighten up the black ghettoes of America, to put a few adventure playgrounds in Watts, but sometimes our reaction to vandalism suggests that we ignore the subject's definition of his environment and imbue him with an artistic or romantic motive selected from a bourgeois compendium.

But if ecologists and psychologists are sometimes insensitive in the way they relate environmental characteristics and behaviour, this is even more true of all those biologists who turn environment into 'territory' and then proceed to account for aggression and destruction in terms of man's inherited predispositions. The evidence that man's immediate ancestors were territorial or aggressive is inconclusive enough to make these types of global claim suspect in the first place, but because of their popularity it may be worthwhile to spend a moment upon the inadequacy of their approach.

One of their fundamental concerns is overcrowding and its terrible consequences.

"Density surreptitiously creeping beyond the tolerance limits . . . may create symptoms which cannot be directly and easily traced back to it as their cause but are often attributed to factors which are merely contributory or symptomatic in themselves. The resulting constant subliminal tension will lower the individual's resistance towards other

58

disturbing factors. Thus I have no doubt whatever that a great number of neuroses and social maladjustments are partially or totally, directly or indirectly, caused by overcrowding".[7]

The subjective nature of the concept of overcrowding can be demonstrated in a variety of ways, but here I will draw upon research by Stanley Cohen and myself into long-term prisoners in a maximum security wing in order to show the range of variables which are involved in any felt discomfort in the presence of others.[8]

The prisoners reported to us that fights broke out in the wings and that there were serious tensions produced by so many men living in such proximity. At first we were surprised at these reports; the actual density of the wing was much less than that which most of the men had experienced in other prisons. However, when we had extensively interviewed the men and examined their letters and diaries we found that their concern with the environment could only be understood by reference to the specific expectations about privacy which are held by individuals in contemporary Western society. These men were not objectively overcrowded but they lacked *solitude, intimacy, anonymity* and *reserve.*[9] They lacked solitude in that they were never entirely alone and unobserved by others; they lacked intimacy because they had no way of creating an environment which would maximise personal affinity between themselves and one other person; they lacked anonymity because they were always identifiable by others at all times, and they lacked reserve in that personal details of their lives were known to everyone within the wing. We may in our own lives intermittently endure the absence of one or other of these states —but unlike the prisoners in a maximum security wing we do not have *continually* to face the absence of all four states of privacy. And most importantly—when such states are lacking we do not feel deprived of them as a *punishment*. In any attempt to understand the prisoner's reaction to his environment, all these factors need to be taken into account—and all such factors have a social and cultural relativity. They did not obtain with equal stress at different times or with different men. This is not to detract from the suffering which their absence in the environment produces, but only to dismiss as worthless the vapid generalisations of those biologists who expect to account comprehensively for deviant behaviour by referring to universal genetic predispositions. Space in prison has a different meaning from space at home or space at work. In each case it can only be discussed with reference to the whole way in which the individual conceptualises his predicament.

There is a certain irony in the revival of naive biological views at the present time, for it is in recent years that sociologists, linguists, anthropologists and psychologists have made great advances in the study of personal and social space and have mapped the sensitive ways in which individuals use the environment in the course of social interaction. The general name given to the study of such matters varies. It has been called proxemics, micro-ecology and kinesics. Kinesics is the more general term and it is this that we will use here. The kinesiologists are less grandiose in their claims.[10] Their concern is primarily with environment as subjectively appreciated. They pay little attention to walls and houses and buildings and instead concentrate upon the spaces which people make around themselves and between themselves and others—personal and inter-personal space. Their investigations have shown that there are preferred distances for particular types of conversations, that there are cultural differences in the size of these distances. We may be embarrassed by those from another culture who stand too close to us—who invade our personal space, and we may express this embarrassment by rejecting the other as an alien, as someone different, although we are unable to describe the source of our discomfort. It has been suggested that failures to maintain personal space may also be interpreted as a sign of abnormality or even madness in adults, or of immaturity in children. There is some evidence that 'abnormal' people can be trained to use personal space and that following such training, they will be viewed by others as more pleasant and attractive.

The idea of a personal environment is an important one, but as with other environmental approaches there is a tendency to play up its inflexible nature and to ignore the circumstances in which men use their mastery of personal space to create favourable situations for themselves. But a much greater danger lies in the assumption that there is nothing much we can do about such micro-ecological conventions. For rooted within such apparently trivial ways of behaviour may be fundamentally conservative values.[11] Keeping our distance from another is not simply an arbitrary convention, it is one which allows the other's importance to be recognised. The interposition of a desk between teacher and taught tells us as much about the relationship between the two groups as any analysis of what is being said. It may be more revolutionary to throw away the desk than to revise the curriculum in these circumstances, for the maintenance of personal space which the desk ensures necessarily influences the reception and transmission of any information which is provided—no matter how objectively radical this may be. Windows, bars, counters and desks describe relationships whilst they also mark off physical space. In this way they are appropriate objects for destruction by anyone who considers a revolution in everyday life to be a necessary prelude to wider structural changes. These apparently neutral environmental objects are saturated with meaning. There have been times when the conventions of everyday spatial arrangements have been challenged. Such challenges have been initiated principally by artists, by groups like the surrealists who attempted to show that the physical world which presented itself to our senses lacked solidity and reality. By distorting everyday commodities in their art, they hoped to suggest to others the arbitrariness of common objects. This attack upon everyday reality has been broadened by such political groups as the Situationists. This group which had a profound influence upon the culture of the May 1968 uprising in France, draws attention not only to the 'unreality' of material commodities, but also stresses the repressing nature of the type of everyday interactional conventions described by the kinesiologist. Situationist groups in recent years have deliberately attempted to distort conventions of the social environment; the sudden shock which they produced by ignoring kinesic expectations is regarded as one way in which the apparently solid conventional world can be punctured. Once again there is plenty of evidence here that men can differ from social scientists in the meaning which they attach to the environment. For according to some of the perspectives we have just been describing, conventions about personal space become not cultural 'givens' which determine aspects of social interaction, but are rather seen as subtle ways in which existing social relationships are maintained.

As a final example of the differences in meaning which the environment may contain, I would like to refer to some research on industrial sabotage. A few years ago, Paul Walton and I set out to investigate this common industrial phenomenon.[12] We had some preconceived ideas about what we would find. In particular we expected sabotage to emerge as a form of political protest, an expression of the workers' lack of control over the factory environment. Indeed, we claimed in an early paper that most industrial sabotage was an assertion of control, that it was a way in which men sought to change the world when other more immediately efficacious methods were not available to them. We were able to draw at that time upon the reinterpretations of Luddite behaviour which showed such machine-smashing to have been an example of 'collective bargaining by riot' rather than the actions of a group of rural idiots fighting progress (see Stanley Cohen's remarks in Chapter 1). But as more of our data was processed we realised that we could not hang on to our original hypothesis. Industrial sabotage was not simply a means by which men gained control, a way in which they collectively asserted their political will over time, it was also a method by which varying statements about the quality of life and environment were made. The behaviour had more than one meaning and its nature was extremely diverse; it was individual as well as collective, funny as well as bitter, spontaneous as well as planned. Identical acts had quite different meanings. Fires were regularly started amongst combustible materials, production belts were regularly twisted and cut, foreign objects were repeatedly introduced into commodities during their manufacture, but one could not attach one meaning to each particular type of act. Instead we found several major complexes of meaning. In the first case workers said that they smashed in order to reduce tension and frustration. This type of sabotage was a 'blind swipe' at anything that was around; it was a response to an intolerable situation which could not be attributed specifically to any one person or group of persons. The environment was at hand for attack, but it was not attacked because of its intrinsic characteristics, nor because of its symbolic significance. This type of sabotage:

1. Did not aim to restructure social relationships, to redistribute power.
2. Did not necessarily make life any easier.
3. Did not *directly* challenge authority.
4. Was not spontaneous.
5. Occurred in a situation in which what or who got hurt was relatively arbitrary.

An alternative reason for smashing or breaking was utilitarian. This type of sabotage 'helped things along', it 'cut through the red tape'. Sabotage of this type involved breaking safety guards and using special although illegal tools to speed up production. The environment was conceived of as manipulable for limited personal ends. It could be used. This type of sabotage:

1. Did not aim to restructure social relationships.
2. Attempted to make life easier.
3. Could directly challenge some levels of authority.
4. Involved planning.
5. Had a highly specific target.

The third major meaning given to sabotage was political. Men told us that they had smashed this or that in order to gain some control, to 'show them who was in charge'. These men saw the environment as belonging to others. It was not 'theirs'. It was alien to them and was perceived as persistently oppressive. Their sabotage:

1. Aimed to restructure social relationships—to gain control.
2. Did not make life easier.
3. Involved a direct challenge to authority.
4. Was planned.
5. Did not have an arbitrary target.

I have described these three types in some detail because implicit within each is the conception of the environment which is held by the actor, and in each case this conception is very different. In the first type, the environment is just *there*, a *tabula rasa* upon which to scrawl obscenities. In the second case it is there to be manipulated, it can be twisted to serve one's ends. In the third case it is *theirs* and must therefore be taken over or commandeered before it can be used by others. When men act against their physical environments as they do in the case of industrial sabotage and vandalism, their activity contains within it conceptions of the origins and meaning of that environment. In the past we have been too ready to assume that the activity was somehow entailed by the nature of the environment (e.g. its drabness, its monotony), or by certain territorial or biological givens (e.g. ideas of maximum density) or by particular proxemic necessities (e.g. the need for particular amounts of personal space). We have thereby paid too much attention to the characteristics of the environment and not enough to the conceptualisations of the actor.

Many men in our society are in the position of 'madmen' locked within padded cells. They have no evident ways to communicate their ideas about the world. In these circumstances they may take to scrawling obscenities with their own excrement upon the walls of the cell. We are doing these people a disservice if we ignore the message and instead concentrate upon the way in which an environmental given (the padded cell) had produced a particular deviant act (writing with excrement). If we concentrate upon the cell and the excrement, we ignore the message of the obscenities which tell us that the individual regards this environment as alien and oppressive. The writing is not a reaction to environmental givens, it is an interpretation of them, a statement about the origins and the relative mutability of this bit of the physical world.

The torn conveyor belts, broken street lamps and smashed schools are statements made by people who have few other opportunities for self-expression. They are as meaningful and as lacking in abnormality as the scrawling done by the mental patient. They are the voices of those rendered dumb by their lack of access to prison and pulpit and camera. We must therefore be especially careful to understand such statements and to resist temptations to fit them into some pre-existing schema based upon a simplistic view of the environment as some element in our lives with intrinsic qualities capable of producing determinate reactions. As our industrial sabotage research showed, quite simple (and even identical) destructive acts may contain within them highly differentiated and subtle statements about the nature of the world in which man finds himself.

3 Delinquency and some aspects of housing

Gail Armstrong and Mary Wilson

The notion that the built environment is an important factor in structuring and directing social behaviour appears to have a certain popularity at the present time, significantly among politicians and some professional groups, as well as the general public. It is not the intention here to explore the whole range of what might be termed 'social behaviour.' or 'social life' and its relation to the built form—probably an impossible task!—but rather to consider to what extent such a notion is useful in explaining how certain forms of *deviant* behaviour are produced in society. In particular we shall focus on the relationship between *delinquency* and the built form, and in pursuing this theme draw on our observations of a 'delinquent area' in Glasgow—Easterhouse. In the following pages we put forward some evidence indicating the presence of the belief sometimes termed 'architectural determinism' and in doing so, attempt to account for its emergence. By presenting the findings of our research in Easterhouse we shall show that certain physical features of the estate *did* provide a setting in which resident youth came to be seen as a delinquent population, but for several reasons such a setting could in no way provide a total explanation of youth behaviour. We shall argue then that rather than being directly a cause of deviant behaviour, the built environment constituted one (and by no means the most important) situational factor in the process of Easterhouse becoming a 'delinquent area'.

ARCHITECTURAL DETERMINISM
The prevalence of the notion within architectural and planning circles that aspects of the built environment structure social life, has been carefully documented by Alan Lipman:

"Architectural social theory contends that the social behaviour of building users is influenced and even determined by the physical environment in which the behaviour occurs; in this context the belief system includes the concept that architects direct social behaviour patterns through their work".[1]

It is not possible for us to indicate how widely this belief is held, nor the degree to which it forms a guiding principle in the everyday professional practice of architects and planners. However, if the themes

64

Manila or Bogota? This embattled supermarket is in fact in the Blackhill housing scheme, Glasgow

taken up in the professional journals in recent years are any indication, we can safely say that many architects (especially those concerned with housing) clearly regard themselves at least as in some kind of 'welfare' role[2], if not in the forefront of social change; with an increasing responsibility for the nature and quality of social life. Indeed, the recent introduction of Sociology into Royal Institute of British Architects undergraduate courses suggests, in terms of the syllabus set, a belief that sociologists can provide a 'blue-print' for the architect regarding the means available to him for structuring the social environment[3]. Nevertheless we must add that from personal teaching experience, it appears that students of the subject can approach the notion with a far healthier scepticism than several of the writers in this field. In one popular work, written by two architects, the belief holds so much currency that we are spoiled for choice regarding quotation:

"Civic beauty, as a whole, is consciously shared and does much to induce feelings of loyalty, pride and patriotism. So strong are these physical features of urbanity, that even a stranger, a visitor, cannot escape their impact."[4]

And again:

"A new physical urban order is needed to give expression and meaning

65

to the life of 'urbanising' man, to clarify, to define, and to give integrity to human purposes and organisation."[5]

Regarding the relationship between the built form and socially deviant behaviour, we can see that the public at large has occasionally been presented with the notion via such articles as the colour supplement feature which appeared to invite the question: "Where have we gone wrong?" The dominant theme of this piece was, briefly, 'here we have a high award-winning housing development which nevertheless harbours juveniles who can kill'.[6] It is interesting to note professional sensitivity to these (sometimes veiled) criticisms, an illustration of which was provided by the discussion as to whether or not some kind of public relations department should be established by the profession.[7]

Although architects do turn to the social scientist for a 'blue-print', there is very little (much to their surprise!) in the way of empirical research in this area—clearly a reflection of the latter's scepticism or lack of interest in this thesis. One careful attempt at measuring the effect of proximity of residence on friendship formation concluded with the statement:

". . . (only) . . . in a community of people who are homogeneous with respect to many of the factors which determine the development of friendships, the physical factors arising from the arrangement of houses are major determinants of what friendships will develop and what social groups will be formed."[8]

Other studies which touch on the thesis 'in passing' are sometimes eagerly taken up by its adherents and severely mis-quoted or mis-applied;[9] but typically research covering the relevant data would appear to support the argument of Festinger *et al*, cited above, that the built environment cannot usefully be seen as a major determinant of social behaviour. Students of urban sociology are generally much more interested in investigating the extent to which certain types of social organisation have consequences for the built form.[10] One student of deviant behaviour, after reviewing the research into relationship between substandard housing and deviance, concludes:

"A careful examination of the high deviation rates of the slums does not indicate that either low economic status or bad housing is the explanation. Although studies indicate that rates of deviation and bad housing are correlated, this fact in itself is not the important variable. One comprehensive report on housing lists as a popular fallacy that 'substandard housing is the direct cause of delinquency and crime and that its elimination would result in a crimeless world'."[11]

Despite the dearth of empirical information, then, the notion appears to persist, and certainly regarding the 'Easterhouse problem' there is clear evidence of its prevalence amongst Glasgow's political figures (and others) who were anxious to cite the 'concrete jungle' arguments as explanations of gang violence in the area. This point will be elaborated below, but at present it is necessary to attempt to sketch the emergence of such a belief on a more general level.

Historical roots of the notion

In attempting to account for the emergence of 'architectural determinism' three broad themes need to be treated: firstly, the structural and ideological changes brought about by the industrial revolution and the shift in emphasis thus brought about from a 'punitive' to a 'corrective/preventive' oriented system of social control; secondly, the emergence of the ecological school of sociology, especially the Chicago school[12] as representing a re-location of the notion of pathology from the individual to his environment; and thirdly, the accompanying changes brought about in the role of the architect.

I. Industrialisation and social control

Explanations of criminal behaviour have, historically, been closely linked with systems of, and recommendation for, social control. Thus in the 'welfare state' we see the emergence of social work agencies such as probation, child care, etc., most of which are heavily influenced by ideas derived from the field of psychiatry. The emergence of such agencies of social control represents a shift to a 'treatment' approach to deviance, and a view of the deviant which suggests that 'it is not really his fault'—he is seen as an individual not capable of moral responsibility being propelled into deviant activity through circumstances often outside his control.

In the middle years of the last century, in the midst of a rapidly urbanising and industrialising society, the poor social and housing conditions of our large towns and cities came to be seen as breeding grounds for all kinds of 'immorality'—vagrancy, crime, prostitution, drunkenness and all the rest. There was, it was felt, a serious threat to the very fabric of our society, and a likelihood that uprisings similar to those experienced on the continent might occur if steps were not taken at least to 'contain' the situation. One author has posed the question 'why *should* housing be seen as a social problem at all?'. His answer is highly relevant to our discussion, and so we quote at length:

"The belief that housing and neighbourhoods were 'social problems' is largely based on the notion that problems arising in areas filled with people are in some way contagious. This contagion is largely confined to such 'diseases' as criminality, poverty, illiteracy, and physical breakdowns. Some people, however, are concerned with the slums because of their suspicion that those living inside the slums are likely to have anarchistic effects upon the society as a whole . . . In the same vein, urban redevelopers in the new nations have said that housing is their country's *number one* problem. Asked why they think this, they say, 'We believe that the people who are have-nots, who are concentrated in these areas, are going to create massive civil disobedience in this society'. In old and new nations alike, the old fear of the have-nots crowded into certain areas of the city is still powerful. The 'haves' see the slums as the bailiwicks of disease, organised crime and revolution. This belief has been largely due to rapid urbanisation, and the development of 'non-citizens' within the urban society as a whole. One origin of the notion that housing is a special problem is the assumption that we *create* outsiders by housing them together in segregated parts of the city. Culturally different and differently rewarded, the successful do not find it comfortable to deal with such people. Therefore the interest in abolishing the slums; it is thought that improved housing increases the outsider's stake in the society, in law and order. The outsider is tied to a house as to a 'social anchor'. (Others, of course, prefer to build walls around the slums.)[13]

On a wider level, then, in terms of the general 'diseases' of the industrialising city, it was argued that dissent would result in Britain from members of the working classes being unable to shape their own lives for the better due to the pressures of industrial life. Thus, where possible, the state should remove these pressures and provide a place for the working man within the existing system. Within this framework, correction as opposed to punishment earned a place, this new 'ideology' owing much to the pioneering work of Rowntree, the Webbs, etc. . . .[14]

Certainly the early protagonists of the Town Planning movement consistently used arguments to this effect.[15] The history of this movement, although demonstrating a lamentable inability to provide better housing, contains numerous illustrations of the belief that the control of housing can restructure and redirect social life, be it the paternalism/commercialism of the pioneering philanthropic housing associations, or the radical idealism of figures such as Owen. Indeed, the emergence of town planning first as a permissive and later as an obligatory function of local government has had far-reaching consequences for the architectural profession, a point we shall refer to presently.

However, it was during this period of rapid urbanisation and industrialisation that housing can be said to have emerged as a 'social problem', that is, the effects of bad housing were seen as threatening to the social order, and consequently, 'something had to be done'. Since deviance appeared most visibly in the worst pockets of urban housing, it currently came to be understood that the control of these conditions would at least go some way towards the control of deviant behaviour, while if the problem were allowed to run its free course such areas would become the breeding grounds of criminality, prostitution, irreligiousness and the like.

II. The 'sick' environment

The observation that certain areas of many large towns and cities produced high official rates of deviance subsequently came to be expressed in theoretical terms via the concept of pathology or 'sickness'.[16] The ecological school of deviance, following largely from Wirth's work,[17] contends that certain relationships *can* be spelled out between the natural or physical environment and the social environment: it is held that in areas which contain high rates of official deviance, something has gone wrong with the 'normal' relationship between man and his environment. A notion of 'sickness' or pathology is often introduced to explain such rates: a part of society is disintegrating, breaking-down, etc. In addition, it is held that once the 'sickness' has taken hold of an area there is a likelihood of its spreading rapidly if something is not done to contain, if not to 'cure' it. Ecological theory still retains a large influence both in urban sociology generally and in the sociology of deviance.

Although some evidence has been supplied to demonstrate that certain residential areas (typically those central ones in large cities) maintain high official rates of crime, mental illness and drug addiction, for example, such evidence is far from complete enough to indicate that there is something in the nature of the physical environment which 'triggers off' deviance, as it were. Both over-crowding and isolation have been found to be correlated with suicide, but we cannot conclude from this that the one 'causes' the other: voting conservative may be correlated with telephone ownership, but the two are not causally related.

This type of research raises more issues than it resolves. Because of its very restricted understanding of deviant phenomena (in terms of a deviant/law-breaking population which is in some way 'different' from the 'normal' population, requiring some kind of 'antidote' to bring it back to conformity), it can make no contribution to our understanding of why certain types of deviance appear in certain forms in society (or alternatively why certain types of behaviour come to be condemned), nor why certain people commit deviant acts, nor in general what it means—and especially what it feels like—to be, and be seen as, a deviant. The errors of such research have been discussed elsewhere.[18] The main point we would take issue with—and this is by no means restricted to ecological theories of deviance—is the notion that the deviant is some kind of defective human being. In the case of Yablonsky's work we are led to understand that the 'socio-pathic' personalities of the New York gang-boys he studied had been produced by the dis-equilibrium of the multi-racial slum; but what of those young slum-dwellers who escaped gang involvement?[19] In other words we are presented with a pathological and deterministic portrait of the deviant.

As Stanley Cohen has pointed out, deviance as a social phenomenon can in no way be conceptualised as some sort of 'social cancer', but rather is a property conferred on behaviour by others—for a series of reasons. Most importantly, the means whereby certain groups *become labelled* as deviant and selected for social control, is basically a *political process*. A detailed survey of the social/psychological characteristics of deviants, including such data as family size, place of residence, school record, etc., does not bring us towards an explanation of deviant status—although as Cicourel[20] has carefully demonstrated, it may provide an explanation of the process whereby some individuals rather than others are likely to be selected for *official control*.

Even where correlations have been found between, for example, over-crowding and criminality, the use of official statistics as an index of 'criminal area' is misguided in the extreme. This is because the process whereby such statistics are collected involves the selection of a criminal class from a pool of law-breakers in a very unrepresentative but predictable way: that is largely by social class and other 'non-criminal' aspects of the offender.[21] Illustrations of this process are provided by recent press reports: in one case it was decided not to take action against the young gentlemen found 'experimenting' with drugs at one of our well-known public schools, and during the same week the top management of Claridges admitted to 'turning a blind eye' to those visiting celebrities who steal from their establishment.[22]

Thus it is mistaken to view the 'official' criminal class as the 'real' criminal class, and being different from the rest of us 'normals' because of some sort of mental or moral defect. In the case of delinquency, for example, studies have shown that as much as 80% of the young male population confesses to having broken the law—such a number cannot be justifiably termed as a 'deviant minority'!

But perhaps most importantly, to suggest that criminals are somehow 'ill' because they break the rules of the State is to suggest that the rules of the State must universally define what is 'good', 'moral', etc., which does not acknowledge the several systems of morality which may be present in one social system, the analytical distinction between law and morality, and, surely, any person's right to dissent. Few sociologists have ventured to pose the question 'Whose morality prevails in our society?', which is interesting, to say the least, when we consider that there are remarkably few acts which are universally condemned regardless of who commits them. The technically criminal behaviour of those at the top of the social pyramid—namely 'white collar crime' as it has been termed—is often ignored.[23] The deviant category has been taken to be that portion selected for control, while the central preoccupation among criminologists has been 'What makes them different from the normal population?', together with 'What is it about working class culture that produces delinquent/criminal types?' since official records are weighted in terms of the working classes.

Until recently the fact that working class criminality is produced by the control apparatus in society, has been largely ignored. The actions of the soldier who kills or the public schoolboy who uses drugs are understood with reference to wider or more dominant social values; the soldier kills for 'democracy' and the public schoolboy 'experiments'

70

with drugs. Yet on turning to the street-corner boy we have typically responded with the question 'What made him go wrong?' without appreciating the situational inducement which may have channelled his behaviour in a certain direction.

The role of the architect

With town planning came changes in architecture as a profession: the decline in patronage as the architect began designing for the masses, and his consequent increasing association with building technology. The social distance between the architect and his client (that is: with the future occupant of a new building) has become wide—occupation, life-style, income and hence needs are at extremes, when we consider, for example, the residents of municipal housing estates. It would seem fair to say that the role or scope of the architect has narrowed considerably —the aesthetic aspects of architecture have perhaps declined with the stress on function and the problem of justifying expenses incurred. It is in terms of this narrowing of the architect's role that Lipman begins to explain the emergent preoccupation of the architect with the social implications of building:

". . . today the profession operates with an unprecedented armoury of technical equipment and knowledge, and in consequence, the traditional self-image as artist has been dislocated. In meeting this architects tend to lean on a similarly traditional but relatively latent self-conception as social engineers . . . The belief can also compensate for the tensions which result from the technological preoccupations forced on architects in recent years. Meeting mass demands for buildings appears to be impossible without utilisation of the techniques of mass-production and immersion in technological know-how; familiarisation with tech-niques such as modular co-ordination, critical path analysis, and systematic design method have become required study for an occupa-tion which remains rooted in its craft origins. Architects can find that tension management is, to some degree, accomplished by their belief that they 'manage' social relationships."[24]

Briefly, then, we have the situation where housing has become an industry like any other, the architect acting more in the capacity of engineer than creative artist. Within this context the profession has come to be justified from a welfare angle, acting along with planners as a type of control agent in so far as the sort of housing produced is expected in some way to contribute to the quality of community life. This is perhaps especially manifested in the case of New Towns, where a better quality of community life is expected to emerge, with the size of units, the placing of dwellings and the provision of amenities— together with the removal of traffic—being seen as its major determin-ants.

So far, we have been trying to explain the presence of the belief termed 'architectural determinism', given that although it appears to have fairly wide currency it is indeed misplaced. We have discussed the belief alongside the general notion that the physical nature of the city is causally connected with social deviation, and have historically located the emergence of the town planning movement and the changing role of the architect along with the general changes in social control as fear of a breakdown in the social order became expressed. We have criticised current theories of deviance and delinquency where the deviant is seen as 'sick' or incapable of moral choice, suggesting that most current research in delinquency fails to acknowledge the social and political process whereby behaviour comes to be *defined* as deviant. For deviance can only be conceptualised in terms of the social system of which it is a part—only in a society where stress is laid on the value of private property, for example, can theft form a major category of crime. We must acknowledge such factors in our attempts to understand deviance as a social phenomenon.

In attempting to understand the behaviour of the individual deviant who knowingly engages in 'deviant acts' we need to recognise that:

(*a*) the deviants who form the institutional population—prisons, etc., do not form the total population of deviants.

(*b*) the deviant may engage in his behaviour through a belief that it is not morally wrong—through being one of a minority group, for example, whose values are at odds with those represented by the state.

(*c*) once a person becomes publicly defined as deviant—typically through being apprehended by the police and processed through the control system—there is some evidence to suggest that his chances of conformity are decreased.[25] This is illustrated in the example of the drug-taker, who, once detected and sentenced, may have problems of obtaining employment; he may as a result turn to crime to support himself, turn to others who share his social situation—a 'sub-culture of addicts'—whose culture is likely to support and increase his original deviance.

It is this stance which has directed our research in Easterhouse, and we now turn to our own data to discuss more fully the relationship between delinquency and housing on this estate.

EASTERHOUSE: A DELINQUENT AREA

In the summer of 1968, Easterhouse became widely recognised in Scotland (and throughout Britain) as constituting Glasgow's worst 'trouble-spot' for gang violence. At that time it seemed the obvious choice for those interested in researching the field of delinquency/gang violence, and our own study of the area commenced in January 1969. As members of the Glasgow public, our knowledge of Easterhouse youth was very largely restricted to information communicated by the mass media, and coloured by such reports as:

"Frankie Vaughan's challenge to the violent boys of Easterhouse has been accepted . . . None of the boys" (interviewed for this article) "can reveal their addresses in Europe's largest housing scheme:—'I don't want another gang to find out where I live, that's suicide'—they said."[26] and banner headlines such as:

"O.K. Frankie, We Will Surrender Our Swords, Bayonets, Knives, Meat Cleavers and Iron Railings: By Four Gangs"[27]

We were somewhat surprised, then, if not confused, when six months later, after a period of close and informal contact with the Easterhouse boys, it seemed impossible to isolate any objective conditions which may have fostered the widespread gang violence purported to exist there. At the same time, however, we came to suspect that the 'public reputation' of Easterhouse gang boys was ill-founded, and represented a distorted view of what was actually happening in the area. This suspicion arose because:

(a) There was a discrepancy between newspaper accounts and our own eye-witness accounts of particular incidents.[28]

(b) Independently of what was happening in the area, a stereotypical view of the Easterhouse gang boy persisted, especially in the media— radical students, strikers and the Viet-cong were a few of the groups with which comparisons were drawn. The area became a source of interest to a whole range of public figures, professional social workers, foreign visitors and the like; so that even at times when the area was of no immediate 'news value' films were appearing on Dutch and American—as well as British—television, depicting Easterhouse as some kind of gangster's paradise. Students of social work were 'treated' to conducted tours.

(c) At times (particularly after the publicising of 'gang' incidents) we observed a marked widening of police definitions of what constituted 'delinquent' behaviour. A pop group returning from an evening rehearsal was charged with carrying an offensive weapon—a pair of cymbals; a group standing at a bus-stop was charged with loitering; and there are many more examples. The discovery that some local families were anxious to conceal their place of residence when making arrangements for holiday accommodation—as were young school leavers when applying for jobs—focussed our attention on what appeared to be a highly significant feature of the 'Easterhouse problem': the emergence and effects of the reputation itself.

By March, 1969 the feeling of being 'ostracised' was so widespread in the area that the residents initiated the 'Easterhouse Fights Back Campaign'. The major source of the discontent was the 'exaggerated and distorted reporting' of a particular Scottish newspaper[29]; but in addition, residents saw themselves as being discriminated against by the local administration and being treated as 'slum-dwellers', as they termed it. An example of the latter occurred when one urban official was reported in the press as saying that he was opposed to the installation of wooden fencing around gardens in Easterhouse because it would only be ripped up and used for weapons.

While we could not deny the existence of gang rivalry in the area, at the same time it became evident that it was by no means as widespread, as highly organised, nor were members as committed to the use of weapons, as was commonly believed. Further, this misconception of the 'violent gang' had served to amplify the phenomenon, both in terms of the *behaviour* itself, and in terms of the volume of *official* delinquency. The public reputation of Easterhouse youth was feeding back into the area and having several important consequences for youth.[30]

Thus, in order to understand the emergence of the reputation, we were directed towards an investigation of the processes of interaction between Easterhouse 'delinquents' and the definers of delinquency. We had entered a situation where the public definitions of Easterhouse youth (albeit misconceived) had been 'translated into reality', to use Jock Young's term.[31] The space available to us here does not permit us to recount a detailed history of Easterhouse as a delinquent area.[32] However, below we offer a brief (and incomplete) sketch of the development of the gang which refers to both the objective conditions prevailing in the locality, *and* the subjective world of the Easterhouse boys which served to structure and direct their behaviour.

The setting
In the post-war period, Glasgow, like any other large city, was confronted by a severe housing shortage. In order to alleviate the problem four large housing developments were planned, and by the early 1950s Easterhouse, the last and the largest, was completed. As is frequently the case, the quality of the environment became a secondary consideration, and 9,100 almost identical dwellings were built. It was some years before such basic amenities as schools, transport and shopping facilities were established. Indeed, even at the time of writing one could hardly suggest the community is adequately provided for in some respects; shopping facilities are minimal while social and recreational needs are solely catered for by the schools and churches, supplemented by one public house. This community, about five miles from the city centre, and housing more than 40,000 people, has neither banks nor public offices.

Easterhouse has been described as "an area which has no heart"[33], perhaps a reference to the dearth of cultural and social outlets available to its residents; but moreover, those which *are* provided have been situated on a 'scheme' basis. Four 'schemes' or neighbourhoods are readily distinguishable, which until recently were divided by areas of undeveloped wasteland, football pitches, etc. Because the shops, schools, churches and so on tend to be local to each scheme, there is little opportunity (or need) for social mixing to take place *between* them.

74

Bus route through a post-war Glasgow estate. Note the poor standards of construction and maintenance and the use of the pavement by the bus

The result has been for residents of all ages to identify with their own neighbourhood, rather than with the Easterhouse area, the most explicit expression of which has been the 'territory' based gang.

Clearly it would be misguided to point to such deficiencies in, or features of, the built environment as causing the emergence of the violent gang in Easterhouse; many middle class suburbs are equally deprived yet do not produce a similar phenomenon. The street-corner group was evident long before violence and the carrying of weapons became a norm in the area: the importance of the built environment and the local demography lies in the fact that it was able to structure the pattern of youth relationships. The transition from street-corner group to violent gang involves a qualitative change in behaviour, and in order to explain this it is necessary to refer to the subjective definitions of the situation held by the actors themselves.

Having discarded the notion that deviant subjects are in a sense propelled into their activity through a kind of 'moral defect', then we must consider their motives to be meaningful. Further, accepting that they are capable of moral responsibility, then we must regard their perceptions of the situation as having at least some basis in objective reality.

For many, the move to Easterhouse represented a substantial improvement in living conditions; for some it was their first 'home of their own', whilst other young families had enjoyed the relative privacy of a room-and-kitchen or single-end[34] in one or other of the city's decaying areas. As one teenager recalled:

"The old lady was always telling us to speak proper and not to swear; I remember getting really upset because we couldn't bring the dog, the Corporation didn't allow it."

Some, it appears, envisaged a 'new start', but it wasn't long before children playing football in the streets and teenagers meeting their friends on the corners, came to be seen as something of a nuisance, both to some residents and to the police.

In 1961 almost half the population was under the age of twenty-one, and for those with little interest in the activities of the Scouts and other church organisations, the only (if not the obvious meeting-place was the street-corner. It was this highly visible and extensive practice of peers meeting at the street-corner 'hangout', indulging in what are considered 'normal' levels of delinquency[35] which came to be construed as an extensive net-work of highly organised and aggressive gangs.

One cannot deny that rivalry existed between youth from the different neighbourhoods, nor that at times it has been intense and has involved the use of weapons. However, in looking at the history of the gang we can see that changes in youth behaviour are closely related to redefinitions of youth behaviour by others (especially control agents, formal and informal, and neighbouring peers), paralleled by the gang boys' redefinition of themselves.

The street-corner gang

The 'territory' based pattern of youth associations seems to have been a likely consequence of the physical lay-out and size of the community described above. Ironically, however, it was residents' attempts to create a community-wide recreational activity which provided a structure which persisted, and around which the gangs later formed.

Easterhouse boys often refer to their peer group as a 'team'. In the early 60s the focal activity of these teams was competitive football—the Rebels, the Pak, the Toi and the Drummy representing each of the four neighbourhoods. (It is interesting to note that residents themselves came to refer to the neighbourhoods by these 'team' names.) According to the local boys the street-corner gang emerged when the older lads began seeking alternative leisure activities:

"It was through playing football that it all started. Used to hang about the corner after the game. After I left school there was nothing do to except hang about, you'd just hang about with the same crowd. If any-one got dug-up (usually a verbal derogation or provocation), you'd all go down; that was classed as a 'gang fight'." (aged 21).

76

And as another boy put it:

". . . well, the only thing you *could* do was play football in the streets, half the streets weren't paved yet, still mud tracks. Used to play football, go for walks and that . . . when I was 15, that was when I started going about. Started playing football with the Rebels. Then I just started going down, y'know going about with them at night an' that. That was me." (aged 20)

The vast majority of gang boys relate similar experiences. At this point in time, so-called gang fights seemed to be an extension of rivalries featured on the football field; it was 'good for a laugh', as the 20-year old quoted above recalls:

"It used to be good going down with them because you thought you were great, y'know, that was you an' that, thought you was a big man. Used to go with them and watch them fight, used to stay at the back at first, shout and throw bricks and bottles, you thought it was great. You really enjoyed yourself. It was great entertainment it was (laughs)."

In this advertisement for polycarbonate light fittings the vandal is distinctly regional in appearance

BEAT THE VANDALS...

with the Extended Coughtrie range of Polycarbonate fittings

Now Coughtrie have extended the range of fittings with diffusers or covers made in *polycarbonate,* the new well-nigh unbreakable plastic. So Local Authorities now have a wider selection in fighting the high cost of maintenance caused by vandalism.

We say "well-nigh" unbreakable because we do not claim they are bullet-proof. At the same time you are welcome to try a 5 lb. club hammer on them. We did, and we didn't have much success! It will pay you handsomely to write for full details of the Coughtrie polycarbonate range.

Asked if there were ever any casualties:

"No, there were no weapons, knives an' that; just sticks to bash them over the head. Used to (laughs), used to be great y'know, everybody used to know each other, say the person on the other side, you knew him from school or something, used to go 'How's it going'? an' that, but you'd still fling bricks at him! I don't know what really made us do it. There was nothing else to do I don't think. We just let off steam, that's all it was. It was better than playing football."

However, it was these activities which came to be viewed in a rather more serious light by local officials and residents. In 1965 a confidential report to the Corporation[36] entitled *Ways of Dealing with Vandalism*, notes that:

"Already, rivalry of a disturbing sort exists between the youth from the different schemes."

It was about this time that a special mobile police squad appears to have focussed its attention on the area:

"Used to walk out your close and the polis would lift you. This was really before any of the fighting had really begun, y'know, as bad as it was. They used to lift you as you was walking out the close; the fighting had all just started and it was just throwing bricks and that, so they brought this riot squad up. And as you were walking out the close they would lift you, go round to somebody's else's close and lift them, until they got about eight of you, then do you for breach of the peace, disorderly crowd or that. That kinda maddened the boys . . . getting booked three or four times in the one night sometimes. That was for nothing, even if you was standing at the corner and they got a lot of you, they would do you for breach of the peace. Wasn't ever doing nothing."

When asked "How do you mean, 'maddened them'?";

"Well, they were all kind a going crazy about it, blokes getting three or four times lifted in one night, names getting took, getting £5 and £10 fines . . . some of them couldn't even leave the scheme after that, they had that many fines to pay. Couldn't go to the dancing or anything like that, paying £3 and £4 away in fines each week."

In 1967 a small local police office was established in Easterhouse, and what appears to be a public relations handout describes the "riot squad" thus:

"One dormobile van operates from . . . (divisional HQ) . . . and is manned by one sergeant and four constables in plain clothes and patrols from 10 am daily. They are better known as 'The Untouchables' or to the Police Officers as 'Echo 10' their radio call sign."

It was clearly hoped that the introduction of this squad would go a long way towards discouraging 'gang activity', their preventative role being described in the same document thus:

"GROUP DISORDERS: . . . Many anonymous phone calls are received from residents in the area that a number of youths are loitering at a particular locus, and they are usually apprehensive about their future conduct. This is deal with by the plain clothes crew of Echo 10 or the Untouchables."

However, it is equally clear that just the opposite effect was produced:

"I can't remember really when they started, but they were running about daft . . . remember a couple of times I'd just walked out the close meet somebody at the close and just stand talking to them; you'd see them coming, you knew the score and you had to go back up to the house again . . . Well you knew they were going to lift you, do you for something so it got to the stage you had to run away from them all the time. And they were just going like that, Aye! And any gang fights an' that wouldn't stand about when the polis came, you'd run away. And you'd see it in the papers the next day about 'they all ran away when the polis came'. But you see, if there was a gang fight, the polis would just lift you off the street after it, anybody walking along, and say you were involved. Even standing at your close an' that, you'd get done for loitering. You'd get done for loitering at your own close and they thought that was breaking up the gang. It was only making them worse."

When asked "How come?":

". . . Well they couldn't get leaving the place they had that many fines to pay off and it gave them a grudge against the polis. See sometimes the polis would lift from —— Drive, charge you with breach of the peace, take you down to the Pak and when there's a lot of them standing around, let you out in front of them all. All the Pak would start chasing you, *one* boy . . . It's happened to me . . . That's the Untouchables . . . After the boys get lifted, they're in a bad mood, cursing and swearing an' all that. They're all going like that: 'I got done for breach of the peace for nothing, next time it'll be something! . . . Might as well get the gaol for something." (An ex-leader of the Drummy)[37]

These feelings were repeated, almost without exception, by *all* the gang boys we contacted in Easterhouse. Objective conditions in the

79

area *had* changed, as far as youth were concerned, and they had to learn to cope with the new situation. They either had to run or hide from the police (in which case a chase and charge usually ensued) or quit the streets altogether: and many clearly did. Some left Easterhouse altogether because life for them there had become almost intolerable. The practice of being 'escorted' home from the youth club at night evolved, since the company of a youth club worker, for example, was seen as providing immunity from police apprehension. However, there were times when even 'escorts' were charged with breach of the peace, loitering, etc., and when sufficient escorts weren't available, the boys ensured that they either got a lift in a car or had plenty of company to walk home with . . . (frequently termed a 'disorderly crowd' by patrolling Untouchables).

The level of antagonism against the police reached such heights during one period in 1970 that gang activity became almost totally redirected towards the police. In one incident:

". . . A fight broke out between the boys, and the polis stepped in. We ended up smashing the van. The boys didn't like the way the polis was kicking one of them. It was the big boys' idea to get the boy away from the polis, we ended up throwing bricks and all that at the van. The boys weren't fighting really, it was just a square-do (fair fight), we all turned on the polis; you don't want anyone to get caught by *them*."

This incident, which was first brought to our attention by a middle-aged woman who witnessed it, became the subject of great amusement amongst the local boys, many of whom later claimed to have participated—and hadn't!—others of whom were encouraged to follow suit—and did.

Our research findings indicate that not only did *official* reaction (police control) result in changes in youth behaviour, but that the effect of informal control agents (such as employers, parents, etc.) accepting the 'official' definition of the Easterhouse gang boy also had important consequences. Certain areas of interaction came to be[38], or were *seen* to be, blocked to Easterhouse boys, such as youth clubs, dance halls and so on. In some cases boys voluntarily withdraw, by avoiding contact with those they saw as likely to apply the 'gang boy' stereotype, especially city youths:

". . . You know, when you're in a new place you don't know, say you were down the Barrows (an open air market in Glasgow) or something, they might come up and say: 'Where do you come from?' . . . We wouldn't say Easterhouse, we'd say a different place . . . where there's not so much gangs. They'd say 'That's okay, then', but if you said Easterhouse you'd probably get battered."

The publicity focussed on the Easterhouse gangs, especially after

Frankie Vaughan's initiative to provide a club in the area (mid-1968) had the effect of supplying a distorted and stereotyped definition of local boys to a much wider public. One ex-gang boy illustrated the self-fulfilling effect of this on his own behaviour:

"When I was sixteen (1967) it was bottles and bricks you threw; then we started pulling off fences, and after a while everyone started carrying blades. It was the done thing to carry one. After a while you couldn't break away; you'd get dug-up in town if you were by yourself, so it was best to have a blade. After that they carried them all the time . . . Sometimes I got dug-up at work, on the building sites, so I always carried it."

Within Easterhouse itself, the limited interaction between boys from the different neighbourhoods, together with the tone and content of media reportage about the gangs in the area, set the scene for shared misunderstandings to be generated. The frequency with which it was claimed that weapons were carried only for defensive purposes, and the ritual avoidance of 'rival' territory and neighbouring peers, are indications of this process. The youth finds that he is increasingly limited (perhaps a self-imposed limitation) to his own peer group as providing the least threat to his own self identity.[39] The street-corner hangout or the club set up for 'gang boys' may provide the gang boy with what Goffman has termed a 'backplace'. But further, as David Matza[40] has lucidly described, he is at the same time entering a situation where he is increasingly at risk of engaging in that sort of behaviour which will lead to his being publicly defined as delinquent.

Some concluding remarks

As Easterhouse gained its public reputation as a violent housing estate, planners, architects, social workers and researchers took up the 'concrete jungle' argument and applied it as an explanation of 'the problem'. Others preferred to explain it in more traditional terms of control, as did the Police Convenor who, after a weekend of purported extensive violence, stated:

"Really, the only answer lies in the return of the birch and capital punishment."[41]

In this chapter we have been trying to demonstrate the need for an alternative stance, both in terms of how a phenomenon such as delinquency might eventually be explained, and in terms of the 'special relationship' the researcher should maintain with the subject of his research. In so doing we have not provided a detailed outline of what we consider useful approaches to delinquency within urban sociology, and it may be contended by some that we have not done justice to the contribution that this area might make to the study of deviance. We do not have the space to provide any such critique of these theories, but we would maintain that a contribution could only come from this field where the arguments we have outlined under the heading "The 'Sick' Environment" above are acknowledged.

Nor have we proposed a framework of social organisation within which the "social forces released by the work of the architect"—to quote the RIBA syllabus—might be causally located. Such a framework could only serve as a heuristic device at present, given the lack of careful empirical research available. Rather, the aim has been to provide some empirical material within this area which might be of some interest to architects. We consider that this material indicates the barrenness of the 'architectural determinism' argument.

We have not directly taken up the theme of vandalism at all. We excuse the omission on the grounds that in the case of Easterhouse, vandalism is not located as a central problem, and thus our data is patchy and largely impressionistic. We would argue that vandalism in the context of the gang can only be understood from an appreciation of the gang boy's social world. The motives for smashing the windows of a school may not be identical with those for spraying gang slogans in enemy territory, for example, but as with other behaviour appropriate to the situation of the gang,[42] a delicate balance is sought between the element of risk and the pay-off in terms of prestige. Other writers have noted[43] the ways in which gang boys exaggerate their numerical strength and emphasise the superior wit and cunning of their fellow gang members. It would seem that attempts to dominate the landscape with gang slogans is seen as perhaps lending credence to such claims. At the same time, an awareness of the self-produced 'fantasy' is reflected in the very honest and very humorous slogan which appeared in letters three feet high the morning after the first US moon landing. It read:

TOO LATE YANKS, WEST REBELS RULE THE MOON!

Defacing public property is perhaps considered the least harmful form of vandalism by those who wish to control it; however, on the basis of our own data we do not pretend to be in a position to elaborate on the phenomenon on a more general level.[44] An adequate theoretical discussion of vandalism has already been presented earlier in this book.

It may be that the reader of this chapter detects a patronising attitude towards the architect, and this from two writers who have no knowledge of architecture as a profession 'from the inside'. Our reply would be that while attacking this facet of the professional ideology of architects, we are well aware that many do not pretend that through their 'craft' they can initiate social change. Indeed there is a growing body of opinion which holds that this can only come through architects entering the political arena. Further, such an attack is not solely directed at architects, as we have tried to make plain. Several sociologists seem to have faith in the power of the built environment to effect social change. Writing on delinquency and 'space', Ann Buttimer states:

"There are, however, certain implications for spatial planning, most notably, the concept of 'delinquency area', which illustrated the relationship between certain ecological conditions and delinquency behaviour. The improvement of certain physical conditions, and the provision of alternative sources of satisfaction within such areas might remove some of the underlying causes of delinquent behaviour and crime." [45]

Although we do appreciate that our argument is based on only limited personal knowledge of the 'workings' of the architectural profession, we have had the opportunity of teaching students who were themselves practising architects. Without such contacts this paper could hardly have been written at all.

In a recent issue of the *Architects' Journal*, a student writes in the form of a letter to the editors:

"AJ editors speak of 'ominous trends', and give 'warnings' of 'threats' to, and 'attacks' on the 'position of the professions' in relation to reports that computer-wielding non-architects are daring to turn their attention towards environmental design. Why must this sort of initiative always be seen as a threat? . . . Architects must be prepared to forget the RIBA and all that goes with it, to lose their present identity, to infiltrate themselves into the places were the running is being made, and to influence these organisations in the light of their unique generalist knowledge of human needs . . . It is only by making themselves indispensable, indeed the prime movers, in the places were real progress is being made . . . that architects . . . will be really influential on a world scale . . . The magnitude of the changes they will have to carry through is equivalent to the scale of the disparity between the world housing problem and present day architecture's capacity for solving it." [46]

Such a letter raises the question: "To what extent can the means of solving the world's housing problem lie within the scope of the profession?" It would seem that, although (at least in terms of what one reads in the professional journals) architects persistently speak of the 'breadth' of their professional role, and their 'wide knowledge of human needs' they are more limited than their specialist colleagues when it comes to the control they can exercise over the built environment. For after all, the architect enters the planning process at the end rather than at the beginning. It is surely only through architects as a group attempting to 'manipulate' the planning process, rather than working individually within it, that they can exercise more power or control over the quality of the built environment in relation to human needs. This, of course, begs the question of the extent to which the role of the architect *is* wide enough to allow an awareness of human needs (not that the role of the architect in society must be seen as 'fixed').

We have already mentioned that the social distance between the architect and the future user of his buildings is often very wide, especially when compared with how things were in the past. Is it possible for the architect to be *really* appreciative of clients' needs in these circumstances? Although (one might feel unfortunately) the sociologist does not typically see himself as prescribing for human needs, this problem of social distance arises in the same way so that he often operates with models of social behaviour which are artificial to the extreme—we have seen this to be the case with 'delinquency'. In fact it is of interest to note that an eminent figure in the planning world accused an established sociologist of this, stating:

"And here is the main difference between us. He is playful about the relevance of my experience in new towns. What much more profoundly influences my views on housing conditions and community growth is that I lived the first nineteen years of my life in a miner's cottage . . . so I know something about working class communities from the inside: about the hope and the despair, the violence and the tenderness, the ambition and the inertia, the love and the hate, the humbug and the honesty that fills these people's lives . . .
"Most sociologists look at these places as they do at goldfish bowls; and manifest the same rapport with the inhabitants of either. How else could they be so sloppily sentimental on the one hand and so infuriatingly patronising on the other?
"Too many, though not all, architects are also making patronising assumptions from a standpoint of even more massive ignorance. For instance, they seem determined to force face to face contacts on tenants of public housing the moment they step out of doors. It may be said that these architects, and sociologists who encourage them, sincerely feel this is socially desirable. But I have not heard or read one who has convinced me that he is concerned above and before all else with the visual result, with the self-induced euphoria of 'impact, drama and excitement'.
"Where is the one who admits his ignorance of the inner fabric of the lives of his prospective tenants: who respects their dignity and regards them as his equals; and who then approaches his task with genuine humility? . . ."[47]

Architects and sociologists could gain from a serious consideration of such criticism.

4 A field experiment in auto shaping

Philip G. Zimbardo

The Sanitation Department reported that over 31,500 abandoned cars had to be removed from New York's streets in 1968 (an increase of 5,000 from the previous year). These are cars which either had been stolen or were abandoned by their owners because they were no longer in good running condition. What is interesting is that most of them are stripped of usable parts and then battered and smashed almost beyond recognition. During the past several years, I have been systematically observing this new phenomenon of ritual destruction of the automobile—the symbol of American's affluence, technology and mobility, as well as the symbol of its owner's independence, status, and (according to motivation researchers) sexual fantasies. In a single day, on a 20-mile run from my home in Brooklyn to the campus of New York University in the Bronx, I recorded 218 such vandalised cars.

Repeated observations of the transformation of a typical car lead me to conclude that there are six distinct stages involved. First, the

A stage-six Corvette convertible—becoming a vandalised refuse container

Stripping our abandoned car before destroying it

car must provide some 'releaser' stimuli to call attention to itself, such as no licence plates, hood or trunk open, or a tyre removed. However, there are also less obvious cues, such as a flat tyre not repaired within a day or two, or simply a car which has not been moved from one place for several days. In a city that is always on the go, anything static must be dead, and it becomes public domain if no one calls for the body. Older boys and men are attracted by the lure of usable or saleable parts, and so the car is stripped of all items of possible value. Either late in this stage or after it is completed (depending on implicit neighbourhood norms), younger children begin to smash the front and rear windows. Then all easily broken or bent parts are attacked. Next, the remainder of the car is smashed with rocks, pipes, and hammers. Sometimes it is set on fire, and sometimes even the body metal is torn off. Finally, and most ignominiously, the last state in the metamorphosis occurs when people in the neighbourhood (and even Sanitation Department clean-up men) use it as a big garbage can, dumping their refuse into it.

In order to observe in a more systematic fashion who are the vandals and what are the conditions associated with their acts of vandalism, Scott Fraser and I bought a car and left it on a street across from the Bronx campus of New York University, where it was observed continuously for 64 hours. At the same time, we repeated this procedure in Palo Alto, California on a street near the Stanford University campus. The licence plates of both cars were removed and the hoods opened to provide the necessary 'releaser' signals.

What happened in New York was unbelievable! Within ten minutes, the 1959 Oldsmobile received its first auto strippers—a father, mother, and eight-year-old son. The mother appeared to be a look-out, while the son aided the father's search of the trunk, glove compartment and motor. He handed his father the tools necessary to remove the battery and radiator. Total time of destructive contact: seven minutes.

"By the end of the first 26 hours, a steady parade of vandals had removed the battery, radiator, air cleaner, radio antenna, windshield wipers, right-hand-side chrome strip, hubcaps, a set of jumper cables, a gas can, a can of car wax, and the left rear tyre (the other tyres were too worn to be interesting). Nine hours later, random destruction began when two laughing teenagers tore off the rear-view mirror, and began throwing it at the headlights and front windshield. Eventually, five eight-year-olds claimed the car as their private playground, crawling in and out of it and smashing the windows. One of the last visitors was a middle-aged man in a camel's hair coat and matching hat, pushing a

Vandalising the abandoned car—fun and games for children, families and observers

"Hit it again, harder, harder!" The awakening of dark impulses at Stanford University

baby in a carriage. He stopped, rummaged through the trunk, took out an unidentifiable part, put it in the baby carriage and wheeled off."[1]

In less than three days, what remained was a battered, useless hulk of metal, the result of 23 incidents of destructive contact. The vandalism was almost always observed by one or more other passers-by, who occasionally stopped to chat with the looters. Most of the destruction was done in the daylight hours and not at night (as we had anticipated), and the adults' stealing clearly preceded the window-breaking, tyre-slashing fun of the youngsters. The adults were all well-dressed, clean-cut whites who would under other circumstances be mistaken for mature, responsible citizens demanding more law and order. The one optimistic note to emerge from this study is that the number of people who came into contact with the car but did not steal or damage it was twice as large as the number of actual vandals.

In startling contrast, the Palo Alto car not only emerged untouched, but when it began to rain, one passer-by lowered the hood so that the motor would not get wet!

Next, this car was abandoned on the Stanford University campus for over a week without incident. It was obvious that the releaser cues which were sufficient in New York were not adequate here. I expected that vandalism needed to be primed where it did not occur with a higher 'natural' frequency. To do this, my male graduate students and I decided to provide a better model for destruction by taking a sledge hammer to the car ourselves and then seeing if others would follow suit.

Several observations are noteworthy. First of all, there is considerable

reluctance to take that first blow, to smash through the windshields and initiate the destruction of a form. But it feels so good after the first smack, that the next one comes more easily, with more force, and feels even better. Although everyone knew that the sequence was being filmed, the students got 'carried away' temporarily. Once one person had begun to wield the sledge hammer, it was difficult to get him to stop and pass it to the next pair of eager hands. Finally, they all attacked simultaneously. One student jumped on the roof and began stomping it in, two were pulling the door from its hinges, another hammered away at the hood and motor, while the last one broke all the glass he could find. They later reported that feeling the metal or glass give way under the force of their blows was stimulating and pleasurable. Observers of this action, who were shouting out to hit it harder and to smash it, finally joined in and turned the car completely over on its back, whacking at the underside. There seemed little hope to expect spontaneous vandalism of this car since it was already wrecked so badly. However, that night at 12.30 a.m three young men with pipes and bars began pounding away at the carcass so intensely that dormitory residents (a block away) shouted out for them to stop.

We might conclude from these preliminary studies that to *initiate* such acts of destructive vandalism, the necessary ingredients are the acquired feelings of anonymity provided by the life in a city like New York along with some minimal releaser cues. Where social anonymity is not a 'given' of one's everyday life, it is necessary to have more extreme releaser cues, more explicit models for destruction and aggression, and physical anonymity—a large crowd or the darkness of the night. A heightened state of preparatory general arousal would serve to make the action go, with less direct priming. To maintain and intensify the action, the ideal conditions occur where the physical act is a gross one involving a great deal of energy, thus producing considerable non-cognitive feedback. It is pleasurable to behave at a purely sensual, physical, unthinking level—regardless of whether the act is making love or making war.

It is only proper to conclude with two final, recently gathered anecdotes. 1. A tank which was part of an army convoy travelling through the Bronx, developed trouble and had to be left in the street while a mechanic was dispatched. He arrived a few hours later to find it totally stripped of all removable parts (which earned it the *Esquire* Dubious Prize of the Year 1968). 2. A motorist pulled his car off a highway in Queens, New York to fix a flat tyre. He jacked up his car and, while removing the flat tyre, was startled to see his hood being opened and a stranger starting to pull out the battery. The stranger tried to mollify his assumed car-stripping colleague by telling him, "Take it easy, buddy, you can have the tyres; all I want is the battery!"

What is being destroyed here is not simply a car, but the basic fabric of social norms which must regulate all communal life. The horrible scene from *Zorba, the Greek* in which the old townswomen begin to strip the home of the dying Bubbalina before she is yet dead is symbolically enacted many times every day in cities like New York where young and old, poor and affluent strip, steal, and vandalise cars, schools, churches and almost all symbols of social order.

5 Hey, mister, this is what we really do ...

Ian Taylor and Paul Walton

Some observations on vandalism in play

"Tell it like it is"—a slogan of the underground in Britain and America —appears to guide the work of many sociologists interested in youth culture, deviancy, delinquency and dissent. This slogan was given methodological status by David Matza, the Berkeley criminologist, in urging on his colleagues 'the naturalistic perspective'—the accurate and truthful description of social phenomena in their own right, rather than the description of those phenomena in order to correct, reform or eradicate them ('the correctional perspective').

But 'telling it like it is' *has* been a central concern for many sociologists interested in understanding the processes and conditions under which people deviate and dissent. A fundamental problem for sociologists of this persuasion, however, has been that they are, in effect, on the outside looking in. The Chicago School of Sociology, in the 1930s, struggled to represent the social processes involved in becoming, for example, a billiard-room hustler, a member of the twilight worlds of taxi-drivers and prostitutes, a con-man, a shoplifter or an alcoholic. The Chicago studies were the result of personal struggles by the sociologist to identify with particular subcultures and to win acceptance in deviant worlds (where privacy and individuality were highly valued). In the 1950s, Albert Cohen[1] and Walter Miller[2], in particular, attempted to focus on the 'delinquent subculture' of American street-corner kids and, again, were guided by the need to depict the subcultures 'naturalistically'. Though not involving themselves so deeply in the deviant worlds as their Chicago mentors, Cohen and Miller began their analysis via an expression of affinity with their delinquent subjects.

What distinguishes the subcultural theorists of the 1950s from their earlier Chicago counterparts is the attempt to place their description of the street-corner in a theoretical framework. This difference of emphasis is indicative of the continuing tension in sociology between 'telling it like it is' and speculating on how it came to be that way. Walter Miller, for example, was taken up with an explanation of why most official delinquency was working-class in origin, and came to see delinquency, not as an activity of particular groups within the working-class, but as a direct reflection of what he calls the 'focal concerns' of most working-class children in the United States. For Miller, these focal concerns are the stress on toughness, smartness, excitement, and

91

autonomy, coupled with a belief in the inevitability of trouble in everyday life and the continual intervention of fate and luck in deciding on one's life-chances. Miller's decision to emphasise these concerns (to the exclusion of possible others) has, however, left him open to the charge of predicting too much delinquency: not all working-class street kids are delinquent and not all delinquency is working-class.

An alternative approach to Miller's, in the study of working-class kids and delinquents, has been to construct 'typologies'—descriptions of types of delinquent activity—and to explain why one type (for example, smashing school windows, or breaking telephone boxes) should be a popular subcultural activity. This approach is heavily dependent on the naturalistic perspective because the explanations advanced by the observer must obviously depend very heavily on the explanations offered by the kids themselves (Stanley Cohen, 1968).[3] But it has not worked out that way in all respects.

A lot of work on 'delinquent activity' in Britain and America has been guided by the conclusion of Albert Cohen (1955) that much delinquency is 'malicious, negativistic and non-utilitarian', in motivation and direction.

What appears to Albert Cohen to be activity of a 'malicious, negativistic and non-utilitarian' nature may, however, be perfectly sensible, constructive and instrumentally creative to the kids themselves. Theories about delinquent behaviour, and social life in general, must bear relation to what is actually happening; in the tension between description and explanation, description must not lose out. Theories are possible—but new theories, and new explanations, should arise out of real action.

Purposive and creative delinquency

Let us look at some examples of working-class activity, accidentally chanced upon, in and around a park in Bradford on a Sunday afternoon. All of them suggest a delinquency that is purposive and creative.

Bradford's Victorian parks, peopled with statues of local wool-merchants from a bygone era, and emblazoned with Latin inscriptions in praise of profit and puritanism, have had playgrounds added to them over the years. A token gesture in the direction of leisure, placed conveniently out of sight of the afternoon strollers. In the winter (which lasts longer in the North) they put locks on the rocking horses and remove the swings, presumably a civic attempt to protect the young from 'danger'. So parks in Bradford need a city key before they can be used.

Walking through one of these parks one Sunday, we observed a small multi-racial group of six-year-olds busy smashing the lock that chained their rocking horse. From the council's point of view, their actions would probably appear ungrateful, and would certainly find their way into the ledgers as an example of 'malicious vandalism'. From the kids' point of view, the action was a real blow for Play Power.

Norman Mailer has characterised the architecture of New York as

Basket riding in a supermarket

'totalitarian architecture'—referring to the physical and material structure of the high-rise office and apartment buildings. Park architecture in Britain in general, and in Bradford and the North in particular, is totalitarian too—but in the sense that the parks are reserved for appropriate 'leisure pursuits', closed at six, locked in the winter, and have the status of 'civic amenities' for which we should all be grateful. They are physical spaces not social spaces: you look out for the "parkie" you can't play here, and we're locking the gate at six. Keep off the grass —an admonition aimed not at the middle-class pot smokers—is merely another dictate from 'public' authority, excluding the working-class from what they have in common of England's green and pleasant land. Two streets away from the playground someone has etched into the wall the slogan "It's a Mean Old Scene" (hardly a central slogan of the Underground, but a true reflection of Bradford's mood, where, as a northern poet has put it, "wool-merchants marry chorus girls, but not one supposes for breeding purposes, to put a bit of salt into the strain; and leave the lass at 'ome to deal with Dostoyevsky".[4] The slogan has been there two years now, outlasting some of the other more contentious (political) slogans. Presumably the council agrees.

Round the corner from the park is a drive-in supermarket (closed on Sundays). Here another multi-racial group of 10 to 11-year-olds were utilising the technological spin-off from consumer society. They had stripped down several supermarket trolley baskets and had perfected their own roller coaster gliding down the car-park slope at hair-raising speeds, all the time spinning round in circles, hanging cheerfully on to

Tag and pallet game

their stripped-down machines. When approached by us, photographed, and a conspiratorial rapport established, one grubby 10-year old off a nearby council estate enquired: "Hey, mister, do you want to see what we really do?"

Around at the front of the supermarket, the kids had constructed a complex game of tag and climbing, using large wooden pallets whose conventional use was to stabilise the loads carried by fork-lift trucks into the stores. Piling the pallets into stacks of various heights, they had erected a chasing game exceeding in its intricacy the games of the park and the wider society. One may note, with Miller, that the pallet game contained fascination through potential danger.

Seen on a Monday morning through the cold official eye of the supermarket owner, these games would no doubt appear to be 'malicious, negativistic and non-utilitarian'. Why should people throw pallets around and destroy the baskets? Child care officers and welfare workers would no doubt express concern at the fact that the children, avoiding a nearby park and its open spaces, should prefer to play (at some danger to themselves) in the concrete world of a supermarket car-park. And some sociologists would no doubt accept these activities as deviant or pathological.

But ready alternatives are not really available. The park, stripped of its playground hardware, is a bore. And it provides nothing in the way of adventure and risk, the core of working-class play. We could multiply instances from other parts of the country .: ". . . the trolleys are taken out of the shopping complex at Wandsworth's Arndale Centre and left near car parking areas by shoppers, and children have been seen by tenants forming the trolleys into long columns and pushing them down car ramps into busy Garratt Lane. 'Local children—not from our estate—collect these trolleys on a Sunday and play trains.' "[5]

Vandalism and delinquency these games may be, but are they without purpose? If the Play Power of middle-class flower children can be seen as a purposive revolt against a consumer society, then the destruction of consumer technology to create objects of play must be seen as a necessarily illegal, but entirely purposive, attempt to use a technology the working-class kid cannot afford to ignore.

Supermarket double-decker in the River Wandle

6 Vandalism and the architect

Alexander Miller

To many architects, the idea that there is a connection between their work and vandalism may seem rather novel. But if a visit to a favourite job some months after completion shows that carefully considered details have been damaged, scrupulously selected finishes defaced, and laboriously studied effects ruined, all by wilful and apparently pointless human attack, it may occur to them that some modifications in design and construction to make buildings and their surroundings less prone to such damage would be worth while on future occasions.

An architect having this experience may of course say, "It is a disgrace that the caretakers and the police allow these young hooligans to behave like this, and what are the parents and the schoolteachers doing about it?" . . . etc.—all of which is quite justified, since the control of vandalism is primarily a matter for those responsible for discipline, law and order. If, however, our architect finds that damage occurs in certain situations in spite of good caretaking and supervision, he may realise that if he wishes his buildings to survive as designed he must take the possibility of wilful damage into account in design and specification in the same way as the possibilities of weathering, wear, decay or corrosion.

It is this practical, *ad hoc* aspect of the design/vandalism relationship that this chapter will discuss, rather than a more abstract one which some architects would clearly prefer.[1] The latter is based on the fairly obvious fact that vandalism flourishes in 'bad' environments and is less of a problem in 'good' environments, and from this it seems to be argued that environments can be designed to satisfy the needs of their inhabitants so fully that vandalism (and presumably other forms of crime as well) will no longer be an attractive pastime. This seems, to this writer at least, to misunderstand the nature of the factors that produce a 'bad' environment in the sense mentioned above; these are more likely to be overcrowding, decaying buildings, and lack of sanitary, recreational and other facilities, than poor design in any aesthetic sense. It is generally recognised that the avoidance of these adverse factors has a beneficial effect on the incidence of crime, including vandalism, in a community, but to go further and assume that particular forms of architectural expression (e.g. good scale and homely appearance as opposed to overbearing size and bleakness) will directly affect behaviour such as vandalism is not justified, though it is an idea dear to architects. Vere Hole, in a recent paper, says:

"Man's behaviour, however, involves a highly complex interaction between the physical environment (natural and man-made) and technology on the one hand and his social organisation and social values on the other. Except in the sense of imposing certain limitations, the physical environment and human behaviour cannot be viewed as a simple cause and effect relationship."[2]

Moreover, even if this approach could be shown to be effective, its result would really be to produce environmental areas which did not breed vandals to damage their own or other areas; it would not prevent other less well-satisfied vandals entering the area from elsewhere and possibly finding it all the more pleasurable to damage because of the perfection of the design. Thus, as a method for reducing vandalism, it could be effective only if applied to a large and self-contained environment—such as a new town.

For these reasons, then, the present discussion is confined to a consideration of possible measures of 'self-defence' for buildings and their appurtenances against wilful damage. The tabulated data which follow were collected by the author in the course of a short exploratory study of wilful damage on housing estates made at the Building Research Station in 1969 and 1970. Typical estates in various parts of the country were inspected and evidence of wilful damage noted. Information was also collected from architects, housing managers and caretakers on measures adopted for countering vandalism by design and selection of materials and equipment, and by management procedures. Although the study was limited to housing, much of the information obtained was of fairly general applicaton, and it is presented here as illustrating the types of precautionary measure which the architect can take to counter vandalism in buildings of various types.

The data are set out under the main headings of Wall finishes, Materials and Design features, and in each case those materials or features which are notably susceptible to wilful damage and are best avoided are listed first; this list is followed by one of items classed as useful. There is insufficient knowledge to enable materials or features to be graded according to their effectiveness in resisting wilful damage, and the lists of useful items are suggestive only; they leave out in most cases numerous alternative items which in many circumstances would be suitable replacements for items on the first lists.

Graffiti on plastered walls of entrance hall and staircase of a block of flats. Mottled black glaze had been applied to make marking difficult, but it had been overlooked that the softness of the plaster, combined with the contrast in colour between substrate and finish, would invite scratching and cutting and result in permanent defacement

A result similar to that shown above. Galvanised steel door painted in dark colour readily scratched

Ceramic mosaic external finish to local authority block of flats

WALL FINISHES

To be avoided	To reduce risk of:	Remarks
Soft textured		
Easily scratched, particularly if of colour contrasting with substrate	*Defacement by writing, scratching, carving*	E.g. black glaze on soft plaster (see example later)
Light in colour		
Requiring renewal, but too expensive for frequent renewal, e.g. glaze		View held by some; cheaper paint frequently renewed preferred

Useful (resistant to damage or marking)	To reduce risk of:	Remarks
Special paints and glazes (of suitable colour in relation to substrate—see above)		
Ceramic mosaic	*Defacement by writing, scratching, carving*	All vulnerable to marking by aerosol paint
Glazed tiles		
Ribbed aluminium sheet		
Roughcast		
Rough-textured bricks		

Useful (cleanable)		
Special paints and glazes	*Ditto*	
Ceramic mosaic		
Glazed tiles		

MATERIALS

To be avoided	To reduce risk of:	Remarks
Glass in large panes and in vulnerable positions	*Breakage*	
Glass bricks	*Ditto*	Opinions vary; better than glass panes, but can be broken; particularly attractive to vandals

Mesh-reinforced, transparent, plastic sheeting replacing glass in staircase window after breakage

Damage to accessible asbestos cement rainwater pipe
Plastic glazing to ceiling light in pedestrian subway. Glazing has been replaced after being burnt by vandals
Damage to cast-iron steet nameplate; probably used as target for stone-throwing or airgun practice
Soft mortar joints in brickwork raked out

Plastic rainwater goods below 2m height	*Ditto*
Asbestos cement goods below 2m height	*Ditto*
Felt on flat roofs, if easily accessible	*Youngsters playing and dancing on roofs; penetration and tearing of felt*
Asbestos cement roofs, if easily accessible	*Breakage; accident hazard*
Plastic control buttons and indicator lights in lifts	*Prising out; burning; dislocation of lift service*
Glass covers to lighting fittings	*Breakage*
Plastics covers to lighting fittings, if accessible	*Burning*
Cast iron signs (eg street names)	*Breakage*
External copper piping	*Theft*
Soft mortar joints in brickwork, where accessible	*Scraping out*

(Glass covers / Plastics covers to lighting fittings) } Preferences between these vary

Useful	To reduce risk of	Remarks
In windows, doors, signs, etc: transparent plastics sheet (polycarbonate considered best; acrylic, unplasticised pvc and butyrate sheet also available)	*Breakage*	Some say sheets easily removed; risk of being burnt appears to be less than in lighting fittings
Armourplate glass	*Breakage*	
Glass bricks		In place of glass panes in windows; opinions vary
Translucent covers to lighting fittings (if inaccessible but may be target for catapult, air-gun or stone-throwing): Plastics (polycarbonate or butyrate)	*Breakage*	
Ditto (if accessible): Glass	*Burning*	But breakable
Cast iron rainwater goods	*Breakage*	Preferred to plastics and asbestos cement below height of 2m
In lift cars: Ribbed aluminium sheet wall lining	*Marking and writing*	Ribbing makes formation of letters very difficult
Plastics laminate ditto	*Ditto*	Particularly if boldly patterned
pvc flooring	*Fouling of lift*	Waterproof cleanable
Metal control buttons	*Prising out; burning; dislocation of lift service*	

101

Lock-up garage with concealed gutter and down-pipe, but with low wall providing easy access to roof

Accumulation of rubbish in space left at end of a range of lock-up garages

Damage to paint finish of tubular steel column at shopping centre; probably started through use of columns as bicycle rests and continued as a destructive pastime.

Damage to tile hanging at low level and in accessible positions. Tiles and cladding units probably broken partly by accident—e.g. during children's play—and partly deliberately

Grating missing from gully in paved area at shopping centre, constituting serious accident hazard

102

To be avoided	To reduce risk of:	Remarks
Open spaces too large	*General*	Lack of supervision
Nooks and crannies in layout	*General*	Lack of supervision
Access to flat roofs (adjacent walls, lower buildings, projections giving foothold, rwp's for climbing etc.)	*Damage to felt or asbestos cement roof coverings*	
Thin concrete (or stone) copings to low walls, particularly if with overhang (unless specially designed—see later)	*Removal of copings*	
Tile copings to low walls	*Removal of copings*	
Brick-on-edge copings to low walls without strengthened ends and corners	*Removal of copings*	
Tile-hanging below ground floor sill level, particularly if adjacent ground is level and open for children to play	*Breakage and/or removal of tiles*	Could be accidental or deliberate
Glass, ditto	*Breakage of glass*	Ditto
Coffin doors in lifts	*Breakage of mechanism*	
Hidden corners in entrance halls	*General*	
Open spaces under stairs in entrance halls	*General*	
Lever handles to doors	*Breakage*	
Painting of tubular steel posts, rails, etc, in play-grounds or public spaces	*Chipping and scratching of paint*	
Unlockable gully gratings	*Breakage*	

Coping prised off

Brick courses progressively removed

103

Damage to garage doors of inadequate strength

Planted plots trampled to provide short cut to shopping centre

Damage to trees, both young and old

Light fitting at ground level where it can easily be kicked in

To be avoided	To reduce risk of:	Remarks
Up and over garage doors of inadequate strength	Youths swinging on them or charging them on motor cycles; distortion, dislocation of balancing mechanism	
Projecting handles on garage doors about knee-height	Kicking off, leading to breaking in	
Glass panels in garage doors	Breakage of glass	
Timber or metal fascias to garages	Pulling off	
Excessive amounts of soft landscaping	Shortcutting; breakage, cutting down or burning of trees; theft of shrubs, plants and turf	
Ranch fencing in white painted wood	Breakage and damage to paint by children climbing	Satisfactory if suitably strengthened and unpainted
Cobbles or granite setts	Lifting and use as missiles	In extremely rough areas
Surface wiring (electric) in public spaces	Youths swing on conduit and detach it from ceiling; exposed cable torn down	
Bad positioning of lighting fittings	Breakage	
Decorative features which may appear out of keeping with the general style and standard of amenity of the buildings and their surroundings	General destruction	Water features particularly popular targets for attack

Damage to bus shelters: glass panels broken
Transparent plastic glazing in place of glass
Sheet-metal roof damaged, probably by being jumped on from adjacent bus-stop post

105

Raised beds with planting; note gap to provide direct route to entrance to flats   *Raised grassed area; probably looks better from above*

Heavy coping without overhang on outer face claimed to be a protection
Concrete stop ends and corner blocks protect brick-on-edge copings

Useful	To reduce risk of:	Remarks
Concealed fixing of fittings and equipment	*Removal of fittings or parts; dislocation services*	
Recessed head or hexagon socket screws instead of bolts or slotted screws for fixings	*Ditto*	
Spherical knob handles instead of lever to external doors	*Breakage*	Except in old people's dwellings, where lever handles may be preferred for safety
Lockable gully gratings	*Breakage; removal; danger to pedestrians*	
Heavy timber garage doors (framed, ledged, braced and sheeted) with robust hasp, staple and padlock; no glass panel	*General damage*	One authority's specification (severe conditions)
Good quality 'up and over' garage doors, with lock at floor	*Ditto*	Another authority's specification (less severe conditions)
Retractable handle for 'up-and-over' garage doors	*General damage, and providing access to roof*	
Car boot type handle for 'up-and-over' garage doors to be in vertical position when locked	*Providing access to roof*	
Concealed or internal gutters and rwp's to garages	*Breakage of gutters, pipes and fittings*	
Garages in rows facing dwellings in preference to garage courts	*General*	
Planted plots raised, with retaining walls	*General damage to planting*	Opinions vary on effectiveness
Roses or other prickly bushes used for planting	*Ditto*	
Copings to low walls, piers, balustrades, etc., specially secured, e.g.:	*Removal of copings*	
Cast *in-situ* with wire mesh fixed to wall with masonry nails		
Precast, flush on one or both faces (in former case may have single slope, towards overhang)		
Brick-on-edge, with *in-situ* concrete stop ends and corners		

Useful	To reduce risk of:	Remarks
Vertical boarding in fences in preference to horizontal	*Damage from children climbing*	
Horizontal boarding in fences (if used) suitably strengthened and left unpainted	*Ditto*	
Stop buttons in lifts	*Damage to mechanism when doors wedged open (eg by milkmen)*	Not all authorities approve; disciplining milkmen preferred, but appears to be ineffective
Provision of lavatory off ground floor lift hall of high blocks of flats	*Fouling of lifts*	Not all authorities approve; lavatories themselves subject to wilful damage, which however, may be offset by special precautions (see below)
Specially designed or selected sanitary fittings for lavatories open to public	*Breakage of fittings*	
Piping and mechanism for these concealed or protected	*Ditto*	
High standard of lighting of interior access areas of buildings, both at night and in daytime if necessary	*General*	
High standard of lighting of external spaces at night (floodlighting in extreme cases)	*Ditto*	
Locked external doors to blocks of dwellings, with telephone communication between tenants and visitors	*Ditto*	Installations mainly in luxury blocks; effectiveness not proved; installation itself subject to wilful damage or abuse
'Office' for caretaker of flat block, with look-out window commanding entrance	*Ditto*	Suggested; two examples seen
Provision of adequate play areas round blocks of dwellings for children of various ages	*Ditto*	Assumed to be an essential for reasons other than reduction of vandalism; may not be wholly beneficial for that purpose; children may be attracted from outside estate, and the playgrounds themselves suffer wilful damage

Wilful damage to footbridge over railway. Screen at end (erected to prevent overlooking of adjacent houses and gardens) produces a virtually enclosed area shut off from public view (foot traffic over the bridge is light). The reinforced asbestos cement sheeting provides a smooth surface for graffiti, and since it shuts off the view of the trains below large holes have been punched in it and have had to be patched as shown. Some forms of unclimbable mesh giving a view both outwards and inwards would probably have prevented these difficulties

Special mention requires to be made of certain other design features or situations which are found to provoke or permit vandalism. These are as follows:

1. Enclosures of any kind which are freely accessible but not open to constant public view or readily open to supervision. These include: lifts; garage courts; ranges of tenants' stores; subways; bridges; hidden or secluded corners in courtyards, entrance halls, or open ground floors of buildings on *piloti*.

2. Shopping centres and buildings adjacent to them.

3. Newly occupied housing estates, particularly where part is still under construction; at this time living conditions are unsettled and there is a plentiful armoury of building materials to hand for window breaking, etc.

Wilful damage to buildings under construction, or completed but unoccupied, can also be very serious. These are, however, in a transitional phase and require special protective measures rather than permanent design or constructional precautions.

Shopping centre where damage to soft landscaping made it necessary to pave the whole area

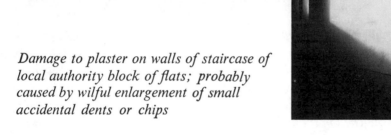

Damage to plaster on walls of staircase of local authority block of flats; probably caused by wilful enlargement of small accidental dents or chips

The relationships between maintenance, appearance and vandalism are important to note. Persistence in the repair of wilful damage and the removal of defacement seems to be necessary if the appearance of an estate or group of buildings is not to decline. Deterioration of appearance can, however, arise from other causes besides wilful damage and poor maintenance, for instance accidental damage, misuse or ordinary wear and tear (or indeed from weathering, decay, corrosion or other forms of failure). If this were allowed to develop, it seems probable that wilful damage would be encouraged, since it has been seen that comparatively minor faults or incipient failure can provide temptation to even well-suppressed vandalistic tendencies. As with all matters concerning maintenance, good feed-back from the management and maintenance side to architects and other designers is of the utmost importance.

Although in some cases the existence of adverse social conditions, or the presence of certain design features or situations as mentioned above, may indicate a high risk of wilful damage to a projected building scheme or layout, the incidence of vandalism is not in general easy to predict. It is not to be expected therefore that expensive technical preventive measures will be widely adopted in new work. It is hoped, however, that the suggestions put forward here will not be regarded

110

General view of gaps in a reinforced concrete fence bounding a children's play area attached to a housing estate, and separating both from a trunk road

Slope from trunk road down which empty tar barrels (left by road repairers) were rolled by youths

This example is illustrated to show how unpredictable the activities of vandals can be, rather than to suggest any particular safeguards of general applicability. Nevertheless it does underline the point that materials or articles which might be used as missiles or weapons should not be left lying about, and it also suggests that where possible fences should be placed at the top of slopes of this kind rather than at the base

merely as unwelcome additions to building costs. If the hazard of wilful damage is kept in mind at the design stage it is often possible to build-in protection against it without extra cost or loss of amenity. Elsewhere the aim should be to keep the options open and ensure that the design does not preclude the adoption of vandalism-resistant arrangements later on if found necessary.

As with cost, some compromise on the question of appearance and amenity may be necessary, since on the whole vandalism-resistant finishes and materials are thought of as being hard and unsympathetic. They need not be so, however, and there is clearly an opportunity for skilful design to maintain a good standard of appearance while avoiding vandalism proneness. Any unavoidable sacrifice of appearance and amenity must be set off against the expectation that one cause of their deterioration is being at least partly removed.

7 The architect's dilemma—one firm's working notes

Farmer and Dark

1. DEFINITION OF VANDALISM

The general problem of damage covers a wide range of causes culminating in vandalism:

Whim However full the client consultation in the design stage, the occupation stage can defeat the design intention by immediate misuse and imposed dross. A devaluation of design effort rather than book damage. Commonly attributed to lack of communication, but also stemming from the root urge to 'do your own thing regardless' which applies all down the line of other categories.

Tough Wear From boisterous behaviour and overcrowding.

Clumsiness e.g. the secondary school age group tends to be naturally clumsy both from growing strength and growing limbs; soldiers may move heavily because of the weight and bulk of their equipment, etc. Cleaning machinery and trolleys can cause damage in highly finished spaces no less than in light industrial ones. Contract furniture removers also take their toll.

Temptation The irresistable fascination to peel off, pick at or break up materials that prove easily vulnerable to such treatment. This includes absent-minded fiddling. Examples: lap joints of plastic cloth; rubber studs under stacking chairs. Non setting mastics, etc.

In a more extreme degree this results in waves of particular forms of damage—once something proves vulnerable it becomes the fashion to bust it; for a time; then the fun goes and the fashion moves on to another type of target.

On schools we note that the least damage occurs in workshop, science and practical areas where there are in fact the most weapons of destruction. This contradiction seems to result from (a) the staff keeping strict discipline in the pupils' physical interests and making this plain to them; (b) interest in making and discovering things (this lines up with the fact that militancy in universities seems to come mainly from the arts and social science students rather than from natural science students.)

WEYROC CUBICLES DON'T CARE

There's no reason why they should. Even the most boisterous of boys would make little impact on the tough, hard-wearing melamine surfaces, the strong plastic structural members, the pvc-protected edges and accessories. But long service is only one of many advantages architects, local authorities, builders and contractors gain. Weyroc Cubicles save time, effort and money — right from the moment you put pen to order. Initial outlay is competitively low. Individual packaging protects against damage en route. The unique clip-in method speeds assembly, thus installation on site is fast and

— self-opening doors with fitted hinges — bolts with 'Engaged' and 'Vacant' indicators — partition walls and fascias in Charcoal fleck (B.S.9.097) — doors in 4 alternative fleck colours, Tangerine BS.0.004, Olive BS.4.050, Mediterranean BS.7.083 or Charcoal BS.9.097. **And now our standard range also includes Junior cubicles, specially designed to withstand extra wear-and-tear and really rough treatment. Weyroc Junior cubicles are ideal for schools.**

Want to know more about these budget-pruning, simple to fix, **easy**

. . . from boisterous behaviour and overcrowding . . .

113

Selfishness	As in removing the spray fittings in taps, to get a more immediate flow; pocketing basin plugs to make sure of having your own; removing valve devices to divert more heating to oneself. Emergency escape devices broken to get a short cut. Electrical improvisation of dangerous ingenuity.
Ignorance	Operating and control systems for heaters, etc., becoming increasingly sophisticated. Sensors and stats in sill line heaters should be very inaccessible. Tendency of staff (as well as pupils) to remove access panels and set up to maximum. Result: overheating, complaints of inadequate ventilation, unbalancing of system.
Mischief	Boredom, frustration, curiosity and a desire for adventure, and to show off, are other causes leading to damage —inadvertent and deliberate, as well as amusement in 'defeating the system' (e.g. a game by fork-lift truck drivers to drive at automatic doors and hit them before they could open).
Vandalism	This is presumably the ultimate degree where quite considerable strength and determination is employed to smash things for the sheer satisfaction of smashing them.

2. BRIEFING

It would help the designer if the degree of likelihood of damage could be faced up to in the client's brief, including what measures may be available to control it, e.g. supervisors, security patrolling, discipline, re-payment on damage, etc. Could not sociologists be used to assess such 'behaviour-patterns' in advance—anyway to some extent? Equally to assess the duration of the behaviour pattern so that the client could if necessary set aside money to make good initial 'attack' on the assumption of it not being repeated. A calculated strategy.

We have had experience of designing to some realistic briefs of this sort. e.g. a boys' club and work for the services. But in other cases, and particularly now in large schools there seems to be a widening gap between the humanitarian, Utopian and adventurous aspirations of educationalists, and increasing evidence of vandalism after occupation.

Architects have long continued to work to, and believe in, the post-war educational hypothesis that civilized and imaginative buildings will 'rub-off' on the children; that the children will end up by respecting the buildings; and that the price in terms of initial damage by the minority is worth paying in the process of education. That the corollary—of designing to penal standards of safeguard is a denial of education, let alone of pleasant environment.

A quarter of a century later—with vandalism on the increase and warnings of even more; with the raising of the school leaving age; with rejection of authority by the young, and with a rejection by education authorities of old fashioned disciplinary measures—we have to question

114

whether this ideological hypothesis can survive in terms of its economic consequences.

Meanwhile the architect is in a cleft stick; if the place is smashed he is accused of undue aesthetic preoccupation—things are not tough enough; if on the other hand he designs against the minority vandals the building is criticized for being institutional.

In the design of buildings for industrial process, mass transport and so on, potential causes of damage from the nature of the activity have long been identified, assessed and acted upon. But in the design of buildings for people, client authorities, no less than architects, prefer to proceed from an assumption of reasonable respect. Current patterns of abuse suggest that this factor should be assessed a a specific item in the brief, not just in relation to a building type, but to each project and site individually.

3 SOME EXAMPLES
Planting
An easy target for destruction and we have had examples in university precincts as well as in schools and low-cost housing.

Peter Shepheard once defined a 'Law of Diminishing Vandalism' on this—that you had to face replanting 75% after the first year, 50% after the second, etc. On a low-cost housing group many years ago we did have some small success by calling a meeting of tenants and allocating individual trees to the care of particular households. Care in selection of landscape materials appropriate to size and use of space is important. Grass and planting will be abused in small, heavily used areas—hard materials are more appropriate. Some species of berberis, acacia, mahonia and holly are prickly enough to protect other planting behind.

Internal Wall Finishes
Sharp sand and cement rendered with a wood float and painted with emulsion paint and glaze can give colour and a scrubbable finish, whilst discouraging smearing and graffiti. Felt pens are a potent new weapon on emulsion paint as the mark is hard to wash off. So are aerosol spray cans.

Wall linings covering insulation, etc., should be in plywood. We have Asbestolux and hardboard linings kicked in deliberately—even in a swimming pool—presumably with bare feet.

One case of 200 mm thick concrete blocks being prized out of a wall—also clay air bricks.

Ceiling Finishes
Acoustic ceilings (increasingly necessary in 'open plan' schools) tend, with money available, to be of easily damaged materials. Lay-in systems invite their dislodgement and crawling in ceiling voids. Problems of security (tuck shops, etc.) which can be entered from above. Need for wire mesh in ceiling voids.

Roofing
Schools Fives Courts. A light translucent sheeting was used to 'win' a

weatherproof roof on the cheap. This was written off by brickbats being lobbed on to it. (Phased occupation meant ample builders' rubble as ammunition.)

Doors

2″ solid timber doors with 6″ brass butts wrenched out of frames. Laminate push panels cut through. Ironmongery, particularly closers, pulls and handles should be *very* robust and difficult to unscrew. Answer may be in pressed metal doors and frames with welded hinges. Narrow wired glass vision panels entirely broken out.

Venetian Blinds

Easy target. Destruction included cutting cords at blind head—60% of blinds destroyed in one school before this vogue palled.

Sanitary fittings and Lavatories

This is the usual 'Public Convenience' problem—fittings smashed, basin traps removed, etc. A row of cantilever basins with single side mixer taps sheared off at mid point by kicking the taps. Normal seats for W.C.s and the fixings of their flushing cisterns are not strong enough. Wrenched off or stood on and collapse. W.C.s seats with plastic hinges not man enough. Mirror screw domes always removed—other way of fixing. Mirrors (even Girls') smashed. Consider stainless steel? Only answer (at a price) would seem to be monolithic assemblies with all pipes, etc., in locked ducts accessible from circulation areas.

Grilles and handrails

Light metal ventilation and convection grilles kicked through, or unscrewed, bent double and thrown out of the window. We really need grilles of equal robustness to a foot scraper with no screw heads (including P.K. heads) accessible. $4″ \times 2″ \times 12′$ long hollow steel handrails welded to $3′ \times 6″ \times \frac{1}{4}″$ ragged plates built into brick wall— whole assembly wrenched out. Aluminium grilles in lavatory doors kicked in. Suggest welded steel.

Electrical

Widespread damage to switches, sockets, draw boxes and electric clocks. Fire alarm and loudspeaker systems put out of action. We have (when briefed to do so) had all switches controlled from lockable strong rooms —External bollard diffusers vulnerable means reverting to pole fittings —Extra tough diffusers needed.

Furniture

Cases of new desks having fires lit in them or slung up in trees (school) and of new chairs being thrown into a lake (university). Curtains set alight. Should be flame proofed as for theatre? Carpet tiles unsatisfactory —thrown about. Lino tops carved. Use melamine? (As compared to old fashioned heavy desks, simple light modern ones show damage the more). Upholstery slashed. Also colours have to be geared to dirty jeans vogue. Stainless steel hot cupboards kicked in.

Miscellaneous

Coat hooks should be very short (had to be sawn off to 50 mm), so they **cannot** be swung on or bent, or have a 'web' to make them more rigid.

116

8 What the architect can do: a series of design guides

Alan Leather and Antony Matthews

Contents

Introduction
Research Procedure

A Overall Planning
p. 121
      Introduction
A (i)   External Circulation
      Pedestrian
      Vehicular
A (ii)   Garages
A (iii)   Play Areas
A (iv)   Boundaries
A (v)   Supervision
A (vi)   Susceptible Materials

B Detailed Planning
p. 126
      Introduction
B (i)   Lighting
      Internal
      External
B (ii)   Circulation
      Internal
      External
B (iii) Fenestration
B (iv) Plan Form
B (v)   Landscaping
      Hard Surfacing
      Soft Surfacing

C Applied Finishes
p. 137
      Introduction
C (i)   Applied Film
C (ii)   Applied Sheet
C (iii) Applied Units
C (iv) Applied Coatings

D Materials
p. 147
      Introduction
D (i)   Glazing
D (ii)   Plaster
D (iii) Hard External Surfacing

	D (iv)	Weatherboard and Tile-hanging
	D (v)	Sheet Materials
	D (vi)	Timber
	D (vii)	Bricks and Blocks
	D (viii)	Self-finished Materials

E Components and Services Introduction
p. 154

E (i)	Signs and Lettering
E (ii)	Sanitary Fittings
E (iii)	Light Fittings
E (iv)	Doors
E (v)	Rainwater Goods
E (vi)	Services
E (vii)	Screens
E (viii)	Lifts
E (ix)	External Barriers

F Detailing Introduction
p. 161

F (i)	Method of Access
F (ii)	Copings
F (iii)	Mechanical Fixings
F (iv)	Gravestones

G Environment Introduction
p. 165

G (i)	Dilapidation
G (ii)	Features of Novel Appearance
G (iii)	Privacy
G (iv)	Character
G (v)	Effect of Height and Density
G (vi)	Zone of Responsibility

Summary Progression of Damage
p. 170

Future Research
Zone of Responsibility
Environmental Factors
Related Aspects
Time Factor
Feed Back
Telephone Boxes
Conclusions

INTRODUCTION

The basic objective of our project was to investigate the nature and extent of the wilful damage to buildings resulting from vandalism, in order to produce a series of guides for designers to enable them to counter vandalism, with particular reference to any precautions that can be taken at the design and construction stages. Originally, the scope

118

of the project excluded wilful damage resulting from attempted theft, or to buildings left unoccupied or under construction. However, during the course of the research, it was occasionally necessary to touch upon these aspects because of the excessive damage that is involved in these three categories. It has also been necessary to widen the scope to include the designer's contribution to the provision of an environment that is not conducive to vandalism.

In the long term we look for solutions to the social psychologists, but we feel that in creating an urban environment, the designer's contribution must not be underestimated or overlooked. The factors constituting an environment produce sociological, psychological and perhaps physical reactions within the user. Therefore teams of designers *do* have considerable responsibility, and their influence may be applied to its maximum effect at the planning stages of the design, for it is at this point that all factors relating to the character and nature of the surroundings and their intended uses should be considered.

Consequently we are concerned not only with the construction of internal and external spaces, but also with their sizes and relationships each to the other, relative to their purpose. We think that to attack the problem at the overall and detailed planning stages will alleviate or even eliminate the later problems encountered in the selection of appropriate finishes, materials, components and details. To consider the relative merits of certain types of finishes to withstand attack, is to consider the final and desperate last line of defence: the problem should never have been allowed to penetrate so deeply into the design.

RESEARCH PROCEDURE

At the outset of the project, we decided to keep our attitude to it as flexible as possible, so that we could allow it to develop along its own course, until such time as obvious paths of research became evident.

As a result of several initial discussions on the means of approaching the objective, it was decided that we should contact numerous authorities and organisations, in order to ascertain the extent and nature of vandalism within selected localities distributed throughout the country. It was considered an advantage to devise a 'questionnaire' type of letter in order to seek out basic information, although this was later amended to allow the informant more latitude in his reply. Over eighty authorities and organisations were contacted, predominantly architects, Direct Works and Borough Engineers' Departments, together with newspapers, insurance firms and other sundry bodies. Under 40% replied, with only a proportion of these being positively helpful.

The research pattern therefore entailed the following up of the leads provided by these replies, in the form of interviews and visits to the localities. The form of the interviews was biased towards the extraction of information concerning the problems encountered and remedial measures, if any. If no remedial action had been taken we attempted to find out why this was so. Often the visits resulted from the recommendations and discussions with interviewees, and took the form of a detailed inspection of specific examples of wilful damage, noting the materials and/or components attacked, local environmental conditions intensity of attack, and suggested remedies.

In order to acquire sufficient information and to broaden the field of the project, we realised that it would be necessary to obtain more information in the form of inspections, other than those related to interviews. This was achieved by the close scrutiny of severely attacked areas of Liverpool and surrounding overspill areas, using the Specific Example Format as shown. Since the project was on a short-term basis it was necessary to use each interview or inspection as a pilot for those that followed—we realised that this was not good practice, since it meant that new factors arising in later visits might not have been considered in earlier ones. However, with hindsight, we feel able to justify the method adopted, by pointing out that one of the striking features of the study was the regularity with which the same problems occurred in different localities. Although we evolved a fairly rigid framework within which to note the specific examples, it was considered to be undesirable for the interviews because of the varying personalities and attitudes of the interviewees.

Having gained what we thought to be adequate information, we then began to 'distil' and correlate it into a series of information sheets, (the form of which was based upon the notation system for the specific examples) which were then used as a basis for the design guides.

Specific Example Format	CI/Sfb	TABLES	SECTION No.
	0	1	2/3 b
(a) Precis	General aspects of the damage		
(b) Locality	Define exact position		
	(1) Town and district		
	(2) Street(s)		
	(3) Internal or external space		
	(4) Level		
	(5) Overall location plan, elevation or section		
(c) Material and/or Component Attacked	(1) Detailed description		
	(2) Extent of damage		
	(3) By what		
	(4) Plans, sections, elevations particularly relevant		
(d) Initial conclusions	(1) Nuisance/benefit to users		
	(2) Motive behind damage		
	(3) Evidence of past avoiding measures		
	(4) Future remedial action		
(e) Summary			

The guides evolved from a discussion and notation system devised to enable us, both individually and collectively, to give deeper thought to the problems with which we were concerned. It was also necessary to adopt this procedure in order to try to generate original thought, because despite the tremendous losses resulting from vandalism, surprisingly little attention has been given to this form of delinquency by sociologists, psychologists, and particularly, by designers.

In his book, *Juvenile Vandalism*, J. M. Martin states that, "an article published in *Federal Probation* as part of a 'symposium on vandalism' noted that although it was possible to build up a substantial library about such subjects as arson, assault, burglary, kleptomania, runaways, sex misconduct, and truancy, the voluminous professional literature on juvenile delinquency was virtually silent on vandalism".

Therefore, since the nature of the project was by necessity exploratory, the design guides presented in the sections that follow are offered for the contribution they may make toward a better understanding of the designer's role in preventing vandalism and wilful damage—they are not intended to be accepted as final and absolute statements.

A - Overall planning

INTRODUCTION

For the purposes of this study the term Overall Planning refers to the stage of the design process where the architect considers the juxta-position of a building or buildings to the surrounding external areas and elements of landscape. The number of topics analysed is not comprehensive by any means, but does embrace all the basic factors considered essential for the initial stage in designing to prevent vandalism. The greatest benefits may be gained by careful design at this stage. Because of the scale involved, any mistake or omission will create problems that at a later design stage will be too great to rectify.

A (i)   EXTERNAL CIRCULATION—PEDESTRIAN

Far too often designers tend to produce overall plans containing much too rigid a system of pedestrian circulation. This is often achieved by actual physical barriers varying from the juxtaposition of long buildings to the use of high brick walls around pathways. It is so unnatural for people to be channelled around in fixed routes that it is not surprising that they are forever trying to find short cuts across the circulation system. This would be quite acceptable if no damage resulted and no privacy were invaded, but alas, this is seldom the case. Basically, therefore, designers should

allow pedestrians as much freedom of movement as possible

provided that privacy is respected and property protected.

During the research it became increasingly evident that areas of vertical circulation which are also used as part of a ground floor,

1

3

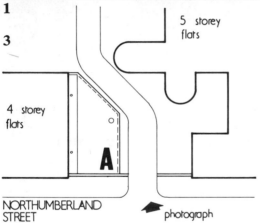

5 storey
flats

4 storey
flats

A

NORTHUMBERLAND
STREET

← photograph

January 19th, 1971		81	90	a

(a) Precis — Derelict courtyard between blocks of flats

(b) Locality
  (1) Liverpool 8
  (2) Northumberland Street
  (3) External space
  (4) Ground

(c) Material and/or component attacked
  (1) Area A used as 'litter tipping ground', fence around this area non-existent, only m.s. uprights left.
  (2)
  (3)
  (4)

(d) Initial conclusions
  (1) Nuisance as cannot use area A for anything else except a tip for rubbish.
  (2) Reaction to space as a whole
  (3) None
  (4) Produce a more interesting and useful space.

(e) Summary

The whole space seems to lack purpose, except for pedestrian circulation and access for vehicles. Large areas of tarmac and the space A which was originally fenced off from the users, are left over with no apparent use after the road is accounted for—people appear to be secondary to vehicles. With a little thought, the road ought to have run straight through area A and without subdividing the space.

The brick wall between Northumberland Street and the area seems to have no use— except perhaps to provide more space for graffiti and damage—the whole space would have felt less restricted and prison-like without it. Admittedly children would run out on to the main road, but this kind of problem is only truly overcome at the design stage to the whole housing layout. As it is, children can still run out through the opening in the wall left for the road and yet have a more restricted vision than if there were no wall.

Many walls such as that mentioned above have been noted, all with no apparent purpose —again a waste of money, and all producing a prison-like atmosphere.

horizontal, or external circulation pattern are attacked beyond all proportion (1). The increase in the number of people likely to pass through such areas caused by the dual use, appears at first to contradict our contention that the possible increase in supervision leads to a reduction in vandalism, but further research shows that it is this very increase which probably produces the extensive wear and tear initially, which is then followed by dilapidation and vandalism. The latter is often the result of children playing while sheltering from rain. More will be found on this matter in the Detailed Planning section.

A (i) EXTERNAL CIRCULATION—VEHICULAR

The layout of roads, particularly in housing estates, has a tremendous effect on the usable spaces left over for the estate inhabitants. In order that vehicular circulation should not dominate any area,
the number of vehicles should be reduced to a minimum
avoiding long straight roads that can become "race tracks" thus allowing pedestrians greater freedom and obviously more safety.

It is important that designers realise that the positioning of a road can have an immense effect on the eventual use and treatment of an area. They should always ensure that, if a road has to pass through a confined space, the areas remaining are useful and interesting for the people who are intended to use them, otherwise such nondescript areas will be abused—perhaps deservedly so (2, 3). The specific example notes that follow are a copy of the original notes taken during the inspection of such an area in Liverpool.

A (ii) GARAGES

Since garage compounds form ideal sheltered spaces in which children can play, often causing damage, and are rarely supervised, least of all by the dwellings that they serve (**4, 5**), the children can create havoc without any fear of being caught. Therefore, do not group garages in large compounds.

The optimum size for garage groups should be four units and it is not sufficient to cluster groups together in long rows. By far the best method to overcome this form of damage is to
locate garages within houses, as far as possible.
Where not possible, for instance in medium and high rise developments, garages should be located on main pedestrian routes so that more supervision is available. It is also an asset if the garage area is on a through vehicular route and is not a "one access" compound.

A (iii) PLAY AREAS—GENERAL

Perhaps the cause of a great deal of damage found in high rise developments is the lack of suitable spaces where children can play safely. However, even where such spaces are provided, children, especially boys, may prefer to play on the hard surfaced areas nearer their homes (**6, 7**).
Large, flat hard-surfaced areas should be avoided where it is not intended that children should play games,
otherwise they will cause damage to surrounding dwellings especially by the breaking of windows, and annoyance to the surrounding residents, especially on the ground floor—who by necessity are usually the ones least able to put up with this type of discomfort—the elderly.

This theory can be extended to service areas. These should not be located close to designated play spaces since they will be used as an extension of these areas particularly if not supervised by passers-by or surrounding dwellings. As previously stated, garage compounds and service areas are ideal places for children to play completely undisturbed, and so to begin the deterioration of these areas by inflicting what is at first accidental damage. Such areas are found to be more attacked if they have a southerly aspect, probably because children prefer to play in sunny sheltered spaces.
Therefore
all service areas should be made non-conducive to the playing of games
by whatever planning means possible.

A (iv) BOUNDARIES

Often the provision of sometimes unnecessary circulation separates properties which could justifiably share a common boundary. This entails the provision of extra fencing and the creation of a public 'no-

124

4

5

6 7

man's-land' pathway—thus producing an unsupervised area (**8**). Dilapidation may then follow since the tenants may feel that they have no responsibility for its maintenance.

Do not provide circulation where it is unnecessary.

While avoiding this form of circulation, it should be realised that privacy must be maintained and that an added advantage is the reduction in means of access, for the would-be thieves and vandals.

A (v) SUPERVISION

Like thieves, vandals prefer to work in areas where they cannot be observed. The provision of supervision should be as much a part of the design process as is the planning of the vehicular network. Basically **there cannot be too much supervision whether it is organised or of an incidental nature.**

This point was repeatedly emphasized by all those interviewed, especially the Crime Prevention Officer of Liverpool. In areas which are foreseeable as being those of a high risk, a major aid in providing supervision is to bring public circulation as close as possible to or through the area since the fear of being interrupted deters many would-be vandals. The disposition of the different blocks can greatly help supervision, but great care must be taken in the layout of the blocks in order to satisfy other planning considerations.

A (vi) SUSCEPTIBLE MATERIALS

Cases have been noted of highly susceptible materials, such as tile-hanging, glazing, asbestos and composite panels, being attacked out of all proportion—this we feel happened since the elevations in question fronted on to areas considered to be of high risk (**9**).

By careful planning, obstacles such as trees, shrubs, fences, embankments and unglazed buildings may be positioned so that they form an effective barrier against missiles. This form of prevention may be particularly relevant to some system-built schools, where susceptible materials are, by necessity, used on all faces.

But basically:

Building complexes should be planned so that elevations constructed from susceptible materials, do not face high risk areas.

If this is not possible and obstacles have to be provided, then care should be taken so that these do not provide cover for the attacker.

B - Detailed planning

INTRODUCTION:

It is at this stage, where the designer gives deeper thought to the size, disposition and function of elements of accommodation while relating them to the whole, that he is able to ensure that the building will have some form of *permanent* deterrent against attack.

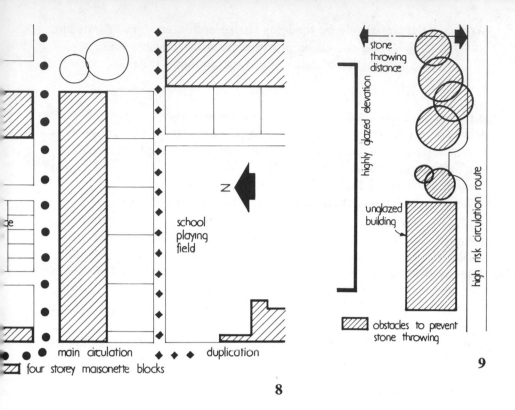

main circulation   ◆ ◆ ◆   duplication

☐ four storey maisonette blocks

8

stone throwing distance

highly glazed elevation

unglazed building

high risk circulation route

▨ obstacles to prevent stone throwing

school playing field

9 *If it is possible to plan a building complex so that elevations using highly vulnerable materials do not face high-risk sides, then obstacles such as trees, shrubs, fences, embankments and unglazed buildings should be placed to form an effective barrier against missiles*

Again, the following aspects are those problems that we encountered and considered that remedial measures should be included at the Detailed Planning stage.

B (i) LIGHTING—INTERNAL

It has already been stated that the vandal prefers to work in areas that are not overlooked, or that are too dark in which to be observed. The designer has the chance during the planning stage to eliminate such areas at least by the provision of adequate lighting. He should always

provide as much natural day lighting as possible

because (a) it provides far more varied and interesting spaces, (b) is generally cheap to provide, (c) allows better supervision—especially of circulation areas and (d) eliminates dark 'nooks and crannies'. In providing a general level of illumination of public areas at night time, the designer should also highlight areas that are considered of high risk, for example recessed doorways, lift lobbies, etc.

Artificial lighting should be made as varied and interesting as possible, and any highlighting should be provided from inaccessible sources,
for instance from within a shop window to highlight the doorway.

B (i) LIGHTING—EXTERNAL

It was pointed out repeatedly during the research that a high proportion of vandalism occurred in places where there was enough light to see by, but not enough to be seen in. It is obviously this dim half-light with numerous shadows that should be avoided.

A high level of illumination must be provided in high risk areas.

The need for better day lighting externally may seem beyond the designer's control, but this is not so if one considers the effect that certain design decisions have upon the degree of day lighting available. The positioning of central vertical circulation areas in blocks of square plan shape results in large dark areas under the building on the ground floor. These areas are ideal for loitering and sheltering and much damage may result.

Large dark areas should be eliminated with the use of natural lighting.

B (ii) CIRCULATION—INTERNAL

During the series of inspections many cases were seen of excessive amounts of circulation area, particularly on the ground floor of blocks of flats. Excess space increases the likelihood of juveniles loitering and resultant damage. Instances could be cited of three storey blocks having as much circulation space on the ground floor as blocks containing twenty-three storeys.

Internal circulation should be reduced to a minimum.

Another design error from this point of view is the use of internal vertical circulation areas as part of a major external horizontal circulation route.

Dual use of circulation areas should be avoided.

The solution may lie in allowing a way through for horizontal external circulation with a separate entrance for the vertical circulation. Better still: the vertical circulation should be taken right away from major horizontal routes.

By careful planning it should be possible to arrange that the most intensively used area in each dwelling looks out on to vertical circulation areas while still safeguarding privacy.

Vertical circulation zones should be exposed to supervision at all levels.

A major error often found in circulation areas is the introduction of extra uses. These include the siting of meter cupboards, switch rooms and bicycle stores, which are severely attacked by vandals sheltering in the lobbies (**10, 27**). Many such cases were seen, often with the doors to such rooms bricked up to avoid further damage. It would seem that the damage starts through misuse and is then enlarged by loitering

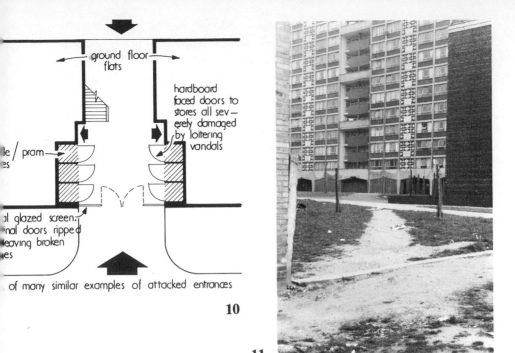

ground floor flats

hardboard faced doors to stores all sev— erely damaged by loitering vandals

le / pram es

ıl glazed screen: inal doors ripped leaving broken es

of many similar examples of attacked entrances

10

11

youths—dilapidation follows and then more serious attacks occur. **Do not introduce extra uses into circulation areas.**

B (ii) CIRCULATION—EXTERNAL

During the past fifteen years, the development of high-rise blocks and certain forms of the Radburn principle of housing layout, have led to large numbers of garages being grouped into unsupervised compounds and thus being open to attack. Lack of supervision arises from the fact that such garages cannot be seen from the dwellings that they serve and that major circulation routes rarely pass through them.

Therefore, relate garages and parking spaces as closely as possible to dwellings and ensure that major circulation routes pass close by them. In fact, where the vehicular circulation is of the cul-de-sac or feeder type,

where the vehicular traffic is very light, additional benefits of supervision of service areas may be gained by the integration of parts of pedestrian circulation with that of vehicles.

Thus, with increased use, such areas may benefit from a reduction in vandalism, due to the greater fear of the vandal of being interrupted.

Pathways

During the interviews and from subsequent inspections it became evident that much external vandalism is attributed to people taking short cuts between lines of circulation (**11**). The solution may lie in more subtlety in circulation planning on the part of the designer and in effect means

(1) avoiding sharp changes in direction
(2) using changes in materials or levels or landscaping to produce interesting but logical and workable lines of movement.
(3) not using feeble items such as litter bins or low walls to change the direction of paths.

Staircases
Throughout the period of research, the damage to enclosed external staircases was found to be immense, especially at ground and first floor levels.
These areas should be treated as an extension of the external circulation by leaving them entirely open, but sheltered possibly by the neighbouring buildings and the flights above.

Supervision
The layout of adjoining blocks should be arranged so as to provide adequate supervision of the surrounding areas (**12**).
Intensively used rooms should overlook circulation areas.
This should also apply to vertical circulation areas in high-rise developments, though the problem of retaining privacy will be more acute.

B (iii) FENESTRATION
The destruction of fenestration is perhaps the most common form of vandalism found in this country. This is probably because the effect for the vandal is so immediate, apparent, and in some strange way, satisfying.

Yet this need not be so. Far too much glazing has been introduced into our buildings during the last generation; often purely for elevational effect rather than in relation to individual room needs. The first guide therefore is to
reduce glazing to a minimum
but still relate it to its purpose. Taken a stage further, the designer in the layout planning stage should
consider the possibility of planning the building(s) so that those elements of accommodation that require very little or no glazing front on to any foreseeable high risk sides (15).
In housing this may be achieved without much difficulty since accommodation such as the kitchen, hall and bathroom naturally face the public service areas, while the living areas front on to the private sides. A simple method of avoiding planning problems, often employed by designers, is to make rooms partially or entirely top lit. Rooflights are very susceptible to attack, firstly from missiles, whether dropped from above, or thrown up on to the roof, and secondly from direct attack with levers, hammers, etc., in order to gain entry. Therefore
provide rooflights only when:
(a) there is no access on to the roof
(b) they are capable of resisting attack
(c) they are really necessary.
130

Here, kitchen windows supervise e public space, while remaining all enough to safeguard privacy

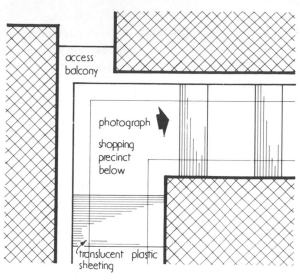

access balcony

photograph

shopping precinct below

translucent plastic sheeting

⬦⬦⬦⬦ buildings with shops on ground floor

13   14

The last comment is made, since examples exist of the ineffective use of rooflights in vulnerable positions. In such instances a co-ordinated system of artificial lighting may have been more beneficial.

The widespread use of translucent sheeting over shopping and other circulation areas has been noted with some apprehension. In many cases where this form of rooflighting was used, it was accessible from upper floor balconies. Not only were these sheets damaged by missiles but also by children playing on them, and the risk of a child fracturing part of a sheet and falling partially or wholly through, resulting in at least severe cuts, can be appreciated (**13, 14**).

Translucent sheeting or other forms of glazed roofing should not be provided if at all accessible or easily attacked with missiles.

131

The present tendency of some architects to devise plan shapes with a large number of recesses has in some cases led to an increase in the damage suffered. The reasons for this are twofold. Firstly, such areas are more often than not hidden from view and so form spaces that are ideal for vandals to damage without being seen. Secondly, such small recesses may form litter traps if not carefully designed as such, may give the building the appearance of being dilapidated and therefore attract attack (**16**).

Small hidden recesses should be avoided

whether inside or outside a building.

Service Ducts

It is advisable at the outset of the design process to consider the allocation of space to service ducts that will contain a system of centralised services (**18**). This, of course, is applicable above all to public conveniences in which

all services should be concealed

but the policy should be applied in all cases within public buildings. The removal of pipework was one item which was repeated many times during the research period as being an incessantly recurrent problem.

"Strong Rooms"

Because of the lightweight nature of modern construction access through partitions is quite easy for a determined vandal. This has been particularly noted in system-built schools throughout the country, where access has easily been gained in order to steal equipment such as tape recorders, television sets and typewriters. Much damage has been caused in the course of such thefts. Therefore in such cases it is advisable to

build a "strong room" into, on to, or closely connected to any building which might be considered susceptible.

Existing strong rooms have a somewhat limited use, since their usefulness depends upon the tedious task of moving equipment in and out of them. Taking the idea to its logical conclusion, however, such rooms should house the equipment without relying on removal procedures. For example, rooms like language laboratories should always be "strong rooms".

Far too often in the research it was noticed that vast areas of hard surfacing are incorporated within housing layouts. Often, too, these large flat areas were accompanied by notice boards proclaiming the penalties

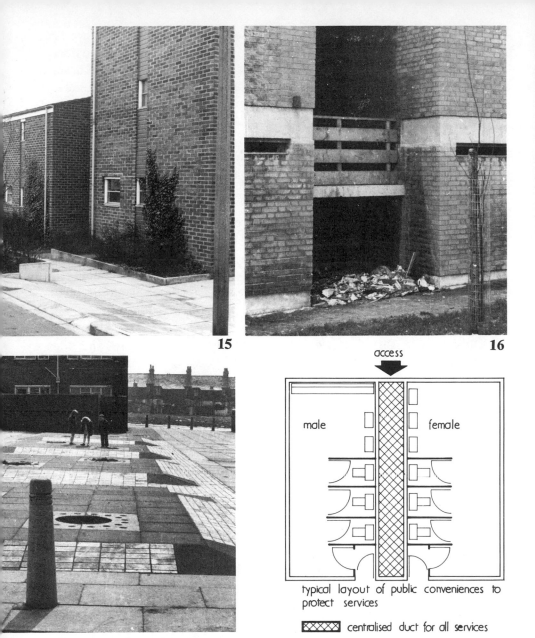

access

male   female

typical layout of public conveniences to protect services

▨▨▨ centralised duct for all services

18

17 *Large flat hard-surfaced areas invite ball games leading to damage: any attempt to break such areas into smaller ones should be done boldly. Here is a meagre attempt which has totally failed. Note: trees have been removed*

for playing ball games in such spaces. If ball games are to be forbidden it is better to provide a series of smaller spaces that are clearly defined and unusable for this purpose as a whole, than just one large area (**17**). Otherwise children will naturally use it as a play space for ball games, leading to misuse, accidental damage and thus dilapidation. The size and type of space must relate to intended use and number of users. **For circulation areas only, reduce the hard paving to a minimum**

133

but still retain a logical and workable circulation pattern, otherwise short-cutting will occur across soft landscaping materials if provided. Soft landscaping is less liable to attack if care is taken over the design and details of the circulation patterns. Above all, monotony should be avoided by utilising changes of level, contrasting materials, etc.

Soft Surfacing

Generally the type of planting that has been, and still is being used by most local authorities, e.g. saplings, hybrid tea roses, geraniums, etc., is either damaged because of people walking across flower beds for a short cut, or wantonly destroyed, or even stolen to be resold or reused elsewhere. Therefore

protect susceptible plants or trees with shrubs that have prickly thorns like gorse, holly, hawthorn and berberis—see recommended planting list.

A few examples of this policy have been seen, and work admirably—especially with a logical circulation progression. Far too much money is wasted on the provision of saplings which in such areas have little or no chance of survival. The normal wire cage is of little use, and does provide a climbing frame for young children. It is more sensible to provide fewer trees surrounded by prickly bushes (**20, 15**), even to the extent of using gooseberry or blackberry bushes, which serve a useful protective purpose.

The principle may be extended to provide protection for fencing or other landscaping elements that are liable to be damaged (**21**). A good example was seen of berberis growing up through a string wire mesh that was attached to a garden fence on an intensively used main circulation route. Such barriers are often attacked.

In order to give any estate or building complex a mature appearance **use plants, shrubs and trees as mature as possible.**

Fewer numbers will be needed since they will provide sufficient coverage. However, since traditional methods of protection such as chestnut palings, wire cages and timber stakes are inadequate (**22**)

saplings, if used, should generally be placed in the gardens of tenants in new housing developments (**19**). Admittedly, a certain number will be abused but the surviving number will be far greater than if they had to grow outside the boundary of a dwelling.

Grass is only successful when used in sufficiently large areas, so that it cannot be destroyed by intensive use, and also

grass should never be located close to sharp changes in the direction of circulation routes

or the sheer number of people walking across it will destroy it (**23**).

Recommended Planting:

The following list of prickly plants was compiled with the help of Skelmersdale Development Corporation and should be read in conjunction with Section B (v) Landscaping.

19 **20**

21 **22 23**

Botanical name	Common name and/or remarks
Berberis aggregata	Deciduous and evergreen shrubs
„ bramptonensis	with small prickly leaves or
„ candidula	stems, usually golden flowers
„ coxii	turning to red or black berries
„ gagnepainii	in autumn—hardy and will grow
„ Julianae	vigorously in most soils.
„ Jamesiana	
„ dictophylla	
„ Koreana	
„ Media Parkjewel	
„ Mentorensis	
„ Morrisonensis	
„ ottowensis	
„ prattii	
„ rubroscilla	
„ stenophylla	
„ thunbergii	
„ suberecta	
„ verrucandida	
„ Robusta	
„ vulgaris	
Crataegus oxycantha	Hawthorn—prickly
Ilex aquifolium	Holly—many varieties available
	—prickly

Botanical name	Common name and/or remarks
Rosa rugosa Max Graf.	Roses—mainly of wild varieties
„ hybrid Fruhlings gold	—all prickly
„ hybrid Fruhlings morgan	
„ xanthia Canary Bird	
„ spinosissima	
„ rubrifolia	
„ gallica complicata	
„ Carolina	
„ moyesii	
„ omeiensis pteracantha	
„ gallica Scharachglut	
„ eglanteria	
Ulex europaeus	Gorse; Furze; Whin—well
„ plenus	known prickly plants of heath
	and moor.

C - Applied Finishes

INTRODUCTION:

The performance of an applied finish to withstand attack relies to a large extent upon the backing and/or underlying construction, and we have therefore divided the vast range of applied finishes available into four basic types, namely:

(i)   APPLIED FILM

(ii)   APPLIED SHEET

(iii) APPLIED UNITS

(iv)   APPLIED COATINGS

and have sought to present the information so that easy and direct comparisons could be made, between the characteristics of the four types. Thus each type is sub-divided into eight sections and evaluated against the criteria for each section given below:

a. *Surface Texture* It has been noted throughout the research, that surfaces having a very marked texture were relatively free from vandalism—and in particular, graffiti—this is more than likely due to the fact that the formation of letters is so much more difficult than on large, smooth areas.

b. *Colour* The colour of an applied finish is of importance, when one considers the effect of exposing the underlying materials as a result of damage.

c. *Pattern* Research has shown that the more strongly patterned surfaces formed by using relatively bold, contrasting colours, are less prone to attack than similar sizes of wall area having a plain, pristine character—again, this is particularly relevant to graffiti. However, the scale of the pattern should not be too large, otherwise writing will still occur within large areas of colour, and of course, will be all the more conspicuous.

d. *Dura-bility* Ability to withstand weathering and particularly normal wear and tear, is the main criterion here, since any form of failure within these properties will lead to dilapidation and subsequently will make the surface more prone to attack.

e. *Main-tenance* Simplicity and cheapness of maintenance are essential for those finishes that are liable to be attacked, but care should be taken to ensure that this will not mean an increased frequency of renewal, as this could lead to higher overall running costs and the justification of an initially dearer, but more durable finish.

f. *Strength in Resisting Attack* Inherent strength to resist a certain degree of attack is essential if the finish is not only to withstand damage, but constant wear and tear—although to a large extent, any resistance to attack will rely upon the bond between the finish and the underlying construction, and the nature of the backing itself.

g. *Form of Under-lying Con-struction*	Stability of the backing or underlying construction is of paramount importance since the finish may be initially damaged by movement of the element of structure. The specifications of the bonding and the construction as a whole are also very important, in order to eliminate any defects that could arise through faulty materials or workmanship and thus produce a shabby appearance.
h. *Sum-mary*	Basically, this is a conclusion formulated from the above performance criteria, in order to produce a form of design guide. The following notes are mainly concerned with coverings to vertical elements, since during research little or no damage was found to floors and ceilings—possibly due to the fact that in order to attack a wall finish, the offender is probably less conspicuous and the object more convenient, than in the other two elements. Our notes are also orientated towards those finishes that we found to be attacked the most, but may be applied in principle, to other finishes.

C (i) APPLIED FILM

This type of applied finish encompasses all paints, varnishes, lacquers, etc., which are normally applied by brush or spray. The main forms of attack encountered are writing, scratching and peeling—the last type usually following some kind of inherent defect within the film, for example, blistering or flaking.

a. *Surface Texture*	Generally, the texture of the film is smooth (although some sprayed finishes do produce a slightly granular effect) due to its characteristic of being so thin and of normally being applied to a smooth backing—thus providing an ideal 'canvas' for the graffiti specialists. Only by applying the film to a surface that is previously markedly textured will this problem be *partially* alleviated since this will make the formation of letters far more difficult—except of course, if the vandal uses an aerosol spray.
b. *Colour*	One of the main disadvantages of the applied film, is that it may be chipped or scratched away to reveal the material below and if the colour of the film and the backing are totally unrelated, the result will be all the more noticeable (**24**). Since the film could be one of literally hundreds of colours, matching this to the colour of the backing could prove to be difficult and restrictive, but as far as possible select colour of applied film so that it is closely related to or completely matches the colour of the underlying material. Examples of this form of accentuated damage are galvanised sheet metal and plasterwork painted in a rich, dark colour—that is, films applied to surfaces of low

24   25

	porosity which do not allow the colour to penetrate to any depth.

c. *Pattern*   Bold patterns formed from strong, contrasting colours of applied film seem to be conspicuous by their absence—this is probably due to the fact that in order to produce a result worthy of merit, highly skilled workmen have to be found and high labour rates paid over a long period. The end result would probably be of a semi-permanent nature and would almost certainly be painted over during the next maintenance period.

d. *Dura-bility*   Due to the thin nature of applied films, they tend to weather relatively quickly, especially under the action of the sun and if not regularly maintained they will soon produce a dilapidated appearance (**25**)—see DILAPIDATION. Their thinness also has other disadvantages, in that there is very little resistance to abrasion or impact inflicted during normal use, major defects on the surface of the underlying construction are not concealed, and any defect within the film itself is soon accentuated by enlargements to unsightly proportions, whether by accident, or with intent.

e. *Main-tenance*   Generally, applied films are easy to maintain, since their cleaning and replacement present few problems and is normally inexpensive—this is possibly the reason why they are so widely used. However, since this type of finish is so susceptible to attack, maintenance should be far more frequent in order to keep up with vandalism, and consequently may be more expensive than with the use of more durable finishes.

139

f. *Strength in Resisting Attack* Since applied films have very little, or no inherent strength, they rely entirely upon the underlying construction for any resistance to attack. It may be appreciated therefore how feeble most of these finishes are, since they may easily be scratched off, fractured, or pulled away in large pieces upon impact, or peeled off following damage or defect of another type. The two types of film that do offer some form of resistance are those that are polyurethane based, or those that colour by staining—the former does have a certain degree of impact resistance, whereas the latter (for example, a timber preservative) not only provides a protective film, but also colours the material to a sufficient depth to make scratching and/or gouging less noticeable.

g. *Form of Underlying Construction* Stability and rigidity are necessary from the underlying construction, otherwise cracking, crazing or flaking may occur and thus provide a 'beginning' for the vandals. The specification and workmanship of materials immediately beneath the applied film is very important since any superficial defect will not be hidden by the thin coat of film. Defects that arise from the interaction of the film and its backing will also be noticed, because of the fact that the film is so thin and lacks inherent strength and will therefore not have sufficient resistance to any expansion or contraction resulting from this process.

h. *Summary*
(i)   Easily defaced—writing, scratching, gouging.
(ii) Weathers relatively quickly
(iii) No inherent strength to resist attack.
(iv) Shows up all types of defects of underlying construction.
(v)   Easy, but frequent maintenance.
(vi) Use in inaccessible places or where colour is impregnated.

C (ii) APPLIED SHEET

This form of finish may be conveniently sub-divided into two basic categories—rigid and flexible—and it is under these headings that the information is presented for the different characteristics.

Of the rigid sheets available, asbestos, sheet metal, ribbed aluminium and plastic sheet in the form of a laminate facing, are the most commonly attacked—the flexible types are limited to the different types of wallpapers. Rigid sheets when under attack may be chipped, cracked, shattered, dented and of course written upon, and with the exception of the graffiti it is generally true that the initial attack is focussed upon the junction between the two sheets or with another material.

Flexible sheets are prone to gouging, writing and peeling off—this again at junctions.

a. *Surface Texture* Rigid: the texture may vary from being completely smooth as with plastic sheet, to the numerous textures available in pre-formed sheet metal. The former have the disadvantage of providing a surface that is easy to write upon, but the advantage of being easily cleaned. The latter, although more difficult to clean, has the added deterrent of making the formation of letters very difficult—unless the vandal uses an aerosol spray, to which there seems to be no answer.

Flexible: since these are generally applied to a flat surface and since their thickness allows very little texture to be formed within it, they generally present a smooth surface to the vandal and are therefore ideal for graffiti or gouging—the latter being a particularly effective form of attack since a contrast in colours usually results between the finish and its backing, while the damage is far more difficult to repair.

b. *Colour* Rigid: it is an advantage with certain types of rigid sheet that in order to make it self-supporting, the thickness of the material, and consequently the depth of through-colour is increased—thus making gouging and scratching far less noticeable than with contrasting colours. Thus with long thin facing sheets, care should be taken in relating the colours of the finish to its backing.

Flexible: as with the rigid type, many colours are available and careful selection of colours (finish and backing) will reduce the unsightly appearance of scratching and gouging—since this form of applied sheet is particularly vulnerable to this form of attack.

c. *Pattern* Rigid: sheets such as plastics may be highly patterned on the exposed face, and during the research it was found that such surfaces apper to be less prone to attack—particularly from writing. Patterns formed from the ribbing or stippling of sheet metal have the same effect, with the advantage that since the pattern is three-dimensional, forming letters on the surface is not easy.

Flexible: these too are manufactured in numerous surface patterns which will be effective in reducing graffiti only.

d. *Dura-bility* Rigid: provided that rigid sheets are applied to a sound and adequate backing and the junctions between sheets and other materials are good, their performance against normal wear and tear and weathering is generally good.

Flexible: vinyl wall coverings are more durable than the ordinary type of wallpaper since they have a certain degree of elasticity and are therefore able to absorb many de-

141

26 27 *The same: a month later*

formations before giving a dilapidated appearance. Thus cracks, blisters and flaking are less likely to occur and to be the target for the initial stages of vandalistic attack. In general though, it is not advisable to use flexible sheetings in areas of high-density pedestrian ·traffic since they are easily marked by impact and abrasion.

e. *Main-tenance* Rigid: generally these are easy to clean and replace and in many cases are self-finished, so that re-decoration is not necessary.

Flexible: these too are easily cleaned, but may be difficult to replace since they are generally bonded to the backing panel.

f. *Strength in Resisting Attack* Rigid: most rigid sheets are able to resist a certain amount of impact (**26**), but still rely basically upon the underlying construction to prevent excessive deflection and distortion when this occurs.

Flexible: due to their characteristic of being very thin, this type of finish, as stated before, presents few or no problems to the vandal and is therefore unsuitable in accessible positions.

g. *Form of Under-lying Con-struction* Rigid: good workmanship throughout and rigidity of the whole is necessary if the opening up of joints is to be avoided, as it is at these points that the attack begins.

Flexible: due to the thin nature of these sheets they have very little ability to hide any defects. Consequently the quality of the underlying materials must be such that any defect should not occur, whether before or after the application of the finish.

142

h. *Summary*   Rigid:

(i) Easily damaged—chipped, cracked, shattered, dented and written on, unless applied to or formed into an intrinsically strong shape; for example ribbed aluminium sheet.

(ii) Vulnerable at junctions, if not protected.

(iii) Adequate texture and patterns available.

(iv) Durable and easily maintained.

Flexible:

(i) Easily damaged—particularly gouging, also writing and peeling off.

(ii) Vulnerable at junctions, if not protected.

(iii) No inherent strength to resist attack.

(iv) Shows up defects of underlying construction.

(v) Not durable—no resistance to abrasion.

(vi) Adequate patterns available, but little depth of texture.

(vii) Replacement difficult.

C (iii) APPLIED UNITS

This form of finish is mainly ceramic wall tiles and mosaics. The main forms of attack are the destruction of the jointing material; the prising out of one unit (particularly at corners) with the subsequent stripping of the rest; cracking and/or shattering by a heavy blow, and writing or scratching.

a. *Surface Texture* Because of the glazed finish the texture is smooth, although the form of the unit itself may provide a moulded profile and thus deter writing.

b. *Colour* Although most units are not easily scratched, because of the heat process involved in the application of the colour and glaze, once scratched or chipped, the effect is easily noticed because of the contrast between the surface colour (and many are available) and that of the backing which is generally white.

c. *Pattern* Since the manufacturing process allows colours to be applied to the surface of the units, these themselves may have their own pattern or be positioned so as to form a large, overall wall design. However, the designer must ensure that the scale of the pattern is not so large as to encourage the formation of words within each block of colour.

d. *Durability* Provided that the underlying construction and bedding are adequate, applied units are quite durable. They weather well, although they may lose some of their colour in strong sunlight and also have a limited scratch resistance. But whether used internally or externally at low level, they will easily be cracked or shattered by impact. Ceramic mosaic

143

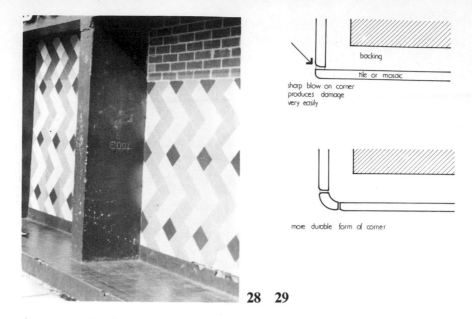

sharp blow on corner
produces damage
very easily

backing

tile or mosaic

more durable form of corner

28 29

28, 29 *Highly-patterned surfaces using bold colours have been found less prone to graffiti. Externally, this is best achieved by glazed ceramic tiles*

is stronger since it is proportionally considerably thicker.

e. *Maintenance*   This type of applied finish is possibly the easiest to maintain since the smooth surface facilitates easy cleaning. (Externally it is self-cleaning in an exposed position) and the replacement of damaged units is also relatively simple although possibly quite frequent.

f. *Strength in Resisting Attack*   Ceramics, whether in tile or mosaic form, cannot resist bending and excessive compression. Their strength in resisting impact, the most common form of attack, lies in their adequate bedding to the underlying construction. Therefore cases where a tile, in particular, is spanning between its fixed edges should be eliminated. One of the most vulnerable positions that occurs when using applied units is at sharp changes of direction as this can leave the edge of a tile or mosaic exposed and therefore relatively easy to lever off—with the subsequent removal of other surrounding units.

g. *Form of Underlying Construction*   Bending and excessive compression are incompatible with this form of applied finish. If such stresses are set up by the movement of the underlying construction, failure may take the form of cracking, shattering and the weakening of the bond between unit and bedding with the possibility of the tile or mosaic falling out. The specification of materials and workmanship is vital if this form of failure is to be avoided.

144

h. *Sum-*
mary (i) Very easily damaged (**29**)—shattered, cracked, levered off, joints destroyed, scratched and written upon, particularly at low level.
(ii) Little inherent strength to resist attack—corners may be very vulnerable.
(iii) Smooth texture, although unit may be profiled.
(iv) Many colours and patterns available, although only superficial.
(v) Easily maintained and relatively durable.

C (iv) APPLIED COATINGS

This type of applied finish incorporates renders, plasters and plasterboard. The main forms of attack are gouging, levering off, writing, or spalling away upon impact.

a. *Surface*
Texture As coatings are generally applied by hand, their finished surface may vary between the smoothness of gypsum plaster to the coarse texture of a rough-cast render. However, their surface textures may be modified for example by an applied film or by small pebbles set in the surface.

b. *Colour* Many coatings are available as self-coloured and are therefore more suitable in vulnerable positions since any scratching or gouging will not be noticed. One of the worst examples noted was the use of a dark-coloured gloss paint on gypsum plaster—whereas a self-coloured Tyrolean render has a surface that is not only difficult to write upon or gouge, but also acts as a deterrent because of its roughness.

c. *Pattern* Only by the organisation and/or repetition of different surface textures can pattern be introduced into applied coatings.

d. *Dura-*
bility Since coatings are susceptible to failure from structural movement, shrinkage, frost damage and defects due to bad workmanship and/or specification this can readily produce a dilapidated appearance and therefore invite attack. Normal wear and tear can easily lead to a run-down appearance due to the fact that they are easily damaged by accidental damage—particularly on corners.

e. *Main-*
tenance Coatings like plaster are easy to replace in damaged areas, but, because of the necessity of an applied film finish, the overall cost may be quite expensive and the finished repair may be very conspicuous if not completely successful. Tyrolean renders are less easy to replace but may not require the additional coat of applied film. If undamaged all types of coatings are relatively easy to maintain, normally with a coat of applied film although the frequency of this operation could produce high overall running costs.

145

30   **31**

It should be pointed out that rough-cast finishes and Tyrolean renders are not easy to keep clean unless finished with coats of applied gloss film.

f. *Strength in Resisting Attack* Because of the granular nature of most coatings they possess little resistance to attack, and are thus easily damaged by impact (**30**) resulting in indentations, cracking, spalling or puncturing (as with plasterboard on studding). Once the damage has been done, it is very easy to continue the process by further impact or the levering off of large segments. The granular nature also allows gouging with sharp instruments (**31**), so that if writing is impracticable, say on a rough-cast render, then gouging of the letters within the depth of the coating is attempted.

g. *Form of Underlying Construction* Since applied coatings rely upon their bonding with the underlying construction for strength and cannot withstand bending or compression, then dimensional and structural stability, and rigidity of the structure or element, is vital for them to remain intact. This is also applicable to plasterboard, particularly on studding.

h. *Summary*
(i)   Easily damaged: gouging, levering off, spalling away upon impact, writing.
(ii) Very little inherent strength in resisting attack.
(iii) Varied textures and through-colours are available.
(iv) Pattern: difficult to achieve successfully.
(v)   Quite durable, but suffer badly from movement.
(vi) Maintenance relatively easy, but frequent.

D - Materials

INTRODUCTION

The term Materials, refers to those elements of substances that are generally used to form parts of components, for example, glazing, timber, etc. They are therefore considered not only in their own right, but also in relation to their location and use, since these two factors have considerable bearing upon their performance characteristics in resisting attack. The following information is related either to highly vulnerable materials or to those which we found to be the most severely and/or consistently attacked.

D (i) GLAZING

As was said in the section of Detailed Planning, the destruction of glazing is the most common form of vandalism, or perhaps the one that is most immediately noticeable. All types of glazing can in some way be broken or disfigured. A material as strong as armour plate glass, for example, can be shattered into harmless pieces with one blow from an engineer's centre punch. Laminated glass, while not actually breaking, crazes badly, and then discolours, and consequently this type of glass, which is often used for shop windows, is rendered useless even though still in one piece. The widespread belief that georgian wired glass is useful in resisting attack appears to be unfounded.

32   *Georgian-wired glazing, foolishly located at foot level*

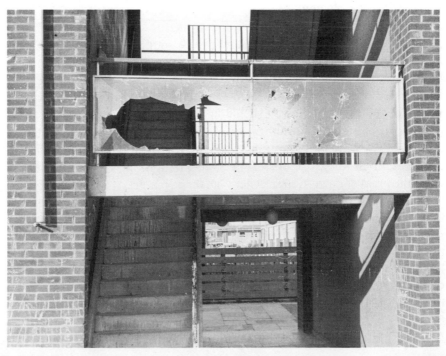

Judging by the amount of it found broken, this type is easily damaged without the vandal fearing injury, since the broken pieces do not fall off, but remain fastened to the wire mesh.

The tremendous amount of glass found damaged is no doubt a result of the high proportion of glazing used in modern buildings. Enough has already been said about the quantity of fenestration and the planning means by which a reduction is possible, but the size of pane used is also extremely important. Small panes are cheaper and easier to replace, and in general have a higher resistance to impact. It is preferable therefore to

use glass in smaller areas

though in some cases this may slightly increase maintenance costs because of the painting of extra mullions.

The theory has been put forward that the use of extremely large panes of glass deters the vandal, since the danger of injury to the attacker is increased, has to our minds still to be proved. Examples for and against have been seen and an attempt was made to analyse the environmental conditions of each case in order to define a pattern of behaviour. No such pattern has been established, though it is felt that the theory could have some validity in cases where the attacker cannot possibly stand out of range of any glass splinters. This may be the reason for the apparent success of the new type of open bus shelters at present being installed in our city centres. It should be pointed out, however, that the designer has a responsibility to safeguard the public from injury as a result of accidental damage.

The high incidence of attack to glass blocks and other forms of structural glazing which was apparent throughout the research, probably stems from the element of competition which is inherent in their destruction. Such forms are often used as target practice for the vandal to prove his worth. The damage is relatively simple to inflict since the blocks, while resisting compressive forces, have little surface resistance to impact. The result is all the more unsightly since as they are generally hollow, a resting place is provided for the missile within the blocks.

No form of structural glazing should be used in high risk areas.

Polycarbonate and similar types of glazing which are claimed to be unbreakable, have until now had a somewhat limited and misguided use. Although they do possess a high strength in resisting impact, examples have been noted where such a material has been badly attacked, because the glazing was taken down to ground level, and was thus within range of the vandal's boot. However, at a higher level, polycarbonate sheeting can be extremely successful and could justify the initial high cost. Therefore

in severe cases use polycarbonate glazing.

Certain qualifications have to be made to this recommendation because of the basic properties of the material. Firstly, because of the inherent flexibility of polycarbonate sheeting the sizes of such sheets should be restricted to no larger than 1,000mm × 600mm, otherwise a great deal

33 *A patent-glazed rooflight at the foot of an external staircase, where it was vulnerable to missiles dropped from the top landing*

of distortion will be apparent. Secondly, again because of this flexibility, more than adequate fixing should be provided or the vandal will be able to spring the pane out of its retaining beads, and thirdly, care must be taken in placing the sheet, as the surface can easily be scratched by sharp objects or burnt through with such things as cigarettes. Most of these reservations can be discounted when the polycarbonate is moulded to form inherently strong shapes, for instance, hemispherical covers for light fittings, rooflights, etc. No matter which form of glazing is used, in certain areas it will be exposed to a greater danger of attack. **The thickness of glazing should vary not only with exposure to wind forces, but also with the degree of attack expected** particularly for instance when glazing is used at ground level (**32, 33**).

D (ii) PLASTER

Unfortunately, for a material with such widespread use, plaster is highly susceptible to any form of damage, mainly because of its smooth pristine nature. Such surfaces are not only easily damaged, but also accentuate the damage and virtually invite the vandal to attack or to enlarge existing defects. **This inherent defect makes plaster unsuitable for use in high risk areas,** especially if a finish of a different colour is to be used. The initial damage to plastered surfaces can be caused by such simple everyday events as furniture removal. This is particularly true on corners. The defects are then enlarged, often by children loitering. Any form of

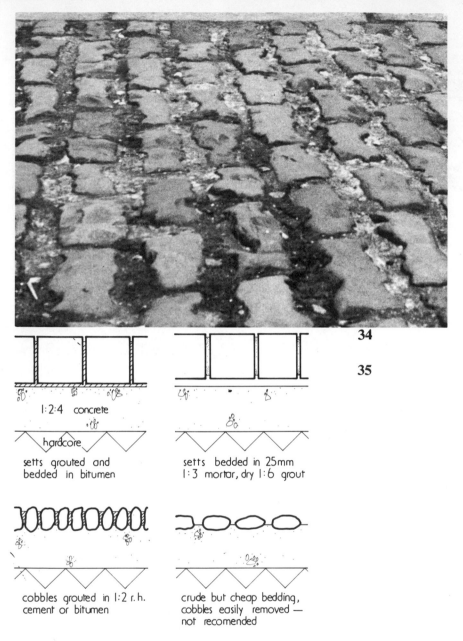

34

35

1:2:4 concrete

hardcore

setts grouted and
bedded in bitumen

setts bedded in 25mm
1:3 mortar, dry 1:6 grout

cobbles grouted in 1:2 r.h.
cement or bitumen

crude but cheap bedding,
cobbles easily removed —
not recomended

plaster or rendering which is less easily gouged, written on or carved is obviously better, therefore the use of

roughcast is preferable especially for circulation areas

since the surface relief reduces the chance of graffiti because the letters cannot be formed easily, and because it does not show up defects as much as ordinary plaster.

D (iii) HARD EXTERNAL SURFACING (SMALL UNITS)

The use of small units of hard landscaping can greatly relieve the monotony of large open areas, but if not securely laid, such materials as cobbles, setts and brick paving are easily removed and provide a

150

ready supply of ammunition. Once the seating of one unit is destroyed, whether naturally, for example by frost, or mechanically by a vandal with some form of lever, the remainder are simple to extract (**34**).

Such small units should be set in bitumen with the larger proportion below the surface.

Furthermore, in order to reduce the amount of leverage possible, they should be bedded as close together as is practicable (**35**).

D (iv) WEATHERBOARD AND TILEHANGING

These materials which are subjected to extensive use in some system building methods are frequently destroyed through insufficient thought concerning their siting. Both will fracture with incessant impact, particularly tiles; both can be levered off without much difficulty; and both can quickly become unsightly. This is especially true when such materials are used at low level where they are in range of attack by kicking or ball games.

Weatherboard and tile-hanging should never be used facing high risk sites.
An example was seen of tile hanging used on one complete elevation of a school which fronted on to the playground. The wall was used as a goal, with the result that all the tiles had to be removed after months of excessive maintenance.

D (v) SHEET MATERIALS

Damage to sheet materials often results from their use in unsuitable situations. Such materials as hardboard, plywood, asbestos, plasterboard and fibreboard are in general highly susceptible to attack, yet these are usually the materials used to make up composite panels for positioning below window sill level. The performance of each obviously depends greatly on the surrounding conditions and the size of sheet used. Often such sheets constitute large flat exposed areas which are an attraction to the vandal for writing or carving. Examples were seen of badly attacked hardboard-faced doors in circulation areas, a position in which the material was quite inadequate. Such materials tend to stand out from their surroundings as they are sometimes used to provide colour and therefore may become the obvious place for graffiti.

Care must be taken in the siting of large flat areas of sheet materials.
A special note must be made about the use of translucent sheeting for roof coverings. Many examples were seen of this type of material being used in accessible positions. Not only is this form of sheet easily fractured but it readily becomes unsightly when damaged.

D (vi) TIMBER

Some timbers are particularly vulnerable to attack especially if of a wide grained variety. Nearly all timbers are vulnerable if moulded into forms on which the arris can easily be gouged or broken off, for example, on door frames and window sills. Unfortunately timber is the traditional

36

material for carving, especially of names, and is therefore highly susceptible in areas in which people loiter. Therefore if it has to be used **in high risk areas, utilise timber of close grained type** with impregnated, stained, preservative finish, rather than with paint or varnish, which would tend to heighten any damage. It has become increasingly evident that any timber painted white is particularly vulnerable to attack. This applies most of all to ranch type fencing, which has been used a great deal throughout many housing developments, and to panels of weatherboarding. Perhaps it is because it stands out so much, or that the vandal prefers his handiwork to be seen. The amount of white fencing used in these estates, while giving a feeling of lightness, did in fact produce an effect of monotony, heightened by vandalism, which could have been avoided.

D (vii) BRICKS AND BLOCKS

These two materials are the traditional ones for counteracting vandalism, and, basically, are very good because of their hard dense nature. Most types also have a rough surface texture which deters the attacker from writing for fear of grazing knuckles, etc., and at the same time their strength prevents gouging and carving. The integral colouring of bricks prevents any damage caused from becoming an eyesore. The smoother textured varieties and the older examples that have weathered badly, do provide a hard suitable surface for writing. This is all the more noticeable as brick walls often constitute large expanses on which to paint immense messages. They are unfortunately extremely hard to clean. If brickwork has to be used in large areas the surface should be given some form of relief, to deter the formation of large letters.

The only form of gouging found in brickwork is that of mortar joints which are scraped out. This is more noticeable on corners and if the

38   mortar is of a light colour. Bricks do form a considerable nuisance after the useful life of the building has ended; hence the damage noticed around demolition sites (**36**). This is because no vandal carries ammunition with him, but relies on a ready supply of missiles in his target area. This the demolition site provides.
All debris should be removed immediately from demolition sites
otherwise much damage will result.

D (viii) SELF FINISHED MATERIALS
Materials which require no surface treatment initially and therefore little maintenance are generally very useful in withstanding wilful damage. This is particularly so if the surface of such materials has a rough texture which can prevent the formation of letters or words. This is important as certain self finished materials do provide large areas of flat surfaces on which a vandal might paint. The extra relief given by rough board finishes, bush hammering, or striated concrete would help to lessen this tendency. This is particularly shown in comparing the relative amounts of attack received by plain sheet and ribbed aluminium. Self finished materials tend to be hard and to have through colour, thus helping to reduce the amount of gouging, carving and defects in construction that are noticeable. Therefore
self finished materials are preferable in high risk areas
providing they have some form of rough surface texture (**37, 38**).

E - Components and services

INTRODUCTION

Components and services may be defined as the secondary elements of the building fabric or external space, such as light fittings, sanitary installations, doors, barriers, etc. During the research it was noted that damage to this type of element seemed to be restricted to a few items, but was repeatedly found in many different localities. All these items are considered here, as well as other components or services that we feel may be made less vulnerable.

E (i) SIGNS AND LETTERING

Although signs and lettering are necessary and can give a lively, bustling character to the urban scene, a large proportion of them are totally incongruous with their surroundings. The advent of enormous flashing signs not only gave the vandals something new to attack, but assisted them, firstly by proclaiming their existence, secondly by providing more than sufficient light at the target, and thirdly by offering such a large area to attack. In order to counteract this, the first consideration is to

reduce the size of signs and lettering to a minimum

while ensuring that they are also in keeping with their surroundings. In reducing the size, it then becomes economically viable to use impact-resistant materials such as polycarbonate, polymethyl methacrylate (PMMA) or a glass fibre reinforced plastic, since the slightly higher initial cost will be recouped on maintenance.

A secondary consideration to reduce the damage is to

make the signs and lettering completely inaccessible

since so many examples (**39**) can be seen of applied lettering torn down and signs defaced and damaged at low level. If it is found impossible to position them out of reach, the only other deterrent is to ensure that,

the front face of the sign or lettering is flush with the face of the wall

upon which it is mounted, since this will reduce the number of locations where purchase could be gained to lever them off.

Finally, we are surprised to find it necessary to point out that the fixings of such elements are as important as the elements themselves, in that they should not only be strong enough to resist a certain degree of attack, and should be of a type that cannot readily be undone, but, most important of all,

the fixings should be concealed

since this will alleviate some of the problems related to their type and adequacy.

E (ii) SANITARY FITTINGS

Together with glazing, sanitary fittings in public conveniences are possibly the most commonly attacked elements—and as we suggested in discussing Glazing (Materials D (i)), this is probably due to the fact

that the damage may be wrought quickly and effectively. The vitreous china from which most fittings are formed is very brittle and a well-placed, heavy blow from a sharp object can produce devastating results. For example, urinal stall dividers can be sheared off, urinal slabs heavily pitted at foot level, wash basins and even WC's severely cracked or broken.

Therefore, specify fittings that are partially or wholly manufactured from a less impact-prone material.

Instances have been noted of the successful use of stainless steel urinals and wash basins, although in the case of the urinals, success depends upon the bonding of the steel to a firm backing—otherwise indentations can be made, particularly at low level.

Secondary fittings that are allied to these appliances have also been widely abused: pillar and bib taps wrenched away, flushing handles torn off, soap and towel dispensers removed, and so on. Therefore **provide the simplest and least exposed form of secondary fittings** such as push-button (whether floor or wall mounted) operation in WCs, lavatory basins, soap dispensers, etc., small, thermostatically controlled mixer taps, captive plugs, recessed towel dispensers or hand driers, etc.

The fixings for these fittings are also attacked, and should therefore preferably be concealed. If they cannot be, they should be of a type that is difficult to undo, but above all **the fixings must ensure resistance to the deformation or removal of all sanitary appliances and fittings.**

E (iii) LIGHT FITTINGS

During the research many instances of broken fittings were found to be attributable solely to the fact that they could be reached (**40**): therefore it is simply common sense to

41 *Recessed light fitting broken in spite of use of plastic sheet (though not a type generally regarded as best for this purpose).*

42

43

44

position light fittings so that they are inaccessible.
The situation is further aggravated by the use of surface-mounted fittings, since these may be levered or knocked away from the surface, even when out of reach. It is therefore advisable in susceptible areas **(40, 41)** to **use flush-mounted or concealed light fittings**
while for both types, the fixings should preferably be concealed.

Also subject to intense attack are the diffusers, since many of them are glass and consequently very easy to break—see Glazing (Materials D (i)). This is another justification for the use of polycarbonate since it has a very high impact resistance and may be formed into inherently strong shapes. In fact, many cases were seen where the surrounding area was dilapidated and devastated, but the polycarbonate light fittings remained intact.

E (iv) DOORS

Because of the very low, and consequently limiting cost yardsticks with which architects and designers have to contend, the selection of materials, components and finishes is normally dependent upon their cheapness. Doors appear to be no exception to this rule, and many instances were seen where the doors were totally inadequate for their purpose or situation. A prime example was noted where a hardboard-faced, hollow-core type was used between a private pram/bicycle/general store and a ground floor circulation area for the flats above. Needless to say a hole had been punched straight through. Others had been so badly damaged that they had to be removed, and some of the openings filled in with brickwork.
It is therefore imperative to relate the construction of the door to its intended use and location (42, 43, 44).

A minor consideration, but one which may have major benefits, is the swing of the door. It is always advantageous (though it may be impossible for other reasons) to design doors for private spaces opening out into the high-risk public area, since it is more difficult to 'spring' or force them open.

Door furniture is also prone to attack, mainly through the removal of handles, levers and closers. It is therefore wise to
reduce exposed door furniture to a minimum.
An oval knob is preferable to either a lever handle which can easily be pulled away, or a spherical knob which elderly people find difficult to grasp.

Again, provide adequate fixings—
no less than $1\frac{1}{2}$ pairs of hinges
which themselves should be concealed.

Garage doors suffer from constant attack. This is probably due more to their location than to their ability to withstand a certain amount of damage. See Garages (Overall Planning A (ii)). However, certain types are more prone to damage than others. The metal "up-and-over" type may first of all be disfigured by scratching away the paintwork, secondly

45   **46**

may have their opening handle kicked off, as most locks are at low level, and can be severely distorted by youths swinging on them while open.

The answer may be to design a framed, ledge and braced door that is sturdily constructed from unwrought timber members and then coloured with a timber preservative.

E (V) RAINWATER GOODS

In most large towns and cities instances may be seen where the last two or three metres of downpipe have been totally removed. The first defence against this is to

conceal rainwater pipes within the building or its external wall

but if this is not possible, they should be recessed, or located against the wall as closely as possible. Square or rectangular sections are better in this case because their shape and fixing characteristics allow very little room for fingers to get behind in order to pull them away. If they do have to be exposed then

position the downpipes so that they are less vulnerable to accidental damage.

For example, do not locate them on corners (**45**), or children will use them in order to negotiate the turn at high speed.

As far as the material of the rainwater pipe is concerned, we have found that the plastic types are more durable, since they are less prone to breakage by impact than the cast-iron or asbestos variety, and do not require maintenance, though they do need extra fixings because of their flexibility and their consequent tendency to 'spring' out.

158

E (vi) SERVICES

Many interviewees told us that one of their most troublesome maintenance problems was the wanton removal of, or damage to, the pipework
to sanitary fittings and other services, since many authorities still
insist on placing exposed pipework in vulnerable and accessible positions. In order to eliminate this risk

all pipework and other services should be concealed

preferably within a centralised duct, especially in circulation areas and
public conveniences.

The type of pipework used is also particularly relevant. Lead pipes
are not only easily damaged, but are valuable for resale by thieves.
Plastic pipes, although inherently more resistant to impact are easy to
dismantle because of the type of jointing employed. Salt-glazed ware,
although seldom removed, is easily shattered since it is vulnerable to
impact by sharp objects. If it is found to be impracticable to conceal
pipework, then the answer may lie in the use of steel, since it has
strength to resist attack and has little resale value.

E (vii) SCREENS

Designers frequently employ glazed screens to create a barrier to the
free flow of public circulation, primarily to prevent the misuse of public
spaces by rampaging children. Such barriers are frequently totally
destroyed (**46**), but more careful planning can often make their use
unnecessary. Therefore, in high-risk areas,

eliminate all glazed screens by whatever planning means are possible.

The positioning of screens can also lead to their eventual destruction
by constituting litter traps and sheltered loitering areas.

E (viii) LIFTS

The high intensity of use of the lifts in high blocks increases the risk of
damage, whether accidental or intentional, and very quickly produces
a dilapidated appearance.

The materials and components in lifts should be durable and capable
of withstanding considerable attack, which normally takes the form of
writing and carving, prising out and burning of operating buttons,
destruction of light fittings, blocking of bottom door guides, and
urination and defecation upon the lift floor.

In view of this we would recommend the use of highly patterned
plastic laminates or ribbed metal sheeting, metal control panels and
buttons. recessed or hidden light fittings, upstand door guides, and
waterproof flooring with integral coved skirtings.

E (ix) EXTERNAL BARRIERS

It is generally recognised that fences and other external barriers are
required to provide security, privacy and the demarcation of boundaries.
However, the amount of attack these elements suffer suggests first of
all, that

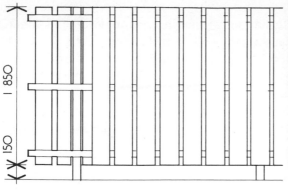

good example of sturdy unclimbable rough textured fencing (s.w. unwrought dark colour impregnated preservative)

200 x 38 uprights at 250mm centres
100 x 100 mm posts at 2 000m centres
100 x 75 mm horizontal rails

47

48

49

fences or barriers should only be provided where essential.
A prime example was noted where a large external circulation area was subdivided into a rigid circulation pattern by a totally ineffective form of barrier, which had subsequently been severely abused and removed to allow more freedom of movement. Where security and supervision are necessary, tall barriers should be "see-through", for example perimeter fences to building sites. This is a provision often requested by the police to help their patrols.
Whether for privacy or security
barriers should preferably be unclimbable (47, 48)
otherwise they will become dilapidated since children will use them as play artefacts.
All fences or barriers, whether permanent or not, should be constructed in a sturdy manner and should deter writing, gouging or general destruction.

The following types are criticised on the basis of the principles set out above, and although the list is not exhaustive, it may serve as a guide to the selection of other types.

(i) *Chain-link*   Climbable, wire itself may be distorted or cut, concrete uprights are readily fractured, although it does provide a good barrier for through-supervision. It also tends to produce a prison-like character.

(ii) *Horizontal ranch-type fence (painted)*   Easily climbed and appears to attract inordinate amounts of graffiti, particularly when painted white. Simply dismantled and quickly deteriorates (**49**). Versatile in providing privacy and supervision.

(iii) *Chestnut paling*   Not easily climbed due to basic instability *but* may be flattened with very little effort and therefore completely inadequate for permanent fences.

(iv) *Larch, interwoven panels*   Not readily climbed. Panels have no impact resistance and tend to look dilapidated if not well-maintained.

(v) *Vertical metal*   Difficult to climb since there are no footholds available; therefore excellent in providing security, but not privacy. Is extremely expensive and requires considerable maintenance.

(vi) *Vertical timber*   Difficult to climb; versatile since it can provide both security and privacy. In an unwrought state, stained with a wood preservative deters writing and other forms of abuse, and when strongly enough constructed is suitable for almost any situation.

(vii) in-situ *barriers*   These generally provide sheer, unclimbable surfaces, good security and privacy, but rarely supervision. Often rough in surface texture but do tend to offer large uninterrupted surfaces for the painting of slogans. They may also be dismantled if constructed from small units—therefore *in-situ* concrete barriers having an exposed aggregate are probably the most successful.

F - Detailing

INTRODUCTION

Most designers appreciate the fact that it is the junctions of elements that are the weakest points and are consequently most vulnerable to attack. This section concerning detailing, considers the ability of junctions, mainly between materials and components, to withstand attack. We concentrate on those which were regularly found to be damaged, or are considered to be very susceptible, or when well-detailed, could contribute to a reduction in the possibility of vandalism.

F (i) METHOD OF ACCESS

Although theft is not strictly within the scope of the project, so much damage is often caused in the furtherance of theft, especially in schools, that access to buildings by thieves and vandals cannot be totally ignored. The weakest point of entry of most buildings is the roof, not only through rooflights but also through the lightweight decking itself. Any building whose roof is in some way accessible is therefore at a higher risk than one whose roof is not.

Window sills

the normal types of virtually flat window sills provide convenient stepping stones for gaining access to roofs, particularly in offering purchase for grappling hooks (**50**).

Window sills should be steeply sloped

in order to prevent footholds and handholds. This is particularly relevant to single storey buildings where the danger from falling is not too great. The traditional method of providing a sloping sill, namely clay tiles, is not considered satisfactory for two reasons. Firstly because they can easily be broken, cracked or removed, and secondly because they cannot be pitched steeply enough since this would put immense strain on the bedding material after, say, an attack of frost. Brick sills are quite useful, especially if specials are used. The typical sloping bricks-on-edge method would be quite adequate if no large overhang were incorporated in the timber or metal frame. Concrete sills are by far the best from this point of view, since they can be moulded to steeply sloping shapes. They also have the advantage that they are

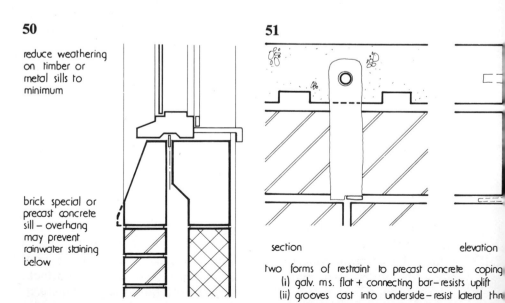

50

reduce weathering on timber or metal sills to minimum

brick special or precast concrete sill – overhang may prevent rainwater staining below

51

section   elevation

two forms of restraint to precast concrete coping
(i) galv. ms. flat + connecting bar – resists uplift
(ii) grooves cast into underside – resist lateral thr...

difficult to remove, or to damage, especially with an exposed aggregate finish.

Overhangs

If for some reason the use of sloping sills is impracticable, for instance, where the glazing extends from ground level to the underside of the fascia

the use of large overhangs is suggested.

These overhangs, whether created by using large reveals to windows and doors, or by large soffits to roof fascias, should be sufficiently large to prevent any vandal standing on a window ledge or rain water pipe from leaning backwards and gaining a purchase above the fascia. Of course, the opposite of this theory can in certain circumstances be equally effective. The production of a sheer surface without any projections, prevents most forms of scaling, but care must be taken in the detailing of parapet walls to ensure that grappling hooks cannot be attached to them.

Rain water pipes

One of the most common methods of gaining access to a roof is by climbing rain water pipes. This is normally attempted only if the pipe is of cast iron, since the p.v.c. variety does not give any element of safety to the climber. In general however,

rain water pipes should be fitted internally

or if this is impracticable, in a recess within the depth of the outer leaf. If neither of these are possible, the rain water pipe should be of square section fitted close to the wall. This prevents would-be climbers from gaining any handhold around the pipe. Pipes should also be positioned away from internal corners as this gives added safety to the vandal while making the face easier to climb.

F (ii) COPINGS

The destruction of copings, especially on low free-standing walls, was one problem which was common to most authorities. The damage seems to start most often at the ends and corners of walls and is more often than not the result of insufficient fixing. It may begin as a result of frost action or accidental damage. The process is then continued by vandals levering the copings from the wall and attempting to break them.

More than adequate fixing should be given to all types of coping at ends and corners (51).

Methods of providing this extra stability vary greatly with each type of wall and coping.

Brick-on-edge copings are generally easily attacked as they are greatly affected by frost action. The ends are particularly vulnerable and should always be reinforced with *in-situ* concrete stubs. This type of coping is not to be recommended for low walls where the coping is in range of foot attack. Concrete copings are basically better because of their heavier weight per unit. However, they do present the vandal with more of a challenge in that more damage can be caused more quickly. One of the main reasons for failure in pre-cast concrete copings is the lack of bond between the top of the wall and the underside of the coping.

Pre-cast copings should always be serrated on the underside in the direction of the wall.

Such serrations when bedded properly would provide resistance to lateral movement which is the normal method of attack. These indentations could be formed quite easily by attaching, say, 25 × 25 mm slats to the formwork.

Since the joints of all types of copings are the weakest point along their length, strengthening may be achieved by the inclusion of cavity ties used vertically to transmit the forces down into the wall construction. Overhangs on copings tend to aid their destruction as they become even easier to kick off or lever off. Flush copings do, however, tend to produce staining on the material below. The designer must therefore decide which is more important in each condition encountered, but the ultimate solution probably lies in free-standing walls of *in-situ* homogeneous materials that do not require copings. Such walls, if used, should have a rough surface texture to deter graffiti.

F (iii) MECHANICAL FIXINGS

The breaking and removal of many components is often attributed to the provision of (a) inadequate and (b) unsuitable fixings. The fixing of any component should be strong enough to withstand any foreseeable attack. Together with this,

as far as possible all fixings should be concealed,

because if exposed, they become an attraction to vandals. If it is impossible to conceal fixings in certain instances they should be of a type not easy to remove without specialist tools, for example Philips or Allen screws.

Many examples were seen of exposed hinges having been removed. This applies not only to doors and gates but also, for example, to the covers of light fittings.

Hinges should always be hidden.

The Crime Prevention Officer interviewed in the course of the research, expressed great surprise at the increase in the tendency of designers to use externally screwed glazing beads. These are virtually an open invitation to any thief and should not be used if at all accessible.

Large quantities of timber, particularly fencing, are removed or destroyed because of the use of normal nailing methods which are often quite inadequate to prevent incessant leverage. Therefore,

in high risk areas use fixings which are difficult to withdraw,

for example, annular or helically threaded nails.

164

52

F (iv) GRAVESTONES

Certain areas seem to have been badly hit by waves of attack on cemeteries, mainly in the overturning of gravestones. Basically the normal shapes of headstones and crosses do in themselves help the attacker as they usually have a very high centre of gravity. They are therefore easy to push over. Coupled with this, the bedding is more often than not quite inadequate to withstand any lateral forces.

Gravestones should always have heavy bases and be properly bedded in concrete,

even to the inclusion of vertical mild steel ties set in the concrete and slotted into the gravestone base.

G - Environment

INTRODUCTION

This section is concerned with the total effect of the surroundings and the question of whether the factors that create the environment are conducive to vandalism. Some of the topics may be dismissed as purely subjective, since no hard and fast evidence is available. However, in spite of this lack of evidence, many of the people interviewed have reaffirmed our conclusions, and we hope that the information gathered here will make a small contribution to further research into the environmental factors related to vandalism.

G (i) DILAPIDATION

One of the most important factors leading to the onset of a wave of vandalism seems to be the overall appearance of the area concerned.

It rapidly became apparent during our research, and was mentioned by many of those interviewed, that an increase in the incidence of vandalism occurs if an area is in any way dilapidated (52) whereas generally when buildings and their surroundings are kept clean, tidy and in good repair, they are relatively free from attack.

It must be made clear that a run down appearance can be caused in many ways; not only by wilful damage and poor maintenance, but also by accidental damage, misuse, ordinary wear and tear or even weathering, decay, corrosion or similar forms of failure. If any combination of these were allowed to develop, conditions favouring vandalism would soon become established. It is important, therefore, that
buildings and their surroundings should be as well maintained as possible. The necessity for efficient maintenance can readily be understood if it is realised that small, almost insignificant, faults in building can provide temptation for even the most suppressed vandalistic tendencies. Many examples were seen of damage originally caused perhaps during furniture removal or similar operations, which had been enlarged to quite unsightly proportions. In each case defects of design, specification or workmanship must have been an important factor in the failure. Deterioration, however, can arise from other decisions taken at the planning stage. The introduction of recesses or low walls around which litter can collect—often caused externally by the spiral flow of the wind —can soon lead to an untidy appearance which if neglected may lead to vandalistic attacks (2, 16).

The decision to phase the development of, say, a housing layout may result in unsettled conditions for the inhabitants as well as a plentiful armoury of building materials for window breaking, etc. There seems no doubt that a mature and tidy appearance helps greatly in reducing the incidence of vandalism, and this the designer must try to create. **New building complexes should not be left with an unfinished appearance.**

Empty buildings
Although not strictly within the scope of this report, the amount of damage done to empty buildings has led us to recommend that **all abandoned buildings should be secured against attack (53).**

The immense rebuilding programmes being carried out in our cities have led to an increasing number of empty houses and schools awaiting the attention of the demolition contractor. The large numbers involved mean that the majority are left a long time before being demolished, and in the meantime, as well as being dangerous but attractive play areas for children, such buildings are considered permissible targets for vandals.

G (ii) FEATURES OF NOVEL APPEARANCE
Care should always be taken over the provision and design of anything which may be considered to be of a novel, pretentious or prestigious nature. Items like statues, clock towers, advertising hoardings and

166

53   54

fountains are focal points. The vandal requires his handiwork to be seen easily, while providing an element of risk for himself (54). Such features are ideal, especially for painting slogans or writing or carving initials. Many examples of this were seen, from decorative park pavilions almost totally destroyed, to immense slogans painted on cathedrals. Features with special lighting or water effects seem particularly vulnerable, though it is especially difficult to know what to do about the latter, since water, wherever accessible, has long been an accepted target for missiles.

G (iii) PRIVACY

The provision of privacy is often regarded as one of the most fundamental contributions that the designer makes to the well-being of the users of his buildings. This important personal right can be safeguarded in two ways; physically by the use of barriers such as fences and screens, or more subtly by the creation of the feeling of intrusion. It is this second method which is generally more successful internally, against vandals. This is particularly relevant for the inhabitants of multi-storey blocks of flats, whose very front doors can become the playthings of rampant children, or loitering areas for sheltering juveniles. The methods of achieving these psychological barriers are many and varied, but the basic need is that the designer should investigate the possibilities of opening up private spaces into public areas of circulation, thereby creating more and better supervision.

The one feeling which is generally impressed on the minds of people touring areas which have a high incidence of vandalism is that of the depressing, spartan atmosphere which pervades such places. No doubt this is connected with the politicians' preoccupation with the question "How many houses can we build"? rather than with "How good should the houses be?" This has done a great deal to create a general feeling of resentment among tenants leading eventually to a lack of pride, to boredom and a tendency towards vindictiveness. The designer's responsibility is now greater than ever before to
make building complexes as pleasant, interesting and varied as possible, making full use of colour, lighting, changes in volume and of levels, and all other planning means.

A point which was emphasised by several of those interviewed was that designers should always use the best materials possible, as this creates respect for the building. This approach has been found to work, for instance, in repeatedly attacked public conveniences which were re-decorated internally with ceramic tiles, giving the building a light and hygenic appearance.

G (v) EFFECT OF HEIGHT AND DENSITY

High density living has, over the years, been blamed for many social disorders, and not the least of them is juvenile delinquency, of which vandalism is just one aspect. The social implications of such living conditions are beyond the scope of this report. However, there are certain planning implications of high density life which, we feel, have had a bearing on the amount of vandalism experienced over the last twenty years, which we can sum up as the concentration of amenities, leading to intensive use of relatively small areas.

This is particularly true of circulation areas, especially on the ground floor of high-rise blocks. The intensity of use of such areas involves an amount of wear and tear which is out of proportion with that of the rest of the building, and these areas consequently rapidly become dilapidated. Such areas are rarely decorated more frequently than the rest of the block, though their use obviously demands higher standards of maintenance. Circulation zones are often made dark and oppressive because of the plan shape of the block—a centralised vertical circulation system in a square block is an obvious example.

The consequences of concentration can also be seen in such services as refuse disposal. Since refuse collection areas are so heavily used they can quickly become untidy and are therefore more prone to attack. This applies particularly to the utilisation of refuse chutes and hoppers, which, if not maintained regularly, soon give the appearance of dilapidation.

Garages are also, by necessity, grouped together. Compounds are used for both economic and space-saving reasons, but unfortunately, they provide areas for the vandal to attack without the fear of being

caught. Signs already exist that the use of multi-storey car parks may accentuate this problem in the future (**55**).

The need for bicycle and pram stores on the ground floor of high blocks has unfortunately too, led to the introduction of dark narrow passages, in many cases providing sheltering and loitering spaces that are completely unsupervised.

Although these observations are made with reference to high-rise developments, many existing low-rise, high density schemes have similar problems. If high density living is with us to stay, there is obviously much scope for skilful design in order to improve on these conditions.

G (vi) ZONE OF RESPONSIBILITY

For many years, designers responsible for rebuilding programmes, have attempted, often in vain, to recreate the community spirit lost in the process of demolition and re-housing. A common approach has been the provision of "terraced streets in the sky" without the social conditions which existed at the time when the original terraces were thought to have been so socially successful. The result of rehousing has often been that people have become introspective, concerned only for the interior of their dwelling, and taking no interest in what happens outside. This has often meant that damage has been caused quite close to dwellings without occupants showing much concern. The feeling that public areas do not belong to them prevents them from taking any deterring action when vandals attack their surroundings. Nor do they take any remedial action when their surroundings become run down. Therefore, designers should always try to

plan so that people within a dwelling or building feel responsible for part of the public space outside,

thereby increasing the two most successful factors in the prevention of vandalism: supervision and maintenance.

This desirable result can be aimed for in many ways, but we feel that perhaps the simplest way is to design housing layouts so that they identify themselves in groups of nine or ten dwellings, thereby reducing the scale of the living conditions. This, no doubt, is the success of the nine- or ten-unit cul-de-sac in which everyone knows each other and collectively looks after the service area which they share.

We believe that there is considerable scope for further research into this topic.

Summary

This summary is not intended to be construed as a final and conclusive statement in which the ultimate and all-encompassing answer is given to the many problems related to vandalism and wilful damage: this would be striving to achieve the impossible.

Conclusions have already been stated and related to the situations to which they apply in the preceding sections. We would like here, to clarify these sections by relating them to a pattern in the progression of damage, to make tentative suggestions as to future paths of research, to consider minor aspects of the problem, and finally to reiterate some of the more important statements.

Progression of Damage
Throughout the period of research, and in particular, when looking for and noting specific examples of damage, thought was given to the possibility of there being some form of pattern in the infliction of damage. We are convinced, though we have very little proof, that the ultimate destruction of an element often begins with an almost negligible amount of damage that is produced either intentionally or by accident.

This damage is then enlarged and/or its form copied nearby, until the element in question has been abused so frequently that it is thought of as an artefact upon which it is almost acceptable and permissible to inflict damage, or is considered to be so dilapidated and therefore useless, that it is completely destroyed or removed. It is at the stage where an element is recognised as an accepted target, that vandalism begins to spread in the form of the wanton destruction which most people find difficult to comprehend.

Therefore, as we emphasised in our introduction, it is the designer's responsibility to ensure that buildings and the spaces between them are not only less prone to damage and attack, but that the resultant environment does not possess any factors that could contribute to the spread of vandalism.

Future Research

(i) *Zone of Responsibility*. At present, in terms of area, volume or distance, this is an almost indefinable quantity that should be consciously designed in the planning and detailing of the relationship between private and public areas. The design of the layout of the buildings and surrounding areas should impart a feeling of responsibility on the part of the private tenant, to ensure the general well-being of a sector of the public space immediately outside or even in the neighbourhood of his dwelling or working unit. This would, by increasing the supervision and general maintenance of the public space, not only provide a more pleasant environment, but possibly one less prone to attack. But we wish to add the point that we consider that this will only be successful when the units (particularly dwellings) are grouped in small numbers around a relatively small public area. Only further research will show whether this is so.

(ii) *Environmental factors*. Here, too, is an indefinable quantity or quality. We feel that some damage may be the result of a reaction against part or all of the environment, and an investigation into this could prove most worthwhile. There are many possible forms that the research could take, but they would all have to relate the amenities, living standards, working conditions and many other factors, to the incidence of vandalism within different selected localities.

Related Aspects

(i) *Time Factor*. Several of the people interviewed were interested in discussing the possibilities of designing parts of a building so that the considerable length of time required to inflict any noticeable damage first of all thwarted an initial attack, and then subsequently acted as a deterrent because of the fear of getting caught. Attempts were made to incorporate this factor within the preceding sections, but it was found to be incompatible with the format of the design guides, and to be so involved, because of the numerous variables, that it was considered to

171

be more worthwhile merely to point out this possibility and leave its application to the designer's judgment.

(ii) *Feedback*. After only a few interviews, it soon became apparent that there is an almost complete absence or disregard of feedback from Direct Works or Maintenance Departments to the designers—with the result that the same elements are incessantly attacked and replaced. In one instance, where the information did get through, the architect discounted the suggestions for a more durable material purely on aesthetic grounds—and the damage continues *ad infinitum*, at the cost of the ratepayer.

Such apathy is complete madness, and to eliminate it, an efficient information channel needs to be set up between Architects' and Maintenance Departments, so that mistakes can readily be corrected and, above all, not repeated.

(iii) *Telephone Boxes*. Since this particular public service is so frequently and severely abused, the reader may question the inconsistency of not including a lengthy appraisal in the Components and Services Section. We feel, however, that because of the long history of damage, sufficient consideration is now being given to the improvement of their design and that it would be impertinent to give a mere paragraph to a subject that has received lengthy and fruitful research, but we would hope that the final design incorporates such features as total supervision, built-in coin boxes, the absence of any projecting instruments, concealed light fittings, etc.

CONCLUSION

Although the preceding design guides are neatly subdivided into their respective sections, the design process rarely evolves in such a rigid framework of thought. However, there is a time when the designer is more aware of the overall and detailed planning implications of the design, and it is our opinion that to attack the problem at these stages will alleviate or even eliminate the later difficulties encountered in the selection of appropriate finishes, materials, components and details. We hope that the design guides will make some contribution to the counteracting of vandalism, but must finally emphasise that they are not applicable in *every* case, even though we have loosely defined each situation. It is up to the designer to evaluate the validity of each guide in relation to the circumstances of each design decision.

9 Planners as vandals

Colin Ward

Above the door, with a nervous and pardonable shuffling of
responsibility (apparently by the architect) were the words,
'This is the Lord's doing.'

MARY WEBB: *The Golden Arrow.*

In the opening chapter of this book Dr Cohen has identified a set of
different manifestations of the kind of behaviour which we usually
stigmatise as vandalism. When we consider the much more serious
destruction of the physical environment by private citizens and public
corporations, governments and local authorities, we can identify a
similar range of motivations. There is vandalism through stupidity,
through neglect, through apathy, through greed, through meanness,
through short-sightedness, through misconceived priorities or through
sheer ignorance.

Thus, in Dan Cruickshank's pictorial survey of the wanton destruction of irreplaceable buildings ,we can identify vandalism by meanness—
the Euston Arch, vandalism by philistine planners and local authorities
—the destruction of the Georgian East End of London, vandalism by
apathy and neglect—the Millman Street story, and vandalism by corporate greed—the demolition of Old Town Farm at Wheathampstead.

But to what extent are we justified in attaching the label of vandalism
to planned modifications of the built environment? At an international
symposium in 1971, C. A. Doxiadis declared that "we are all committing
architectural crimes" and submitted to his fellow penitents a comprehensive list of six of the gravest of these offences, which ranged from
"the construction of high-rise buildings" to "the anti-human city".
The discussion that followed his *Confessions of a criminal*[1] is relevant
if we want to establish the criteria by which we can fairly describe
architects and planners as vandals. These are the points which were
made by the participants, Roger Gregoire, E. F. Murphy, Joseph
Watterson, Buckminster Fuller, Margaret Mead, Gerald Dix, Peter
Shepheard and Gustav Gusti:

There is no crime without criminal intention. Who had the criminal
intention for the crimes which have been described? Certainly not the
architect, the builder; nor even society. All these crimes are the consequence of economic necessity.

Crime implies (1) that someone has the intent to perpetrate a crime;
(2) that it is possible to choose between crime and non-crime; (3) that
there is a clearly defined norm against which the crimes can be meas-

Tearing the insides out

Publicity about the squatters' occupation of houses in the East London borough of Redbridge (which includes Ilford) has played down one item, namely the council's new policy of ripping out the insides of empty houses to prevent any more homeless moving in. Such destruction amply demonstrates the point made by several sociologists that judgements concerning violence to property are relative. Apparently authority decrees it right for councils to destroy houses, but wrong for students to destroy gates.

from *New Society*, 13 March 1969

A family in the ruins of the house they once occupied. They were evicted by men from a private detective agency, and the house demolished by Redbridge Council.

ured. Our purpose is to draw up the norm and establish internal controls among architects.

There is a criminal in the ethical sense. The criminal is usually the promotor or developer, not the architect. Developers are not beneficent nor are they under any municipal or governmental control. Their motive is not economic necessity, but in most cases, pure greed for a quick and easy turnover. The developer pulls out and has no responsibility for the people living in the buildings he has promoted. This is a criminal motive.

The crime is political or economic gain from the exploitation of the ignorance or hardship of others.

In discussing crime we are leaving out the question of time. We are now told that it was criminal to put artificial fertilisers on the soil to increase agricultural production because the run-off in the rivers pollutes the water. But we did not know it earlier. We have been talking about the evil effects of high-rise living on children for almost 50 years and nobody has done a thing about it because we have not been asking the right questions. We have not asked how to make a high-rise habitable, nor have we related high-rise buildings to the needs of the people who live in them. But from now on we can easily call ourselves guilty of criminal negligence because now we do have enough knowledge of how people live.

A lot has been built with the best information available at the time. If the results were wrong, it was not a crime. The crime is the failure to have feedback and the failure to learn from the lessons from the past. Like a doctor, the builder cannot say: "I am sorry. I need to go back and do some more research." He cannot wait to act. But it is a crime if he ignores available information.

The problem is more stupidity than crime. But stupidity does far more harm in the world than crime.

Most of the things we have been talking about are not crimes, stupidities or mistakes, but a lack of consciousness of the whole collectivity, and of the future effects of present planning and building.

Faced with the testimony of the pundits, whom shall we call vandal? The *mea culpa* of Dr Doxiadis was theoretical. I don't know if he has been responsible for any actual buildings, but if he has I am sure he would be rather hurt if we described them as vandalism. The same is true of any architect. He will certainly blame his brief, his client, his budget or the accepted standards of his time, before he blames himself. Thus the RIBA, in the evidence it submitted to one of the working parties for the Stockholm UN Conference on the Human Environment, declared that "It is not generally appreciated that the prime determinants of the built environment are not in any sense architectural: economic, political, commercial and social factors control most of the major design decisions to such an extent that the actual 'designer' has, all too often, to devote his ingenuity to making the best of a bad job, finding a way to bend the rules to create something which is remotely humane—an obvious example of this is the Housing Cost Yardstick, a bureaucratic cost control tool which has been inflated into the principal determinant in public sector housing."

In the private sector the principal determinant is all too obvious. As one disillusioned architect wrote, "Most of the problems seem to stem from the misuse of the word 'architecture.' If the agent of a prostitute is a pimp, what is the agent of a property developer? Can we continue to call ourselves architects when our *raison d'etre* is maximum lettable area and carparking for 5000 cars?"[2]

The 'restorers' of ancient buildings, like Viollet-le-Duc or Sir Gilbert Scott were convinced of the value and necessity of their work, and so of course was the designer of the municipal tower block, replacing the cosy but substandard artisan dwelling. Even the systematic destruction of Bloomsbury to make way for the monumental sub-architecture of the University of London must have appealed to somebody at his drawing board. I never walk down Gower Street without reflecting on the transitory nature of aesthetic judgments. William Morris, who amongst other things, founded the Society for the Protection of Ancient Buildings, hated Gower Street and wanted to blow it up.

The difficulty of course is that one man's improvement is another man's vandalism. Were Baron Haussmann, Stevenage Development Corporation, the Forestry Commission and Colonel Siefert, improvers or vandals? If you are a Canuter (Leslie Ginsburg's word for the indiscriminate resisters of change) the answers are simple. Farmers were vandals when they enclosed the English countryside; now they are vandals when they grub up the hedges. The railway builders of the 19th century were vandals; the railway dismantlers of the 20th century are vandals. The coal-mining entrepreneurs of the 19th century were vandals; their residuary legatees, the National Coal Board, are vandals for closing down and sealing off the pits because of the temporary supremacy of oil. Nash was a vandal when he plastered his jerry-built facades across the West End of London; those knighted Royal Academicians were vandals when they pulled them down again. Used in a blanket fashion to cover any environmental change, the word loses its denunciatory effect. Is there any yardstick for evaluating environmental change? Nan Fairbrother categorised the conservationists in three progressive categories: Reversers, Shunters and Translators.

"Reversers are simple: they want to put the clock back. They would like us all to live happily in a beautiful pre-industrial world, despite the fact that no one would tolerate the pre-industrial life. The Shunters are more realistic but less sympathetic: they accept that modern living means unattractive developments like cement works and pylons, but propose to shunt these into someone else's territory. (We are all to some extent Shunters in private.) The translators are the most advanced and therefore the most useful: they appreciate the past but accept the

176

Demolition contractors had set fire to the 135 year-old Rodmersham Mill in Kent in order to demolish it. Listed as a grade 3 building, it was recommended for upgrading to Grade 2 after Kent County Council had given planning permission for its demolition, thus alerting the public to its possible destruction

"Two villagers, who in a last attempt to save the mill barricaded themselves in it, were badly knocked about by the contractors' men. The local police made no attempt to prevent one of the villagers having his teeth knocked out and no attempt to stop the subsequent manhandling which occurred, off the owner's property, on the village green."

future, and aim to incorporate the inevitable changes with least harm, or even with benefit, to the environment." [3]

For the 'Translators' the means of assessing alterations to the environment is summed up in the idea of "minimax"—a word coined by John von Neumann. "As he worked it out, 'total gain' in any life situation is never a realistic objective. What we must strive for is to achieve the maximum gains that are consonant with the minimum possible losses." [4] This is of course the same criterion for change as the "conservative surgery" of Patrick Geddes. But if the result is minimum gain and maximum loss, if, as Joni Mitchell's song puts it, we have "paved paradise and put up a parking lot", we can surely use the word vandalism. Dan Cruickshank's chapter gives example after example of just this: the Euston Arch may not have been the gateway to paradise, but it gave way to nothing more than a car park. At the public enquiry before the demolition of half of Eldon Square, Newcastle, the government inspector said that it was only because the square was to be replaced by a building of outstanding architectural merit that he was prepared to countenance its destruction. Finally, after demolition, what took its place was not an architectural masterpiece; it was . . . a car park.

In the layman's eyes of course, there is no distinction between the architect, the planner, the developer, the highway engineer, the public utility or the industrialist. The names and functions are simply different functions of *them*. We fear them because we know their handiwork. There can hardly be a city in Britain whose inner residential district has not been ripped open in the last ten years by an Inner Ring Road or its equivalent, with the predictable result that, at fearful cost, traffic problems have been shifted rather than eased. There can hardly be a city where the planned and systematic destruction of working class districts in a policy of 'raze and rise' has not left the residents stacked in concrete megaliths, dispersed heaven knows where, or surrounded by deliberate dereliction in a 'clearance area'. The latter phrase is well-chosen, with its overtones of the Highland clearances, the archetypal vandalism of the homes of the poor and helpless by the rich and powerful.

"The Corporation takes no notice of the opinion of people like us," despairing families in Sunderland told Norman Dennis, and he concluded that in objecting to demolition and rejecting alternative accommodation, they were expressing "sound and rational preferences". And how was the decision to demolish taken? The "monolithic policies of clearance" arose from the planners' mis-perception of the situation:

"No written criteria had been prepared, and the classification of each particular dwelling was the result of a visual external inspection, frequently from a moving vehicle, by personnel with little formal training in the relevant housing legislation, and with only a layman's knowledge of building materials and structures." [5]

Clearance area, Liverpool

When Sir John Betjeman, back in the nineteen-thirties, wrote the lines "Come lovely bombs and fall on Slough / It isn't fit for humans now", he was expressing his contempt for the speculative builder's semi-detached paradise (which he has since learned to love) but he was voicing the dream of the crudely trained planner, seeking a *tabula rasa* on which to practise his art. When the dream came true, it was not so much Slough on which the bombs rained, as on the poor streets of the inner city. Hitler, the planner used to say in the confident days of post-war reconstruction, has provided an opportunity which generations of slum-clearance could not have achieved. Comprehensive redevelopment became possible, and when we ran out of bomb sites, the planners made their own. Battle-tested in the blitzkrieg strategy, pull it down and start again was the only philosophy they knew. Conservative surgery was strictly for the private patients. Ruthless amputation for the public wards.

This approach to urban renewal (a phrase which has become a dirty word in the United States where it has come to mean running the blacks out of town) has still not come to an end. It is seen, in John Barrie's words, "at its most poignant along the Scotswood Road in Newcastle, where a real community has been destroyed to be replaced by some of the most brutal high-rise housing in the country",[6] but it can be seen at its most ludicrous and terrible in Liverpool where the urge to raze has outstripped the financial capacity to rise. In a publicity handout for worried citizens, the Corporation explained,

"Liverpool residents and visitors to the city alike are disturbed to see so many acres of rubble-strewn wasteland in the inner areas of the city. Needless-to-say members of the City Council and officers of the Corporation are similarly concerned by their continued presence, and take this opportunity to explain how the situation has arisen, and to describe the action which is being taken to alleviate the worst effects of the problem.

In recent years, the rate of redevelopment has not kept pace with the rate of slum clearance, which means that some areas will remain clear longer than is desirable. There are many reasons, often outside the control of the City Council, why this is so, although the basic problem is one of finance."[7]

This could be described as the soft sell of the century. Three hundred acres of devastation have to be explained away (scheduled to be 450 acres by 1975), in a city which is proposing to spend at least £10m. on a civic centre. The City Planning Officer himself, "has expressed doubt about the centre, so much so that he has said that he will not defend it at a public enquiry."[8] It is in fact no secret that he is opposed to the policy of destruction pursued by his colleagues in the housing department. What this policy means in practice is described by Alan Stones:

"Life in the new urban deserts is rapidly becoming unbearable for

180

those who remain. Half-demolished houses and broken drains harbour rats, which make their way into still-occupied dwellings. The small number of residents leaves many areas unsupervised and hence subject to vandalism and crime, for which the empty buildings are ideal. Bricks are thrown through windows by children, who find the crumbling ruins a dangerous playground. The wide open spaces have been colonised by gypsies and tinkers, many of whom are running scrap metal businesses. (The Corporation recently spent £20,000 on dumping rubble to make it difficult for caravans to park, a sum which would have been better spent on providing a properly equipped camp-site.) The cleared spaces also double as public lavatories and scrap-heaps for old cars and other rubbish dumped by suburbanites." [9]

Under such circumstances, have we the hypocrisy to complain about juvenile vandalism? But this is not the last word on the destruction of communities which the vandalism of properly constituted authorities implies. In the evidence he gave to the Covent Garden Enquiry in London in 1971, David Triesman argued that

"Central Liverpool had succeeded in producing a social illness problem which had increased by over 750 per cent from the end of the old settled community to the 'redevelopment' of the new. The figures for other city centres had not doubled where the old communities were intact. This report does not mention growths of delinquency rate, the breakdown of marriages, the dispersal of sons and daughters from parents, nor sibling from sibling. It seems unlikely that an area with the highest schizophrenia rate for men in the country, with the highest rates of depressive psychoses among women, had escaped other social traumas. It is not enough to record bleak figures in a landscape of despair. Fortunately we are able to go much further in documenting some of the relationships between various mental and social illnesses and particular forms of incidence. Professors Robert E. L. Faris and H. Warren Dunham in their work *Mental Disorders in Urban Areas*, have established a number of facts indicating a definite and unmistakable relation between the incidence of the chief psychoses and the mode of organisation of the city. And that when areas are re-organised, this results in a change of incidence such that a change to a type of area which is known to have a high correlation with a particular disorder actually causes that disorder to appear where it hadn't formerly been noticeable . . . The impact of this research is that it allows us to make a certain number of predictive statements about the type of redevelopment proposed for Covent Garden." [10]

There is in fact a terrible arrogance about the concept of planning as we have seen it in the last twenty-five years: a branch of municipal enterprise which aims at nothing less than usurping history:

"In planning schools, beginner students usually argue that people's

181

lives in time are wandering and unpredictable, that societies have a history in the sense that they do what was not expected of them, so that this device is misleading. Planning teachers usually reply that of course the projected need would be altered by practical objections in the course of being worked out; the projective-need analysis is a pattern of ideal conditions rather than a fixed prescription.

But the facts of planning in the last few years have shown that this disclaimer on the part of planners is something they do not really mean. Professional planners of highways, of redevelopment housing, of inner-city renewal projects have treated challenges from displaced communities or community groups as a threat to the value of their plans rather than as a natural part of the effort at social reconstruction. Over and over again one can hear in planning circles a fear expressed when the human beings affected by planning changes become even slightly interested in the remedies proposed for their lives. "Interference," "blocking", and "interruption of work"—these are the terms by which social challenges or divergencies from the planners' projections are interpreted. What has really happened is that the planners have wanted to take the plan, the projection in advance, as more "true" than the historical turns, the unforeseen movements in the real time of human lives."[11]

The story of the Category D villages in County Durham is a perfect illustration of this contention. Over twenty years ago the county planners graded these old mining villages from A to D according to predictions about their future economic viability. A village in Category A, like Escomb, has been rehabilitated sensitively and intelligently, without avoidable dislocation of the lives of its people, but Category D villages like Witton Park, with an absolute ban on new building and on improvement grants, have been left to die without regard to the wishes of the inhabitants or to changing prospects of local employment. Officially dead, but unwilling to die, the Category D villages have fought for survival. A few have been upgraded, but most have been kept in the condemned cell, even though as at High Spen, new industry has provided more jobs than the closed colliery. But the decisions of twenty years ago remain more 'true' to Durham County Council than the subsequent activities and aspirations of the people who live in the condemned villages.

By a coincidence which is not so strange, the victims of planned vandalism belong to one social class. For sound economic reasons the urban motorway ploughs through the cheapest property, and the wholesale demolition involved in comprehensive redevelopment does not occur in middle class districts. The professional classes do not live in Category D villages. Similarly the spectacular disasters of vandalism by neglect affect just one class of people. Aberfan was not a commuter village. Ronan Point was not a luxury block. ("For the first time a new

182

architecture, which in all previous epochs had been reserved for the satisfaction of the dominant classes, is directly aimed *at the poor*"[12]). Strange to say, it is these very districts, whether deliberately run down or ruthlessly rebuilt, which are most closely associated with the ordinary common or garden kind of juvenile vandalism. The fathers have eaten sour grapes and the children's teeth are set on edge.

10 Developers as vandals

Dan Cruickshank

"I weep for you," the Walrus said:
"I deeply sympathise"
With sobs and tears he sorted out
THOSE OF THE LARGEST SIZE,
Holding his pocket handkerchief
Before his streaming eyes.

"OYSTERS" said the Carpenter,
"You've had a pleasant run!
Shall we be trotting home again!"
But answer came there none—
And this was scarcely odd, because
They'd eaten every one ! ! .

In a sense, Lewis Carroll's profoundly observed episode of the Walrus and the Carpenter, with their apparent sadness but inexorable appetites, epitomises one type of contemporary large-scale vandalism. This is official vandalism in the name of 'development', or more euphemistically 're-development' which is very often full of regret for the fact that it has been destroying, and is threatening always to destroy, structures which are not only of architectural and historical value, but of considerable worth as environmental assets. As very real assets such buildings should be carefully and lovingly conserved but, some may ask, is their official destruction really vandalism? From the developers' viewpoint could it not be slum clearance? After all, development, which always implies *improvement* when it is by no means necessarily so, does demand land, and sometimes sacrifice. Our case is that in too many instances, after specific examples have been thoroughly examined in their context, what has happened *is* vandalism and this chapter consists of a series of case histories which illustrate our contention. All but one of the cases are drawn from London, but they typify what is happening throughout Britain and indeed, throughout the world. They illustrate vandalism, often almost tearfully carried out, allegedly only because of the pressing needs of 'the many'—for the so-called 'public good'. But the 'public' is made up of 'persons' and it is now becoming fairly clear that much of our new urban environment is increasingly less suited to the all-round needs of human beings. Because of that, any environmental asset which may have been handed down from our predecessors must be conserved, not for pleasure only, but because of genuine psychological necessity and those who destroy such assets, for whatever reason, must be classified as vandals. Part of the problem is that not enough people, including the vandals themselves, recognise what constitutes vandalism. A youngster who pulls a telephone kiosk to pieces, or rips up a railway seat, or wantonly carves his name on an ancient monument, or runs berserk over a building site smashing everything that can be smashed, is readily and universally classified as a vandal. But developers who employ a demolition firm to bulldoze historically and socially irreplaceable structures are seen as business men, or as a democratically responsible authority, carrying out legitimate business. Moreover, the vandalism of the frustrated youngster who for no apparent reason seems intent on smashing up his own immediate environment, is seldom related to the vandalistic model set by the developers, or to the unacceptable environment so widely provided by development.

And that brings us to another aspect of the problem. It is not yet widely appreciated how important environment is; what effects it has on people and their behaviour; or to what extent actual structures may significantly influence environment and people. To illustrate this last point, let us take an example which because of its extreme nature may serve to reveal the truth. Ask yourself, what would the City of London be if St Paul's and other churches were destroyed, if the Mansion House and the Tower of London and the Monument and many smaller but no less significant structures were all demolished? Without them, would there by a City of London as we know it?

True, they are only buildings, but with the passage of time how much more they have become. And, particularly because so much of the City has been lost, have they not become symbols of continuity whose existence give us a certain environmental solace and sense of security? Fine old buildings in other places do the same. It must be added, too, that mostly they are pleasant, and even beautiful, to look at, which is surely an added reason for their conservation.

But when we ask which buildings should be conserved, and why, there is in fact no real problem. In Britain the government itself has faced and dealt with the matter. It has laid down that structures deemed to be of public importance may be listed as being of Historic or Architectural Interest and once they are listed may not legally be destroyed or altered without official permission. Similarly, provisions exist in Europe and America, but for the sake of example let us look at the British scene.

Most buildings dated before 1700 if in anything like their original condition are now listed. Buildings dated between 1700 and 1840 are also generally listed if they have remained more or less in their original condition. Exceptional buildings constructed after 1840, or those that are the work of well known architects, are also listed. There are three grades of listed structures, and the vast majority are listed Grade 2. Since the 1968 Town and Country Planning Act the penalties for destroying these listed buildings are:

"(a) on summary conviction to imprisonment for a term of not more than three months or a fine of not more than £250, or both; or
(b) on conviction or indictment to imprisonment for a term not exceeding twelve months or fine, or both:
and, in determining the amount of any fine . . . the court shall in particular have regard to any financial benefit which has accrued or appears likely to accrue to him in consequence of the offence."

185

Remnant of Woburn Square during demolition in 1970

Less than one sixth of one per cent of the area of Greater London is occupied by listed buildings, so one would think a very good reason would be necessary before a listed building could be destroyed.

But what could be a 'good reason?' This all-important subjective qualification is best illustrated by an example. In 1970, half of Woburn Square, Holborn, was demolished by the University of London which wanted to expand into additional buildings. The University owned the square, and although it was one of the last complete early 19th-century squares left in Bloomsbury, it was not officially protected. (In fact it was not listed precisely *because* it was University property.) Amid public protests the square was pulled down. On the one hand it is difficult to

186

Woburn Square before demolition
Bedford Way, Bloomsbury, during demolition

Euston Station when first built, from a drawing by Philip Hardwick

call the destruction vandalistic because of the nature of the replacement buildings, but still there remains the simple question: Did it have to be Woburn Square? Did they have to expand on to that land?

Call the re-development of Woburn Square what you will, and agreeing it was carried out with the general intention of public benefit, nevertheless, by its example, the University set a precedent which has led to the destruction of much of early 19th-century Bloomsbury. Bedford Way, parallel to Woburn Square, has been completely destroyed for re-development as a hotel. An historic group of buildings, forming an environment which has given pleasure to countless people over many years, and could have given many more people pleasure, was destroyed for the financial gain of a limited number of individuals.

Although the private developers may provide the most blatant examples of vandalism, it must be stated that the public authorities

The propylon before demolition

Photo-montage of the arch on the present station concourse

insofar as they have greater opportunities and power are responsible for the greatest volume of vandalism—they are its true Walrus and Carpenter. Their guilt falls into several main categories: one, calculated and contrived vandalism; two, vandalism arising from sheer short-sightedness and inadequacy and made more socially vicious by a good deal of ignorance; three, vandalism carried out by the evasion and indecision endemic to the bureaucratic system.

Calculated and contrived vandalism: the Euston Arch

As an example of this category, the story of the destruction of Euston railway station arch needs a lot of beating. It was an example of incredible philistinism on the part of authority with power, in the face of informed, but powerless, individuals.

The story of the Euston arch is well known but its re-telling in the context of this chapter will serve to illustrate to those unfamiliar with the subject how the vandalistic destruction of a national monument— let alone a mere terrace of listed houses—may be brought about by those very authorities which should be responsible for its preservation. In this instance the agents of destruction were the owners of the arch, the British Transport Commission. But responsibility must also be laid at the feet of the London County Council and the government itself— the authorities, ironically, responsible for the preservation of such ancient monuments in London.

In retrospect it is incredible that the British Transport Commission could even have considered destroying the arch, let alone actually doing it. It was a monument not only of considerable architectural worth, but also it was part of the history of British transport, originally built as a symbol of the great railway age emerging out of the industrial revolution. That was the inspiration which produced the arch. The Greek revival style of the structure was basically an expression of contemporary fashion but it perfectly suited the intent behind the arch.

189

What could be more appropriate for the symbol of a new age—the railway age—than a monument in the style of what was then considered the birthplace of civilisation, the 'Golden Age' of Athens. That is what the Euston arch was. Tarnished with grime, and crushed between later additions, but a structure which was a spiritual as well as an historical reflection of the age, and which expressed the optimistic vision of the early Victorian railway builders. Now it has gone, forever, but its story is a classic example of how such treasures are made and lost. It began, in 1836 when Philip Hardwick, one of the ablest architects of the time, designed it, and it ended in November 1961 when it was demolished by those who were supposed to be its guardians and protectors, in the teeth of the united protest of many organisations and individuals.

London County Council and the British Transport Commission first met in 1959 to discuss the reconstruction of Euston railway station. At the meeting a model was displayed and this showed that in the proposed reconstruction Hardwick's original station buildings would be destroyed—*all but the arch*. The plan was to preserve the arch, and re-site it on the Euston Road and what a splendid, pivotal environmental asset it would have been to a particularly nondescript and diffuse stretch of thoroughfare. Some months passed and in January 1960 the BTC gave formal notice that they did intend to demolish the existing Euston station buildings. The LCC Town Planning committee raised no objection other than to stipulate that the arch would be preserved and would be re-erected in an appropriate position. The BTC estimated at that time that the re-erection would cost £180,000. The Royal Fine Arts Commission had taken some interest in the reconstruction project and had made efforts to have some say in what decisions were taken but it had not been very successful. Bureaucratic evasiveness had made it difficult for the Commission to make its views effective, or to act in its proper role as watchdog in such matters, on behalf of the public. The LCC in fact had sought 'specialist' advice elsewhere. By May 1960 the formal notice to demolish Hardwick's buildings had become a definite decision—but the plan still was to *remove, re-site and re-erect the arch*.

However, it was also at this point that the idea was first floated that the arch would have to go as well as the rest of Hardwick's station. The reasons? Purely financial, of course. Both the BTC and the LCC wanted to preserve the arch, and had announced their plans and their avowed concern about it may have made it that much easier for them to get general agreement to demolish the other Hardwick station buildings. But having got that agreement, the idea suddenly emerged that perhaps the arch, too, would have to go after all. From then on the fate of Hardwick's arch became not a matter of principle, that of preserving a structure of architectural and historical value, but a matter of who would pay. The LCC asked the government if it would pay. The reply was that the government had no powers to make a contribution—a most extraordinary statement when one realises that the arch was officially listed Grade 2 as a building of architectural and historical interest

190

and, as such, was eligible to be financially provided for by the government.

About a year passed—a period of lull. Then, in July 1961, came the announcement. The Minister of Transport declared that because of the expense which would be involved in moving it, the arch would have to be demolished. It would seem that the lull had been on the side of the public only. In private the BTC and the LCC had been hardening their decisions. The BTC had moved increasingly to a viewpoint from which the arch was seen only as a nuisance. In the reconstruction plan it could be moved to one place or another but really the easiest and cheapest thing to do with it was to dispose of it altogether. Sadly, the LCC, instead of resisting that viewpoint, endorsed it. When the Royal Fine Arts Commission asked them to explain their position they replied that they proposed to take no further action.

As things stood then, demolition could begin at any moment. Those interested in saving the arch tried desperately to find a way of postponing its destruction. The Victorian Society set up a rescue committee and the Chairman of the Royal Fine Arts Commission appealed in a letter to the Prime Minister to save the arch. A Canadian firm competent to move the arch on rollers was found, and their estimated cost was less than half the BTC quotation. A letter in *The Times* of October 20th pleading on behalf of the arch was signed by the President of the Royal Academy, the Georgian Group, the Society for the Protection of Ancient Buildings and the Victorian Society.

Four days after the letter a delegation of the signatories was received by the Prime Minister, Mr Harold Macmillan. A week later the Prime Minister announced that the demolition of the arch would be carried out. No answer was given to the arguments for its preservation. Thus the decision to destroy the arch was reached. But still the protest went on. Even as the arch was being taken down appeals were made to have the stones numbered against the possibility of future re-erection. The demolition firm itself was astonished that it had received no orders to number the stones. The arch was irrevocably dismembered and destroyed. Those responsible for the destruction of the arch can never be forgiven. Although they pleaded that it was too expensive to preserve, the arch was an object whose existence and importance could not be measured in financial terms.

Vandalism by short-sighted inadequacy: London's Georgian East End

The destruction of the Euston arch was a conscious and contrived act of vandalism, but the public authorities have been vandals in many other, different ways. In East London there are examples of vandalism by *sheer short-sighted inadequacy* on the part of the authorities involved. In Stepney, Swedenborg and Wellclose Squares stood side by side, a short walk from the Tower of London and just north of the London Docks. Wellclose Square was laid out in 1678, and Swedenborg at the beginning of the 18th century; both were built in an early stage of the

Swedenborg Square in 1944

26 Wellclose Square in 1905. This house was one of the very few weather-boarded examples left in London.

20 Spital Square in 1944. The ground floor of this 1730 house was altered in the 1780's when it was the residence of Lord Bolingbroke. The building was demolished in the early 1960's.

19-25 Wellclose Square

City of London's eastward sprawl. The original residents were probably well-to-do merchants and seamen—for a while in the 18th-century Wellclose Square was known as Marine Square, and both the squares formed a residential centre for Scandinavian timber merchants. There was a Danish church in Wellclose and a Swedish church in Swedenborg Square.

But during the 19th century, in common with much of the East End, the houses in the two squares became tenements. They fell into disrepair and were so neglected that early in this century they were considered simply as fodder for slum clearance. They survived, and even throughout the last war when bombs destroyed so much property around the London docks the two squares remained virtually untouched. After the war, Swedenborg Square was certainly largely derelict but Wellclose, which had never really fallen into quite the same slum condition as that which existed in surrounding streets, was still lived in, and the houses neatly kept. However, regardless of their state, the point is that at the beginning of the 1960's two squares, both of which contained unique architectural features, and both of which had become more

Elder Street in 1970 after nearly 7 years dereliction

uniquely interesting and worthy of preservation because of the blitzed condition of so many of their contemporaries, still stood. True, they were battered and decayed but they were, marvellously, essentially complete. At this stage one might think that the scene was well and truly set for the restoration of two such squares. A logical course would have been for planners to make use of their obvious qualities, both physical and historical, to make them centres around which to build the necessary comprehensive re-development on sites vacated by both slum clearance and bombing. Assuming that the persons who decide what is to happen in such projects lacked the ability to appreciate the intrinsic architectural qualities of the houses in the two squares, one would have thought that after so much of the old had been arbitrarily destroyed by enemy action they would have at least felt the need to preserve some memory of what had existed before: a thing essential to the creation of a properly balanced environment.

Looking back, how fortunate those East End planners were to have at their disposal not merely houses but two complete Georgian squares —residential units of the kind which are deservedly most famed and cherished. Around them a new neighbourhood environment could have been created, the best of the past linked with and influencing the present and the future. But it did not happen. Presumably the graceful Georgian squares were seen only as slums, and the old slum clearance mentality got to work. Both the squares were swept away, in the early 1960's,

Elder Street in 1971 during restoration

but time has given a couple of double-edged twists to this pathetic but enraging story of destruction. One twist is that neighbouring slum dwellings, much more desperate than the squares were, have been allowed to remain. The other is that the recent re-development plans for turning the nearby St. Katharine Docks into a luxury amenity, with hotel, conference centre, marina and so on, has thrown a new light on the area. Increasingly, properties of the same period as the square are being sought after and restored. Clearly if the houses in the squares had been spared for only a few more years, persons with the means, as well as the inclination, would have come forward to acquire them and restore them—attracted particularly by the St. Katharine Dock development and the growing fashion for residences in the East End.

A case which serves to drive home this point is that of Elder Street, less than a mile to the north of the squares, at Spitalfields. Here there are houses of the same date and of a similar size as those that were in the squares, but in a somewhat inferior residential environment—heavy market traffic lumbers through the street. They were emptied in 1964 and consequently fell into an extremely decayed condition. At that time similar houses in Spital Square, and Folgate Street, which adjoins Elder Street, were demolished to provide car-parking space and to give the market lorries better turning areas! Elder Street was to follow.

Mercifully, however, the Elder Street houses were not knocked down

195

Site of 20-25 Wellclose Square. Number 19 survives with a chunk of frieze from Number 20 still attached

Late 18th-century detail on 21 Wellclose Square taken in 1944

Mayflower Street, Rotherhithe

Houses in Rotherhithe Street before demolition

and today the street has been restored. The work was carried out as a speculation by a private builder. The selling price of the restored houses was put in the £20,000 range and the builder discovered that he could have sold each one "twenty times over". What happened to Elder Street could and should have happened to the squares. They would have been a much sought-after oasis in what is at present something of an environmental desert. But today—well, Swedenborg Square at least lives again, but in the startlingly different form of an estate of council dwellings known as Swedenborg Gardens. All trace of the original line of the square has been obliterated. As for Wellclose Square, at the time of writing it is just rubble, as the demolition left it. In the place where once stood a terrace of houses, two of which were embellished with remarkable cherub panels, there is now nothing. As if to mock the memory of the square, one house, on the corner of the square and Grace's Alley, has been left. It is propped up by a stick against its scarred side like a corpse on a gibbet, adding a touch of horror to the scene of desecration. So public planners, perhaps well-intentioned, but certainly short-sighted and inadequate, are tackling problems far beyond their competence, and examples like this are the wasteful result.

Of course, what happened to the squares may be desperately justified by arguing that the restoration of the houses would have been too expensive a job for a local government authority to spend public money on, in terms of the number of families they would accommodate. But there *was* other land to use, and the restoration of the square need not have been undertaken out of the funds of the local authority; and, more important, it is now becoming increasingly obvious that, in terms of an environment suitable for human beings to live in, we simply cannot afford to lose such inherited assets as the squares represented. If this story was limited only to those two squares it would be bad enough but bearable; but they are only one example among many. In East London itself there are many more examples. In Mayflower Street, Rotherhithe, for example, a few years after the squares had gone, a really fine group of early 18th-century houses went under the bulldozer to make way for a concrete strip on which a local firm parks its lorries. Then, nearby, there was Rotherhithe Street where the houses, overlooking the river, were in good condition because they had been acquired by tenants sufficiently well-to-do to maintain them. In spite of strong and articulate opposition by these occupants, the houses were cleared away to provide space for a dismal little green from which strollers may view the river. This was probably considered to be a pleasant idea, the greatest good for the greatest number, but why, in an area where there was so much derelict property, did the only lived-in houses of architectural and historical worth left on the Rotherhithe riverside have to go for it to be realised?

After the destruction of these two groups of buildings, the only groups left in Rotherhithe, the area was at last officially 'recognised' as possibly having a character worth preserving. It was made into a

191 Stoke Newington High Street, built about 1715
187 and 189 Stoke Newington High Street

conservation area when practically all the elements that formed its character had been destroyed.

Vandalism through apathy and indecision:
Stoke Newington High Street and 18th-century Holborn

We come now to another face of vandalism—vandalism through apathy and indecision. This is probably the most unwitting kind of vandalism caused by good intentions going awry, but amongst those concerned about conservation it fosters the deepest feelings of pessimism. If, because of apathy and indecision, so-called responsible authorities, even the Department of the Environment itself, allow historic, listed buildings under their own protection to decay and crumble to a condition where they are fit only to be regretfully demolished, can the private developer who does the same for his own purposes, be blamed?

This was the case with a property at 191, Stoke Newington High Street. Paradoxically, because this house was the property of the Department it was more vulnerable than it would have been in private hands. As Crown property it was not officially listed for protection and, in effect, the Department could do as it liked with the building—unlike the private person, who must get written agreement from the local planning authority and the Minister if he wishes to demolish a listed building, and who can be heavily fined and imprisoned if he acts without permission.

191 Stoke Newington High Street was one of a group of three large, early 18th-century buildings. The other two in the group, not Crown property, were listed as Grade 2. Since the last war, until 1968, the house had been used for government offices, then it was emptied. It stood empty for three years, and in February 1971 the Department announced that because of its condition it would possibly have to be demolished. While empty, and neglected, part of the roof and back of the house had been taken down, as being dangerous, and although the house's future was dependent on a final structural assessment, nothing had been done to keep out the damaging effects of weather through the gaping roof. Apparently because of apathy, and indecision, the house had been allowed to crumble towards destruction. As it happens, however, the house at the time of writing, has not been demolished. Public interest aroused on its behalf resulted in a temporary roof being put on, and the erection of supporting scaffolding. An important factor in this case is that the fate of number 191 will also affect what happens to the other two houses. Number 187, for instance, belongs to Hackney Council and has been empty for ten years. Offers have been made for it but, despite all the optimistic statements by Lady Dartmouth in her GLC booklet, the house remains empty and gradually decaying. Unless the right attitude is taken in time this could be another case of demolition by disinterest.

At the time of writing it does seem possible that these houses in Stoke Newington may still survive despite all; but they could, and still can, easily go as have the houses in another part of London, Millman Street, in the area of Holborn known as Bloomsbury. The story of Millman Street is among other things a classic example of vandalism by apathy and indecision. The houses involved were in fact 2-12 Millman Street, and 1-4 Millman Place. They were ten early 18th-century houses which stood to the northern end of Great James Street, off Theobalds Road, and which is known to those interested as the most complete street of early 18th-century houses in Holborn. Although of the same size, date and architectural quality as Great James Street, and virtually a continuation of that well-maintained street, the Millman Street and Millman Place houses were decaying tenements. After the last war the Great James Street houses were listed as being of historic or architectural interest, as were, indeed, those in Millman Place—but not those in Millman Street. Not only were they unlisted but the land on which they stood was allocated to the Inner London Education Authority as the site for a new school. At that time it seemed that the fate of Millman Street was sealed. All the houses were lived in, but because of their apparently limited future prospects, they were not well maintained.

In 1966 the Ministry of Housing and Local Government confirmed a Clearance Order on the houses, and this Order included the Millman Place houses. All were then emptied and they stood forlornly open to be used or misused by any tramp or vandal, waiting, it would seem, for the demolition man.

But, as time passed, there was a change of heart about Millman Street. It began to be asked, if Bloomsbury was a conservation area should not these houses in Millman Street and Millman Place, which visually linked the remaining early 18th-century streets of Bloomsbury into one homogeneous group, be conserved? So, in October 1969 the houses were officially listed as buildings of historic or architectural interest and henceforth they could not be demolished without permission from the appropriate Minister.

By this time three of the houses had lost their doorcases, and all had lost their balusters and fireplaces. Rumour had it that these were taken by persons who wanted to save something from the demolition company's ball and chain. As it turned out, how wise they were, but back in October 1969 their actions appeared to be anti-social. Workmen came to the empty Millman Street houses, opened doors, poked around, and went. Men wearing dark suits surveyed the houses and it was feared that perhaps it was too late and that the houses were irrevocably decayed. Suggestions were made that perhaps they should be razed and replaced with new 'Bloomsbury style houses'. However, the District Surveyor reprieved them from destruction on the strict proviso that restoration work begin at once.

During January 1970, a small group of workmen turned up with some rusty scaffolding, enough to go across one house. Mostly they waited, for bricks, for ladders and for lunchtime. They moved the scaffolding from house to house, repaired a small piece of facade here and there,

Millman Street and Millman Place before demolition

Doorcase of 12 Millman Street which was removed some time before the demolition of the building
10 Millman Street propped up after the demolition of numbers 6 and 8

The new view of Millman Place revealed by the demolition of Millman Street
Millman Place levelled to the ground floor to reveal its timber construction and panelling

put up a drainpipe, laid strips of roofing felt across the holes in the roofs, put them back the next day because they had blown off overnight, and then didn't bother. Breeze blocks arrived and were used to seal off all ground-floor windows, and all doors but one. At about this time parts of the rear of the houses began to be dismantled. Bricks from this work were either thrown into the back yards of the houses, or brought into front rooms and left lying around. Was this the restoration work which the District Surveyor six months previously had insisted should comence immediately?

Meanwhile, whilst this desultory and entirely inadequate activity was taking place at the houses themselves, the Maunsel Metropolitan Housing Association, a non-profit making body, had been negotiating to purchase the houses from their owners, Camden Council. These negotiations continued until May 1971 when it was finally agreed that the houses should be converted into flats, some of which were to be offered to families waiting on the Camden Council's housing list, and some members of the Maunsel Association. But long before that agreement had been reached, the workmen had ceased coming to the houses even though rain was still seeping through the roofs. Even so, early in 1971 a notice had been attached to the house railings announcing that they were to be converted to flats.

Then, on 12 June 1971, at about one o'clock in the morning, and with considerable noise, the shared chimney stack of numbers six and eight Millman Street fractured and fell into the street below, taking part of the facade of the houses with it, and crushing a car parked in the roadway, fortunately empty at the time. This incident triggered off a month of feverish, destructive chaos. Classified as 'dangerous structures' the two houses were speedily and efficiently smashed down to a pile of splintered wainscote, joists and old red bricks. Amazingly, the apathy and indecision which had characterised all the activity directed towards preserving the houses was apparently shaken off. Rapidly the houses were surveyed and almost immediately the demolition men were given the order to move in. Ball and chain thumped its way, and within a few days the rest of the Millman Street houses were a red brick scar. This left the interesting early 18th-century facade of Millman Place revealed in a way that had never been seen before. But, then, after a few days, a hole appeared in this facade—and although Millman Place had not been affected by the collapse of six to eight Millman Street, presumable just to make a job of the demolition it too was cleared away.

And in all this there was nothing illegal, for when a listed house becomes a 'dangerous structure' the law provides for its removal. Part 5, section 40, paragraph 8 of the Town and Country Planning Act, 1968, says: "It shall be a defence to prove that the works were urgently necessary in the interest of safety or health, or for the preservation of the building, and that notice in writing of the need for works was given to the local planning authority as soon as reasonably practicable". With a paragraph like that in the law it is perhaps fortunate that many

203

The two houses on the left were also demolished and their destruction has had a sad effect on Great James Street
The opportunity was taken to demolish the early 19th-century remainder of Millman Street

more listed buildings have not quietly disappeared since 1968. It provided a solution for the vandalistic apathy and indecision of Camden Council who had dithered through £2,000 of public money inadequately patching up the houses—but it should always be remembered that the houses were not dangerous structures when they first came into the possession of Camden Council. Emptiness is a hazard to any building and leaking roofs, the buffetings of the weather, the lack of a 'stitch in time'—these were the factors which made sound structures dangerous. In these circumstances, however, the GLC Historic Buildings Division gave its blessing to the demolition. It claimed that restoration would have been too expensive and that the Millman Street houses did, after all, block light from the windows of Millman Place in a way that contravened present building regulations—a problem that was solved, of course, by Millman Street's demolition. To finish off, the GLC added that, because Bloomsbury was a conservation area, buildings of a similar scale and material as the demolished houses should be erected. In the past the Maunsell Metropolitan Housing Association had offered to build flats with reproduction Georgian facades to fill gaps left by bombs. Since what was not bombed has now also gone, it has the chance to build a complete street. But no matter what is done, Bloomsbury is much the less.

The bureaucratic machine as vandal: Deptford, Bow and Wapping
Like Millman Street, Albury Street, Deptford, was a typical victim of that vandalism for which no individual is directly indictable—the vandalism of the 'system' in which the bureaucratic machine blocks original good intentions, defers, debates what is to be done and who is

to pay, whilst the very thing it's all about is falling to pieces.

Emptied by the local council, Albury Street was allowed to stand deserted and rotting for year after year while decisions were made, rejected, considered, laid on the table, and not made at all. As with Millman Street, the Albury Street houses were built in the early 18th century, but they had unique features. Their proximity to the Deptford naval yards must have influenced their original construction, and they were probably originally occupied by high-ranking seamen. They were simple houses but their doorcases were remarkable, probably the work of the same shipwrights who carved the superb figureheads of sailing vessels. By the early part of this century, in common with much of Deptford they were in a slum condition. They survived the bombing of the last war and in 1960 were the only group of houses of their period remain-

This side of Albury Street has now been restored. The house in the centre was gutted by fire

ing in Deptford. Each was individually listed Grade 2, and the street as a whole was likewise listed (of the approximately 19,000 listed buildings in Great London only about 600 are listed Grade 1.)

Around 1960 the process of emptying the houses began, but the intention was not to destroy them and numerous suggestions were made about their future. One of the most destructive ideas floated was that the terrace should be gutted but the facade retained as the frontage for a hospital—not a very fortunate suggestion since the facades which

205

would have been kept, were in part badly re-fronted in the 19th-century, and the panelled interior of the rooms which would have been destroyed are among their most interesting features. By 1969 it was literally as if a vandal had been let loose on the houses. By that time only six of the original 24 houses were lived in. Four of the empty houses on one side of the street had disappeared and on the site was a rubbish dump. One house on the other side of the street had, as part of an inconclusive experiment, been re-faced in an original style and then had been boarded up again. Another had been gutted by a casual fire. There were mutterings that as the houses had been allowed to get into such a poor condition they would have to be destroyed. However, all credit to them, the GLC Historic Buildings Division resolutely demanded that they be preserved. For safe keeping they carefully removed the door-cases and stored them away.

Since then, four of the houses have been restored as a pilot scheme to assess the cost of restoration. The work was carried out on a lightish budget but with a degree of sensitivity about the original facade and panelled interiors. The four houses have been let as unsubsidised council accommodation but the cost of the restoration was such that there was again hesitation about the others, so they continued to stand empty. One night in August, 1971, another one went up in flames, and the intensity of the fire was such that before the Fire Brigade arrived it had gained sufficient hold to reduce the house to a shell; further, in their efforts to get at the fire the firemen had to smash their way into an adjoining house, through the panelled doorway. After the fire the facade of the house was taken down to the first floor level and the party walls with the adjoining houses were shored up and left at that.

At the time of writing another plan has been put forward—it is for the restoration of what is left of the whole street in one operation; which is, of course, what should have been done years ago, before six houses had been lost and when all the houses were in that much better condition and would, therefore, have cost less to restore.

The main cause for concern following the decision to restore, is, of course, how long it will again take to get the work going, and how many more houses will be lost before it commences. As with so many, the survival of these unique houses has become a matter of luck—the chance, for instance, that none of London's depressed homeless, will hop over the back wall and start a bonfire of the wainscote.

Apathy on the part of the local authorities concerned, ten years of indecision, a complete lack of urgency in the face of unique buildings threatened with destruction . . . vandalism, in consequence, if not in intention. Over the river from Deptford in Priscilla Road, Bow, stands the 1706 Drapers Almshouses. Owned by the GLC, but empty and allowed to stand rotting for ten years because it is realised that such buildings should not be destroyed, although a decision cannot be reached as to what to do with them—their facade crumbling. In Raines Street, Wapping, is a 1719 school which the GLC claims it is keeping

This group of restored houses was in as bad a condition as those in the preceding photograph
The early 18th-century school in Raine Street, Wapping

in 'moth-balls' until the best opportunity to use it arises. Ideally, a community organisation should take it over, but so far, the best-suited organisations who want it have not been able to afford it. At the time of writing the building is structurally sound—but how long before it crumbles into the same condition as the Drapers Almshouses?

The Drapers' Almshouses in Priscilla Road, Bow, built in 1706

Vandalism by private opportunism

Public authorites, in so far as they are responsible for the greatest volume of re-development, are involved in the greatest number of instances of vandalistic destruction of buildings which should be preserved. Even where the agent of destruction is a private person or organisation, the local authority almost always plays some part in the proceedings. But, whereas most cases of 'official' vandalism are the result of apathy and indecision resulting from the cumbersome system of administration, cases of sheer, calculated, opportunistic vandalism are mostly perpetrated by private developers, to whom the qualities of environment are of little concern.

In Hanbury Street, in East London, Truman's brewery demolished a terrace of 1700 houses which formed the eastward border to a network of early 18th-century streets, and by doing that rendered less attractive a whole area, thereby jeopardising its possible restoration. The demolished houses were in poor condition but they were an essential part of a distinct environment and, restored, they would have made a very pleasant and important street. To enlarge their brewery Truman's knocked the houses down and replaced them, virtually, with a brick wall, which is a sure way not only of ruining an individual street but also of casting gloom over a whole residential area by creating a hopelessly industrial atmosphere. This was an almost criminal act in an area which desperately needs exactly the opposite for its environmental resuscitation.

The demolition of early 18th-century Hanbury Street
Truman's replacement building

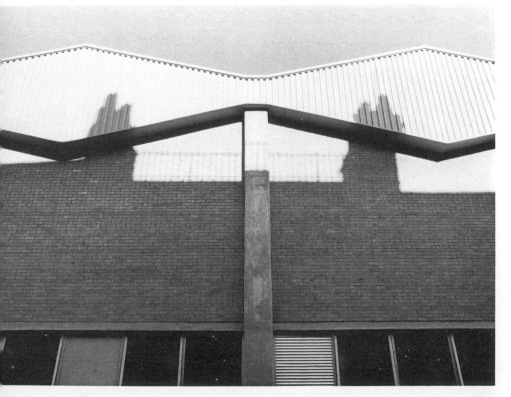

The terrace of 1727 in Wilkes Street
Listed building demolished without consent in Wilkes Street

210

At right angles to Hanbury Street is Wilkes Street, which consists of fine early 18th-century houses. It forms an essential part of a complex of streets, but as far as preservation is concerned it is in a very precarious situation (made more so by the destruction of Hanbury Street). The houses are privately owned and at the time of writing are being allowed to 'run down'—it is understood that for development purposes the idea is to destroy them for their site value. The situation is complicated by the fact that officially they are both under a Slum Clearance order and listed Grade 2 and the fate of these houses could well influence the fate of the whole area. (Incidentally this case illustrates the schizophrenia of developers in the area—in Elder Street fighting each other to get houses to restore and in Wilkes Street to get more houses to demolish to provide sites for office buildings.)

The pressure of developers has already made an imprint on Wilkes Street. Of the two listed buildings in London which the GLC admits were destroyed without proper sanction under the 1968 Town and Country Planning Act, one was in Wilkes Street. Following a fire in the house it was quickly demolished as a dangerous structure. Presumably once a building has been knocked down it is difficult to prove that it was not in a dangerous condition, and perhaps it was for that reason that the GLC took no action. But, since this is an example of the classic method employed to get rid of an unwanted listed building, the GLC's lack of action can only encourage the private developers concerned to hurry the rest of Wilkes Street along the same destructive course.

The other listed building in London demolished without 'listed

Gap in Sekforde Street, Clerkenwell, where the ironworks once stood

building consent' was in Sekforde Street, Clerkenwell. Demolition men working in a street parallel with Sekforde Street, apparently became confused and went on in error to bulldoze Myerson's Iron-works, an early 19th century factory. The demolition was being carried out on behalf of the Woodbridge Estate which owned the site when the Ironworks was first built. It had called in the demolition men to knock down the few houses to provide space for a car park—but the factory went too! Informed by the GLC that they had caused an historic building to be knocked down, and were liable to be prosecuted, the Estate apologised, pleading ignorance. The apology was accepted by the GLC, again no action was taken, and the matter was closed with the Wood-bridge Estate tentatively suggesting that they might put back a replica of the Ironworks, a thing which could be done successfully.

Besides these two cases other listed buildings in London have been destroyed or mutilated with very feeble excuses made by the perpetrators. But still the GLC has not implemented the 1968 Act: a state of affairs that must undermine its deterrent value. However, outside London, at Wheathampstead, Hertfordshire, the local council prosecuted a private development company guilty, for selfish financial reasons, of the flagrant and grossly vandalistic act of destroying a building obvious-ly important to the community in which it existed.

The Old Town Farm was bought by the Maltglade Development Company early in 1971. Their plan was to demolish the farmhouse and to build eleven houses on the site. Although the building was of late 15th-century origin, the developers' plan seemed feasible at the time they acquired it, because despite its age and important central position in the village, the farm was in no way officially protected. However, when Maltglade announced their intentions the St. Albans Rural District Council refused them planning permission and, on 4 May, 1971, took out a Preservation Order on the farm, thus securing for it the same protection as the statutory list provides (that is, that the building cannot be demolished without the written consent of the Minister and the local council). Also this Order should have insured that no works were undertaken on the farm for at least six months. In the regulation manner the Preservation Order was forwarded to Maltglade by regis-tered post, and a copy of it was sent to the farm.

The following Saturday, without notice to anyone—even with the services to the farm intact—demolition men began the work of speedy destruction. The word quickly went around and villagers, local council-lors and the police, rushed to the scene, astounded. The Preservation Order was shown to the man in charge of the demolition gang. He would not cease the demolition work—and, it seems, *it could not be stopped*. He maintained that the Order was not his concern; that on the contrary, his orders were to demolish (perhaps to demolish come what may). Further, the work had to be carried out with all speed because he and his gang wanted to get to a TV set and watch the Cup Final!

Brutally and strictly illegally, and in the teeth of considerable protest,

Wheathampstead, Old Town Farm, before and after demolition

a major act of vandalism was committed in Wheathampstead that Cup Final Saturday afternoon. The historic farm buildings were destroyed and cannot be replaced—all that can be done is to ensure that similar happenings do not take place elsewhere. The Maltglade Development Company were called to account for their actions, and their almost naive reply was that because they had moved their offices and not left a forwarding address they had never received the copy of the Preservation Order. That excuse appeared to throw the St. Albans Rural District Council, and their immediate reaction was that no legal action could be taken. Perhaps for a while it seemed to them that the rights of ownership were such that it could not actually be illegal for a company to destroy its own property.

Fortunately the reaction of the public was more positive. It became apparent that the incident would not be allowed to slide into obscurity but rather would take on the nature of a test case and become the first prosecution under Section V of the 1968 Town and Country Planning Act. The bold front of Maltglade Development visibly cracked. Their architect, who had drawn up the original re-development plans, sought to save his reputation by claiming that he had no idea of the antiquity of the farm—an incredible claim when one knows that he was a resident of Wheathampstead. On 14 May 1971 it was announced that Maltglade Developers had issued a writ against their architects for negligence and slander. The St Albans Rural District Council resolved to prosecute, and issued twenty-three summonses. These were under the 1968 Town and Country Planning Act and also under the Company Act, 1947, Section 107 and 108 of which relates to the fact that the Maltglade Development Company did not have a registered office to which mail could be delivered, and that they did not display a company name— they were, in fact, operating behind a closed door marked 'Private'.On September 17 the directors of the Development Company appeared before the St Albans Magistrates. They pleaded 'not guilty' of the demolition of a protected building and to the charges under the Company Act, but 'guilty' to the charge that the demolition had been undertaken without informing the council. The Queen's Counsellor for the defendants submitted that really there was no case to answer since the Preservation Order had not been received. The Magistrates rejected that submission and the case was adjourned. On October 1 the development company was fined £100 for having destroyed the farmhouse, including a £5 fine for not having given notice of demolition to the council.

The director of the company said, by way of explanation, "There were broken windows and it was a very old and dilapidated building which could easily cause damage to the public."

However, the first step had been taken and by its example similar outrages may be prevented. The St Albans Rural District further announced that it was most unlikely that the Maltglade Development Company would ever be permitted to develop the land which had been cleared by the destruction of the farm buildings. Instead it would be acquired by the council by compulsory purchase, and the price would be that of the site of a vacant lot. And what of the future of the site when purchased by the council? Most likely it would become a car park, they said.

11 Campaigning against vandalism

Stanley Cohen

Social problems can be seen to have both *subjective* and *objective* elements: the former is the awareness by society that the behaviour or condition *is* problematic, the latter is the evidence—as far as it can be ascertained—on which this awareness is based. Social problems can be studied by concentrating on the ways in which society sees a certain condition as threatening or in some way counter to its interests, and then decides that something should be done about it. This is the strategy I would like to adopt in this chapter, concentrating on the subjective elements in the awareness of vandalism as a problem and the various campaigns to elevate it to problem status and then try to control or prevent it.

THE THREAT

The first question to answer is "What exactly is it about the condition which could lead people to define it as problematic at all?" In regard to vandalism, the answer is less obvious than might first appear; the answer would be simpler, for example, for conditions or behaviour such as murder, organized crime, air pollution or traffic congestion. The issue is already over-simplified by using terms such as 'people' or 'society': one cannot assume a consensus about the definition of vandalism as a social problem, nor can one assume that the problem will be seen in the same way by everybody. In addition, some forms of vandalism are very clearly dangerous or threatening, while others are not. Put in this form, then, the question can only be answered on a fairly abstract level.

In the first place, vandalism is behaviour which violates important rules. Under certain conditions, this rule-breaking is defined by significant groups—sometimes speaking for themselves, but more often speaking in the name of 'society'—as being against their interests or as threatening the values they cherish. These interests and values concern both the real and the symbolic value of the damaged property. The real value is measured by such indices as the cost of repairing the damage or replacing the property and the cost of preventive measures. The symbolic value is represented by the threat to the ethics surrounding the possession of property. An assault on property is an assault on these ethics, which in our society involve a complex set of rights, statuses and obligations. Certain forms of vandalism in addition threaten values surrounding the orderly resolution of racial, political and religious differences.

215

ELIZABETH II

1971 CHAPTER 48

An Act to revise the law of England and Wales as to offences of damage to property, and to repeal or amend as respects the United Kingdom certain enactments relating to such offences; and for connected purposes. [14th July 1971]

BE IT ENACTED by the Queen's most Excellent Majesty by, and with the advice and consent of the Lords Spiritual and Temporal, and Commons, in this present Parliament assembled, and by the authority of the same, as follows:—

1.—(1) A person who without lawful excuse destroys or damages any property belonging to another intending to destroy or damage any such property or being reckless as to whether any such property would be destroyed or damaged shall be guilty of an offence. Destroying or damaging property.

(2) A person who without lawful excuse destroys or damages any property, whether belonging to himself or another—

    (*a*) intending to destroy or damage any property or being reckless as to whether any property would be destroyed or damaged ; and

    (*b*) intending by the destruction or damage to endanger the life of another or being reckless as to whether the life of another would be thereby endangered ;

shall be guilty of an offence.

(3) An offence committed under this section by destroying or damaging property by fire shall be charged as arson.

2. A person who without lawful excuse makes to another a threat, intending that that other would fear it would be carried out,— Threats to destroy or damage property.

    (*a*) to destroy or damage any property belonging to that other or a third person ; or

There are more specific problems which vandalism poses. Some forms of property damage are simply inconvenient and annoying: broken chains in public lavatories, street lamps not working or slot machines jammed. The consequences of vandalism are sometimes more than inconveniencing: loss of life or serious injury might result from objects being placed on railway lines or lifebelts being torn from their fittings. Calls for medical aid may be delayed as a result of public telephones being damaged.

Aesthetic values are also threatened by many forms of vandalism especially those involving the defacement of properties such as public buildings, monuments, war memorials and statues. Such defacement is particularly demoralising if the property is newly constructed and in a prominent position. If in addition the property is sacred (such as places of worship and cemeteries) the damage or defacement is particularly abhorrent and may be described by the term "sacrilege". The feelings of demoralisation that defacement of public buildings often evoke are well captured in the reaction of Salinger's Holden Caulfield on seeing obscenities scribbled on the wall of a public museum:

". . . while I was sitting down, I saw something that drove me crazy. Somebody'd written ' — you' on the wall . . . I went down by a different staircase and I saw another ' — you' on the wall. I tried to rub it off with my hand again, but this one was scratched on, with a knife or something. It wouldn't come off. It's hopeless anyway. If you had a million years to do it in, you couldn't rub out even half the ' — you' signs in the world . . ."[1]

Because of its stereotype as being wanton, malicious and pointless, vandalism presents further emotional threats. Even the mischievous, play element in some vandalism is part of the threat, because it appears to be a perfect example of the 'fun morality'. Vandalism is seen as an inversion of the Puritan ethic which demands that actions should be carried out for a recognizable, utilitarian reason. Thus, some sociologists have chosen vandalism as the archetypal act of the delinquent subculture: it is 'malicious, non-utilitarian and negativistic'. These terms conjure up something like the behaviour of the original Vandals. For the public, vandalism is very much part of the stock image of delinquency. Burroughs' horrific vision of uncontrolled adolescent behaviour captures this image perfectly; note how many acts of vandalism he includes:

"Rock and Roll adolescent hoodlums storm the streets of all nations. They rush into the Louvre and throw acid in the Mona Lisa's face. They open zoos, insane asylums, prisons, burst water mains with air hammers, chop the floor out of passenger plane lavatories, shoot out lighthouses, file elevator cables to one thin wire, turn sewers into the water supply, throw sharks and sting rays, electric eels and candiru into swimming pools . . . in nautical costume ram the 'Queen Mary' full speed into

New York Harbor, play chicken with passenger trains and buses, rush into hospitals in white coats carrying saws and axes and scalpels three feet long; throw paralytics out of iron lungs . . . administer injections with bicycle pumps, disconnect artificial kidneys, saw a woman in half with a two-man surgical saw, they drive herds of squealing pigs into the curb, they shit on the floor of the United Nations and wipe their ass with treaties, pacts, alliances . . ."[2]

Vandalism, then, presents threats which give it a high *potential* for being defined as problematic. This potential has certainly been realised in this country, and over the past few decades vandalism—usually associated with such constellation as 'the youth problem' and 'the problem of violence'—has been a prominent focus of public concern. My own survey of the mass media during the 1960's shows a high amount of attention given to vandalism relative to other recognised social problems. Scarcely a day passes in local papers or a week in regional television or radio news, without an item reporting a dramatic incident of vandalism, a 'shock report' or a feature about a 'new' solution announced by an enterprising local figure.

It is interesting though, that the victim organisations I studied—the Post Office, local authorities, British Rail—are *less* likely to define vandalism as a problem than the public as a whole or the mass media. This applies to even the most threatening and highly publicised forms of vandalism, such as railway or telephone vandalism. There was a clear tendency among most organisations to 'put the problem in perspective' and to deplore extreme and hysterical statements made about vandalism in various public arenas. This does not mean, of course, that they were entirely 'right' and the public 'wrong': there are many complex reasons why organisations should want to play down their problems. They might, for example, perceive (often realistically) that scare-publicity would make things worse; they might also simply want to deny the problem in order not to reveal defects in their own organisation.

Almost invariably, victim organisations start defining vandalism in problematic terms because of some pressure being placed on them. This pressure might come from moral enterprise (by one of their own members or an outsider) or as a result of publicity in the mass media. One of the conditions for social problem definition is a perception that the condition is remediable. Somebody must see that something can be done to prevent, control or eradicate the problem. The very absence of this condition among many victim organisations leads to their apparent apathy or refusal to see vandalism in problematic terms. Unlike the mass media, the politicians, the moral entrepreneurs, and the control agents who talk in terms of 'an urgent need to do something about the problem', many victim organisations (again, realistically) do not think that anything can be done or is worth doing. The following example of this attitude may be quoted from a survey on the cost of vandalism to local authorities:

"The bulk of replies and additional letters indicated a defeated acceptance of vandalism as an incurable nuisance. Very few authorities have actually set about tackling the problem. The cost of preventive measures is often as great if not greater than the cost of vandalism. One smart Alec suggested that vandalism might cost them less than answering the questionnaire!" [3]

This report was compiled by an organisation determined to define and publicise vandalism as a problem. The organisation's comment on the above summary of the attitudes of the 922 local authorities which completed its questionnaire, shows how social problems typically get defined and presented:

"The cash cost is surely not the only aspect of the problem to be considered. The cause of vandalism is a serious social matter and until early education attached more importance to a child's appreciation of the public services than to his knowing which is the longest river or the highest mountain, no hope can be held out for tackling the problem at its roots." [4]

Such statements asserting the relative unimportance of objective elements (the 'cash costs') are typical and it can be demonstrated easily that there is a substantial exaggeration, particularly in the mass media, of the amount, seriousness, cost and novelty of vandalism. Popular judgment consistently over-estimates the actual magnitude of the problem and gives it disproportionate attention compared to other offences. But while such discrepancies between objective and subjective elements can be shown, this distinction is not always easy to sustain. On the one hand, an objective index of behaviour such as vandalism is difficult to obtain and on the other, the so-called subjective elements do not exist apart from reality in some numinous world of their own. We are back to asserting that social problems are what people think they are.

CONDITIONS FOR PROBLEM DEFINITION
Given the basic 'problem potential' of vandalism, how does it become generated into a fully fledged, headline social problem? I would like to suggest three conditions for such problem creation: *awareness and visibility; enterprise and publicity* and *favourable beliefs.*

(*i*) *Awareness and visibility*
The need for somebody to become aware of a certain condition as dangerous, troublesome or threatening is both the first stage and the most necessary condition in the development of a social problem. This awareness, in turn, is dependent on the condition being visible: it must be seen, heard or read about before anyone can start defining it as an actual or potential threat.

Most types of vandalism start off—relative to other forms of deviance and problems—with a high degree of physical visibility. The target of most damage is public property, public not just in the sense that it is publicly owned, but that it is prominently accessible and visible to the public. One can see the ripped-up seats in a railway carriage and a broken pane of glass in a telephone kiosk in a sense that one cannot 'see', for example, the results of blackmail, white-collar crime or shop-lifting. The consequence of many forms of deviation are connected more with the symbolic violation of cherished values than actual physical damage. This means that ways of increasing visibility and awareness such as spotlighting 'horror stories' about individual incidents or publishing statistics showing 'dangerous' increases in the amount of deviance, are somewhat less needed for vandalism. In other words, vandalism starts off with some advantages in the initial phases of problem definition.

Visibility and awareness can be increased by real and objective changes in the extent or seriousness of the condition. This effect is by no means easy to establish, nor is it as straightforward and automatic as first appears: people can become aware of a condition as problematic without any real change having taken place. The reverse is also true: a real change can take place without anyone noticing it. As I've suggested, the 'real and objective' changes in regard to vandalism are somewhat ambiguous: the awareness of change was greater than most of the significant changes which did take place.

The visibility of certain types of vandalism has been increased in recent years by certain technological innovations which have made new techniques of vandalism possible. In regard to writing on walls, for example, a notable innovation has been the use of the felt-tipped pen. In the past it was fairly easy to rub out slogans on bus shelters, lamp posts and walls: these were written with chalk, pencil or crayon, all of which instruments are less indelible than the felt-tipped pen. Added to this factor has been the introduction, especially in new towns, of smooth, highly receptive surfaces such as plastic, terrazzo, high finish concrete and mosaic which make wall writing much more difficult to get rid of and hence more visible. An example of an area which suffered this problem is the Precinct of Coventry's rebuilt city centre where it was estimated that it would need six men working full time for a week to clear up the defacement. The Vice-Chairman of the Coventry Education Committee was quoted as saying:

"It was all very well for a courting couple years ago to spend a whole afternoon carving "Jack loves Judith" on a tree. It took them a long time and the marks grew out anyway. With a felt pen on some of these new surfaces you can do a lot of damage in a few minutes and nothing will wash it out."[5]

A technological innovation of similar importance has been the aerosol spray. All poster and advertising companies contacted drew my attention to the effect of this invention. Aerosol sprays are much quicker and easier to apply than paint, and fairly long slogans can be sprayed on posters in a matter of seconds. This decreases the chances of detection even in busy public settings and allows a number of offences to be committed in a short time.

A major factor in increasing visibility is the dramatic and spectacular nature of the condition or event. Tragic cases such as those in which calls for medical help might have been delayed because of a damaged telephone, although very few in number, are played up by the media and defined as if they are almost commonplace. Dramatic consequences are represented as if they were frequent consequences. Thus, a local paper in Birmingham—an area which was seriously affected by telephone vandalism and had high problem-awareness—carried the following editorial:

"The man who breaks open a telephone coin box and steals the money from it is guilty of more than theft, criminal though such action is. He is also guilty of acting without any decent regard for the distress and even the tragedy that he may be causing by depriving people in the vicinity of an essential public facility. He is cutting them off from emergency services required at times of accidents, fires, sickness and childbirth and his action makes him an enemy of the community."[6]

Similarly, a columnist dealing in *News of the World* with vandalism in general, wrote:

"They are known as vandals. I call them potential murderers. They are the lads who wreck telephone boxes for the sheer hell of it, and so hold up emergency calls to doctors, hospitals and ambulance services."[7]

Figures about the number of telephones out of order were quoted to increase the visibility of this threat. Commenting, for example, on an incident in Oxford in which a father was delayed in obtaining medical help for his sick child, the *Daily Mirror* informed its readers that ". . . louts and petty thieves . . . are putting nearly half Britain's 75,000 phone boxes out of action every year.".[8] This information is misleading for two reasons: firstly, although it may have been true that half the phones were damaged at one time or another during that year, *at any one time* the total "out of action" was about *one in thirty*. Secondly, nearly all phones "out of action" are usable for emergency "999" calls.

School vandalism is also of interest here. The type of school vandalism that almost exclusively is visible and shapes society's conception of the problem, is the spectacular type of incident in which a school is broken into one night and an 'orgy of destruction' takes place. This type of incident invariably sets off the process of problem definition (for example, by local education authorities). The more pervasive type of school vandalism (routine or organisational rule breaking) is in many senses more serious. An American study some years ago of school vandalism confirms my own information in this country:

". . . everyday damage to school property—breaking windows, cutting desk tops, gouging walls, damaging washroom equipment, etc—was more costly in the long run than the occasional more spectacular acts of vandalism in which one or two rooms may be extensively damaged."[9]

Another factor which increases awareness and visibility is the type of property that is damaged. It is not always damage to the most expensive type of property which gets noticed but to property which has an important symbolic value. One might compare—simply using the index of number of incidents reported in the mass media—the amount of attention given to damage of religious property on the one hand, and local authority property on the other. Between 1965-67, the national press reported 45 separate incidents of damage to churches and cemeteries and 112 separate incidents of damage to local authority property. This reporting ratio of 1-2$\frac{1}{2}$ is grossly inaccurate, the correct proportion being something like 1:100.

The distinction between rule-breaking and deviance is again relevant. Although rules are by no means automatically enforced when someone becomes aware of their infringement, it is obvious that enforcement cannot occur unless the rule-breaking is visible. Heightened visibility and awareness often combine with other factors to increase the likelihood of certain forms of property destruction being labelled and processed vandalism offences. As an illustration, one may take the case of the vandalism at the Kennedy Memorial at Runnymede. In June 1965 there was a great deal of public indignation about the memorial being defaced. A number of names ("Glyn", "Dell", "Andy") and obscenities had been carved or scribbled on the stone of the memorial. This damage was noticed after a middle-aged couple had disturbed "four young hooligans" breaking shrubs and bushes near the memorial. The boys ran away and the husband went to the National Trust Warden and called the police, who apparently were "amazed" at the shocking condition of the memorial. The damage was widely publicised: a long article in the *Sunday Mirror* for example, headed "Britain's Shame", talked about how vandals had done their best ". . . to deface the monument, desecrate the memory and so dishonour the name of Britain".[10] The offenders were labelled as "the mentally disturbed and the childish who cannot resist making an exhibition of themselves". From all sources there was a call for greater vigilance to prevent this sort of damage. In fact, the damage had taken place throughout the whole year since the monument had been built; this type of vandalism is common and entirely predictable, especially on monuments and similar property in isolated places. Incidental vandalism became defined as problematic, through a combination of : (*i*) heightened visibility resulting from a single incident, which in itself was trivial; (*ii*) the fact that the property damaged was sacred and of highly symbolic value; (*iii*) the suggested association of the vandalism with ideological reasons, for which there was no evidence at all.

(ii) Enterprise and publicity

Sociologists have recently paid attention to the role of *moral entre-preneurs* in the generation of social problem awareness.[11] These are individuals or groups who, with varying degrees of personal interest and commitment, work to create new parts in the "moral fabric" of society. They sometimes fight to create new rules, to enforce existing rules more rigidly or—like the current crusade against pornography (moral filth) in Britain—do both these things and draw public attention to a condition they see as threatening.

Vandalism, because of its high visibility and problem potential (compared, say, with certain forms of drug taking), needs less active enterprise of this sort. It is of interest to study, though, enterprises connected with local authority vandalism; a form which is less dramatic and visible. The Local Government Information Office, for example, waged during the 1960's a successful crusade to make the public aware of such vandalism. It condemned defeatist attitudes in local government and urged that the problem be 'tackled at its roots'. This spirit of moral crusade was illustrated in the Office's distribution of a text of a sermon about vandalism delivered by a Congregational minister.

A similar enterprise by the Council of British Ceramic Sanitaryware Manufacturers was less noteworthy for its moral message than its combination of commercial interests and sophisticated publicity techniques. In 1964 it commissioned a survey about washing facilities in public conveniences and the findings highlighted vandalism as a major impediment to adequate facilities.

". . . Public conveniences are clearly a necessary part of our lives. Yet this basic necessity is threatened because of the attitude of what can only be a small minority—vandals. Evidence would seem to indicate that vandalism generally is on the increase and the time is approaching when a really concerted drive is going to be necessary."[12]

Vandalism was specifically blamed for the poor conditions and low standards of public conveniences and its threat was defined in familiar terms: ". . . until the problem of vandalism is tackled as an urgent national problem it is difficult to see how conditions can be changed".[13] The survey was summarised as follows:

"The Survey has revealed in all its starkness the frightful and fearful growth and impact of the vandals on public conveniences and the way in which the activities of these people interfere with the well-being of normal citizens. A determined effort must be made by all concerned to stamp out effectively the activities of vandals and the public should co-operate with the police to a far greater extent than now appears to be the case to be ruthless and efficient in ending vandalism . . ."[14]

A professional public relations firm arranged for the survey to be launched at a Press conference intended to ". . . bring together at any one time a greater representative gathering of parties interested in Britain's health and hygiene than any other comparable conference". Part of the invitation read:

"SANITARY POTTERS INVITE LOCAL AUTHORITIES TO MEET YOU TO LAUNCH THE FIRST EVER COMPREHENSIVE STUDY OF BRITAIN'S PUBLIC CONVENIENCES.
You, too, must have suffered; you have used a toilet and found no toilet paper; smashed wash basins; broken seat; the walls a mess of artists' design. The reason, vandalism of course. And "come spring, come the vandals". The vandals who seem to have spent the winter months wrecking telephone kiosks, smashing railway specials, now prepare to launch their annual attacks on the conveniences of Britain. . . . Frankly, we have facing us as a nation a frightening picture, horrifying in some cases.
The time for action is now and suggestions will be put forward for a rapid improvement in the standard of Britain's public conveniences."[15]

The conference was attended by journalists and representatives of local authorities, manufacturers, health officials and public health inspectors. The highlight was the unveiling of a full-size model of a public toilet, constructed on the floor of the Conference Room. The model bore various examples of vandalism, and after the unveiling an official of the CBCSM demonstrated (with realistic aggression) the action of a typical vandal; ripping out the chain, wrecking the toilet roll, kicking the seat in and scribbling on the wall.

The emphasis of those attending the conference was very much on their public duty and responsibility in getting something done about vandalism in public conveniences. The CBCSM, too, were emphatic in disclaiming any commercial interest in trying to expose vandalism (for the obvious reason that the more damage that occurred, the more equipment they would be called upon to supply):

"On the face of it, some may say that vandalism indirectly aids the industry because of replacements. But this is short-sighted and certainly it is no part of the manufacturers of ceramic sanitaryware to divert a good proportion of their output in replacement of fitments in public conveniences due to the activities of vandals. Indeed, the demand due to increasing calls upon their output could be embarrassing. The industry is actively engaged in meeting demands from new housing, from conversions, from industrial requirements as well as local authorities and replacement of fitments because of vandalism is output which can ill be spared. Furthermore the calls of the export market and the desire to co-operate in the Government's scheme for exports, makes it all the more necessary in the national interest to reduce the incidence of vandalism."[16]

Again, as with the LGIO efforts, we have an example of a condition previously ignored or reacted to in such a way that it is institutionalised, being elevated into the status of a national, moral and social problem.

The most interesting types of enterprises are those by individual local authorities. These invariably follow an identical sequence. In the first stage, an awareness has to be created of vandalism as a local problem. This occurs in one of three ways: (*i*) a magistrate, judge or similar public figure draws attention to the increase in vandalism throughout the country and calls for it to be "stamped out" in the area; (*ii*) a local government official or politician, influenced by the heightened visibility of vandalism given in the mass media or from a personal sense of public duty, takes the initiative in having the subject raised in some way: by writing to the local newspaper, calling on the council to set up a 'working party', or making a speech on school prize-giving day; (*iii*) a dramatic local incident of vandalism (often misleadingly reported) or the publication of figures showing the extent of the problem locally, provokes someone in the community (such as a local politician, clergyman or newspaper editor) to take up the issue.

The problem is then given considerable publicity and opinions voiced —in the council, from the pulpit, in newspaper columns, by headmasters on speech days, by mayors at inaugural lunches—about its possible causes and solutions. Some temporary body like a Council working party or sub-committee is set up to investigate the seriousness of the problem, or a conference convened of interested parties and 'experts': the Chief Constable, a couple of vicars, local authority officials, headmasters, social workers and businessmen. In about a quarter of the cases the enterprise does not get further. In the rest, some more permanent body is set up and given responsibility to publicise the problem and to formulate, and in some cases to carry out, policy decisions. Invariably, the campaigns peter out or else reach their climax with ambiguous results, it never being quite clear whether the enterprise was successful or not in reducing vandalism. At these later stages in particular the enterprise is faced with what Becker has perceptively identified as the unique dilemma of the rule enforcer: on the one hand, to justify his position, he must demonstrate that the problem still exists and is perhaps worse than ever, but on the other hand he must show that his enterprise has been worthwhile, and that the evil is being dealt with and approaching an end.

By far the most advanced and interesting of the efforts of individual local authorities was that by Birmingham Corporation in 1966-67. Again some background factors—not peculiar in themselves but unique in the particular combination they took in Birmingham—must be sketched in to understand the way in which the enterprise was generated. There was to begin with the fact that among British cities of a comparable size, Birmingham had more than its fair share of vandalism from about 1963 onwards. With not more than the usual journalistic hyperbole, the local newspaper referred to an incident of vandalism in 1966 as ". . . typical of a problem that has been eating like a cancer at the heart of the new Birmingham for the past few years."[17] Characteristically, the incident which could spark off such sentiments was highly dramatic and visible: a Roman Catholic Junior School was broken into, equipment incuding two pianos and a radiogram wrecked, and the annex of the school eventually set on fire. A member of the Education Committee reacted by saying that he would raise the subject of vandalism at the next committee meeting. This particular incident had left him speechless: ". . . I cannot coin the words to describe this senseless and wanton damage. It was nothing but a blatant and disgusting act of hooliganism. In this case it amounts to arson and sacrilege."

Incidents of this sort served to increase public awareness. The cost of vandalism to the Council during the previous year was estimated as between £30,000 - £50,000. Among the most important reasons for what seemed a disproportionate amount of vandalism in Birmingham during this period was the rapid re-development that had taken place in the city. Apart from the presence of much derelict property waiting demolition, there were new sights such as the Bull Ring, escalators, vast areas of plate glass, tiled subway walls and water fountains. While these factors could hardly be said to have made the city "a vandals' paradise"[18] they probably did increase the range of targets usually damaged, the visibility of the damage and the emotive reaction the damage would evoke ("We build new things for them, and look how they treat them"). Types of vandalism that occurred on a national level appeared to be especially acute in Birmingham. Public telephone vandalism, after the introduction of the S.T.D. system in Birmingham in 1965, was particularly prevalent and the target of a separate campaign for higher penalties introduced by the Recorder of Birmingham. Vandalism in the city was an issue that was raised in both local and national politics at the time.

Against this background and in view of the national publicity that the vandalism problem was receiving, it is not particularly surprising that at various times in 1965 and 1966 individual departments of the Council started paying attention to vandalism. In August 1965, after some agitation from the Health Committee, the Town Clerk was asked to ascertain the action taken by other departments to prevent vandalism to their property. In a report in December, 1965, he summarised the replies received from various departments together with statistics from some departments on the amount of vandalism in the 12 months preceding 31st May 1965. Three interesting points arise from this report: (i) He notes that in a calculation made in April 1963, the cost of damage to the Corporation in the previous year (1962) was approximately £37,000. This means that the figure quoted at the beginning of 1967 (when the anti-vandalism campaign actually got under way) of £50,000 damage in the previous year, was not an excessive increase. (ii) Other figures provided in the report and supplemented by more up to date information in 1967, suggest that some types of vandalism (for example, in parks) had actually *decreased* rather than increased in the two years immediately preceding the campaign. This decline was later attributed (by the same people who, caught up in the rule enforcers' dilemma, had to argue at the same time that vandalism was getting worse) to the introduction of patrols by mobile Park Rangers. In initiating the campaign, it was argued that such schemes had a great deterrent value and should be more widely implemented. (*iii*) This claim, however, should be evaluated alongside a particularly significant sentence in the Town Clerk's report:

"It would appear from the views expressed by the General Manager of the Building Department and the General Manager of the Parks Department that the measures taken to prevent vandalism are tending to be more costly than making good the acts of vandalism, and your sub-committee may wish to have regard to this aspect of the matter."

The gravity of the problem evidently impressed itself on the Special Purposes Committee who resolved that:

"the Chairman of the General Purposes Committee be authorized to give the widest possible publicity to many cases of vandalism suffered by the Corporation to property in their ownership in an endeavour to ensure the co-operation of the general public in an effort to eliminate this anti-social behaviour."

This recommendation is characteristic of the early stages of problem definition: the condition must be exposed, publicised and made visible to as wide an audience as possible. The Committee was determined to do this, even if it involved setting aside one of the most important points made in the Town Clerk's report, namely, that measures to prevent vandalism might be more costly than the damage itself. Their comment on this point was:

"Whilst this may be a valid statement your Sub-Committee is strongly of the opinion that vandalism, not only to corporation-owned property, but to property in private ownership, is reaching such serious proportions that there should be no relaxation of any of the measures taken to secure its elimination."

Such statements reveal the uncompromising nature of many moral crusades: the problem is getting worse, one cannot relax until it is completely eliminated.

Acting on this report, the General Purposes Committee decided to publicise the vandalism problem, to convene a Conference of all Committees affected by wilful damage to property under their control (Education, Health, Public Works, etc.). The Conference took place in November, 1965 and consisted mainly of a discussion of various ways and means to prevent vandalism: closed circuit television, alarm systems,

IF YOU LEND A HAND WE CAN
STOP vandalism

If you are a:

RATEPAYER

PROPERTY OWNER

PARENT

YOUNG PERSON

TEACHER

YOUTH WORKER

VANDAL

Do YOU realise that it costs over £50,00 of YOUR MONEY each year to make goo the damage done by vandals to Corpora tion property alone. The cost to everyon in the City is far greater, and in the lon run YOU PAY.

We ask that YOU take all precau tions to protect your property an not to place temptation in the pat of a potential vandal. If YOU ow any dilapidated buildings whic serve no useful purpose, pleas have them demolished. Remembe that even if YOU are insured YO PAY in increased premiums an inconvenience.

Please do everything YOU can to impres on your children how futile it is to wrec other people's property. Please help ther to use their leisure time profitably. Don blame the authorities if they are caugh and punished, because in the end YO PAY.

Please think before YOU wrec something. Think about how muc more fun it may give YOU an others if YOU help to protect rather than break it. Even if YOU are not caught, it is YOUR parent who will PAY for the damage, an if YOU are caught YOU *will* PAY

Please impress on every member of you class how silly it is to destroy the thing which are provided to make their live more pleasant.

Please try to widen your net an give as many young people a possible the opportunities whic your organisation is able to giv them.

Someone will be watching YOU — an have YOU thought that if YOU wreck public telephone — it may be **YOU** **MOTHER** who wants a doctor in a emergency.

YOU may not always be able to stop an act of vandalism yourself, but YOU can dial 999 — because it does concern YOU

Remember if we don't stop vandalism

you will pay

Issued by CITY OF BIRMINGHAM PARKS COMMITTEE   P101618 (Y)

Display card from the Birmingham 'Stop Vandalism Week'

Park Rangers, heavier penalties by the courts, etc. Eventually, the proposition that commended itself was the inauguration of a 'Stop Vandalism Week'. It was further recommended that ". . . in view of their current success in reducing vandalism to property under their control" the task of organisation of the 'Stop Vandalism Week' be given to the Parks Committee. At this point the enterprise moved rapidly to its final stages. The Parks Committee took over and in the beginning of January, 1967, the 'Stop Vandalism Week' was launched with the most extensive and successful publicity of any similar campaign. I will describe later the actual content of the campaign, which was defined less in terms of the 'elimination' of the problem than increasing the community's awareness of vandalism as its responsibility.

Groups other than local authorities, of course, also campaign against vandalism. These are usually groups whose immediate interests are threatened, for example, hotelkeepers, the Licenced Victuallers Association or entertainment and sporting firms. Vested interests can be an important factor in the redefinition of certain types of rule-breaking into social problem terms. An interesting example was the outbreak of an anti-smoking campaign which took the form of daubing the word "Cancer" in red paint on posters advertising cigarettes and tobacco. The British Poster Advertising Association asked Scotland Yard to help fight the campaign, one large tobacco company carried out a survey of its posters when reports of the vandalism began, and the sales manager of one poster advertising contractor was quoted as saying: "I have been out trying to catch someone, and if I do I shall see that they are charged. This is serious wilful damage. This seems to be a campaign against smoking, and it means a lot of work for us . . .". Another element that worried the Advertising Association was that the print was sprayed with aerosol, a speedy and effective method of defacement. ". . . the culprits appear to be a couple of student types who are dashing about the place on a motor cycle". Now poster-daubing is among the most tolerated and incidental types of property damage; it is very rarely defined in problematic terms. A combination of three new elements led to its temporary redefinition as a problem, meriting such attention as a *Daily Telegraph* headline: *Vandals' War on Cigarette Posters:*

(*i*) the switch from 'harmless' graffiti (such as painting moustaches on the girls in the cigarette posters, or even scrawling obscenities) to messages which had a very obvious ideological component;

(*ii*) the presence of groups who had to interpret the message (cigarette smoking causes cancer, therefore don't listen to the advertisements) as a target to commercial interests;

(*iii*) a technological innovation—the use of aerosol sprays—which increased the magnitude of the threat.

There are two incidental comments that should be made about the attempts by vested interest groups to get vandalism defined in social problem terms. The first is that it is either not realised or else deliberately ignored that in virtually all instances the cost of preventive measures exceeds the cost of the damage. This point weakens the case for problem-definition on purely financial grounds. The second point is that much illegal property damage does not get defined as problematic for the very reason that this definition would be more expensive in the long run. This is the case with much 'chartered rule-breaking'; for example, a hotel keeper who regularly has rugby teams staying in his hotel and causing about £20 worth of damage over a week-end, would rather put up with this than ban the team from his hotel, press charges or try to reclaim the damage. I traced a number of instances where hotel managers made strenuous efforts to counter any attempts by the press to give publicity to this type of vandalism.

Publicity is clearly an essential aid to a successful campaign, but in addition the mass media often act as entrepreneurs in their own right, when, for example, they campaign against a particular evil or attempt to 'expose', 'probe' or 'uncover' a particular condition—out of public service or commercial interest.

Exposures—feature articles in newspapers and programmes on the radio or television—consist mainly of a digest of the statistics and a presentation of horror stories. The statistics tend to be selective and the distinction between real increases and increases in attention seldom made. There are often wide disparities between figures quoted by different sources and distortions occur, for example, by quoting rough estimates as if they were accurate figures. In the case of telephone vandalism mistakes of up to £300,000 were made in quoting the annual cost of damage. No distinction is made between the cost of vandalism and the cost of loss from other sources such as theft.

Both in campaigning and exposing, the mass media are an integral part of the process of problem definition: they heighten the visibility of a problem simply by drawing the public's attention to it and also by emphasising its more dramatic aspects. The conscious use of certain techniques emphasises the threatening aspects of the vandalism problem and give the public a peculiar and often distorted image of it: unnecessarily emotive language ("The vandalism death tract"), unrealistic threats ("The whole public telephone service could break down"), and a subtle screening device to pick out particularly noteworthy items. When vandalism is in the news, related areas of interest are scanned to select items about vandalism, however vaguely connected. During such times, stories about the crime rate, youth clubs or schools are presented as if they specifically refer to vandalism. A dramatic example of such screening occurred in a report of one day's hearing of the Aberfan Disaster Tribunal. Evidence was heard about some crucial telephone cable having been stolen from the tip; the Chairman of the Tribunal commented: "These people ought to have heavy hearts and a lot on their consciences". Despite the fact that this was a case of theft and not vandalism and that a great deal of more important evidence was heard on the same day (for example, about previous representations by the villagers about the safety of the tip), the *Daily Telegraph* chose to head
230

its report of the hearings "Judge Criticises Phone Vandals on Tip No.7 'Lot on their Consciences' ".[19]

In ways which are not yet fully appreciated, the media play a crucial role in heightening problem-awareness, spreading the beliefs favourable to problem-definition and transmitting the images and stereotypes about the nature of deviance and social problems.

(iii) Beliefs favourable to problem definition

In tracing the stages through which various types of vandalism emerged to be defined as problems, one repeatedly comes across the same sort of statements about the nature of the problem. The mass media, the victims, the moral entrepreneurs and the public at large, express a number of beliefs which seem to function to ensure that the condition *is* in fact defined as a social problem. In addition, the beliefs or opinions justify certain ways of dealing with the problem. Three themes always come up: firstly, that the condition under consideration is not an isolated or particular one, it is part of a broader social or national problem and is a manifestation or symptom of somthing more "fundamental"; secondly, that the condition is remediable: something can be done about it: and, thirdly, that something *must* be done about the condition or else it will deteriorate. A corollary of the last belief (because of the first) is that the responsibility for doing something lies with "society" or more specifically, the Government.

Thus in regard to vandalism, the following sorts of assertions were made:

(*i*) the particular form of vandalism being considered—say, damage to telephones—was part and parcel of the general vandalism problem;

(*ii*) the general vandalism problem was itself part of a broader problem, variously defined as: 'the delinquency problem'; 'the problem of violence'; 'the youth problem'; 'the problem of the general decline in values (or morals, or respect for property)';

(*iii*) if not dealt with soon, vandalism would 'get out of hand' or 'get beyond control'. It was up to society as a whole, or the Government, and not the organisations affected to do something.

The problem was thus conceptualised in terms of a pyramid of scope, effect and responsibility: visible at the top, was merely one aspect— say, damage to telephones—but at the next level down there was much more—slashing seats in railway carriages, bricks on railway lines, broken bottles on football grounds—while at the base there was an ominous and solidly rooted social problem. The pyramid could only be demolished by attacking the base.

This sort of image has obvious functions for successful problem-definition and variants of it have been used to expose the evils and dangers of prostitution, alcohol, drugs and masturbation. In regard to vandalism, there is, in addition, a less obvious function for some victim organisations: it allows them to deny—sometimes quite reasonably and at other times less reasonably—that vandalism is in fact 'their' problem. Such organisations take pains to point out that they are not responsible for the situation: it was not their fault in the first place, and they could not solve the problem themselves. Thus local authorities—even when they are trying to do something about vandalism—do not want to be labelled as a 'high vandalism area' and soccer clubs do not want their supporters to be stigmatised as a 'bunch of vandals'. The result of such denials means that it is not only the moral entrepreneurs and those really worried about vandalism who define it as a social problem; others uninterested in enterprise and publicity project exactly the same pyramidal image of the situation.

A good example of this pyramid can be found in the evolution of the football hooliganism problem. From the beginning of the 1960's there was a steady build-up of an image of football hooliganism as a massive new national problem, one that was increasing and becoming more intense. Although some increase had, no doubt, taken place[20] there was clearly much exaggeration owing to the attention given to other types of vandalism and the 'creeping menace' image through which this was viewed. At the height of each publicity wave, reporters were sent to football matches to cover the incidents and not any details of the game. They were instructed to report anything on what the *Daily Sketch* called 'The Hooligan Front'. This meant that in order to justify a reporter being sent, *some* incident had to be reported.

The resultant impression was not just that football hooliganism was increasing, but that it was also something totally new: that suddenly, at about the same time as telephones were being smashed and the Mods and Rockers running riot, the vandals descended on the soccer terraces. This impression was reinforced by the somewhat unconvincing attempt to present the problem as somehow 'imported' from foreign countries, particularly on the Continent and in South America. Violence at football matches was not really British at all, it had been picked up through contact with foreign teams and reading about foreign crowds. To quote two press comments after a particularly violent Saturday afternoon:

"Hooliganism among English soccer crowds moved another step nearer Italian style rioting on Saturday".[21]
"British fans have a long way to go yet before Roman standards of violence, but each season sees them moving a little nearer."[22]

As one might expect, very few people with any knowledge of the game could honestly endorse this sort of stereotype: but the probability of football hooliganism being accorded full social problem status was heightened by presenting the situation as a potential threat to Britain's national prestige. When the 'good name of the British sporting public' or 'national pride' was at stake, one could be sure of a receptive audience for appeals to end " . . . the creeping menace which is blackening the name of soccer."[23] Such appeals were particularly prevalent in the months preceding England's staging of the World Football Cup in July 1966. The following two comments were made after incidents in January and April of that year:

" . . . soccer is still reeling and stunned by this ultimate in shame and humiliation. The human garbage have plummetted our national sport to its lowest ever depths of viciousness and wanton hooliganism."[24]
"It may be only a handful of hooligans who are involved at the throwing end, but if this sort of behaviour is repeated in July the world will conclude that all the British are hooligans . . . Either the drift in violence must be checked or soccer will be destroyed as an entertainment. What an advertisement for the British sporting spirit if we end with football pitches enclosed in protective wire cages."[25]

After the World Cup had taken place and England had won, comments like this were made during the next season: "The proud banners of Britain's soccer triumphs are being trampled in the mud of such violence."[26]

Various agencies were blamed for this state of affairs: the players, the supporters, hooligans in the crowd who were not 'real' supporters, the standard of refereeing, the clubs, the Football Association, the police and the courts (for not being tough enough) and—to get to the top of the pyramid—the Government for not giving the police and courts enough power and generally for not 'tackling the problem at its roots'. This pyramid emerges clearly if one looks at the statements of those closely associated with the game: directors, players and managers. They would continually deny that the problem had anything to do with them.[27]

"There is no such thing as soccer hooliganism. It is a suitable occasion for the manifestations of general lawlessness and violence that is appearing in society in all its aspects.
"The root of the problem is not inside, but outside the football ground . . . when hooliganism is reduced in society generally, it will also disappear from the football terraces."
"Someone will call me a fascist or a reactionary but I shudder to think what things will be like in a few years unless this is treated as a national problem. It is a Government problem . . . more discipline and heavier penalties are needed. Football of course will be blamed for all this, but it isn't just our problem."[28]
"I think this is something that has gone beyond Everton and football and even court. This vandalism is a national problem and as such I think we should try to tackle it at Government level."[29]

By the beginning of the 1970's, such statements were less extreme as the clubs—out of commercial self-interest and under public pressure—

began to assume more responsibility. Headlines such as "FA Must Clamp Down on Soccer Violence", "Clubs Must Curb Their Hooligan Element" began to take effect. But the pyramidal picture remained intact, and the more widespread the problem seemed—and at present, it shows no sign of disappearing—the more severe were the sanctions urged from all quarters and the more likely was the theme of football hooliganism as part of a wider social malaise to be repeated. Relatively new forms of deviance such as large-scale disturbances by students and political activists were simply absorbed into the pyramid: it was all part of the

An appeal to the "NORTH BANK BOYS"

So you have done it again. Not only did the behaviour of some of you at Ipswich make us feel thoroughly ashamed, but the result of your train-wrecking activities on the way home was seen by millions of people on Television. It must have filled them with utter disgust.

Why do you do it? If you consider yourselves to be supporters, then quite frankly, yours is the kind of support that both the game and this Club can well do without.

As we understand the term, a **supporter** is one who is proud of the Club and its record, proud of the team, and so proud of its reputation that he would do nothing to tarnish it.

Until you (dis)graced us with your presence two or three years ago, West Ham supporters were voted by British Railways as the best-behaved travellers in the game, **and they still are—apart from you.**

A very few of you are the ring-leaders, and we know who you are. So far you have exercised your "authority" in the very worst possible way, with your punch-ups, obscenities, and train-wrecking. Why not be different from the rest of your kind up and down the country? You could just as easily use your influence to bring this about.

Why cannot you follow the example of your seniors? Why cannot YOU be jealous of our reputation? **Why cannot YOU become known as the best-behaved young supporters in the country?** You would undoubtedly get just as much publicity—probably more!

Appeal from a West Ham United programme

same problem. At the beginning of the 1966 season one official in the soccer hierarchy was noted as insisting that ". . . soccer is suffering from an international malaise which has also expressed itself in Grosvenor Square, American draft-dodgers and Continental universities." Football hooliganism was still just a symptom and moreover a symptom that society had now begun to expect as part of the contemporary scene and which had to be ritualistically denounced:

"Bad behaviour among football fans is now accepted as an almost inevitable part of the Saturday sporting scene. Which means that the situation has surged long past the danger level."[30]

Once problem status is accorded to vandalism, what actual methods of control and prevention are campaigned for?

Because of the problems of definition I discussed in my earlier chapter, private responses to vandalism show wide variations. At the one extreme there is the refusal to label certain illegal forms of property destruction as vandalism at all or the overt encouragement of certain forms for ideological or aesthetic reasons. At the other extreme there is straightforward punitiveness and in the middle, there is ambivalence and inconsistency, shown, for example, in adult nostalgia for the pranks and escapades of their youth.

The common basis for organised social control, however, could not be other than the assumption than vandalism is an undesirable form of behaviour which must be eradicated or at least controlled within manageable proportions. I will deal here with the variations which arise from this assumption and how it is modified by the features of specific types of vandalism.

The following are the main approaches to prevention and control. These are by no means exclusive of each other—although in some cases they do incorporate contradictory conceptions about the problem —and are often advocated or used in various combinations:

1. Defeatism: what can you do?
2. Deflection: understand and channelise
3. Utilitarian prevention: protect and detect
4. Education and publicity: bring the lesson home
5. Deterrence and retribution: clamp down hard
6. Primary prevention: strike at the roots.

1. Defeatism: what can you do?
Many forms of vandalism are seen as endemic to particular situations or settings and the damage is simply written off as being inevitable. These are the forms covered by many of the conditions under which institutionalisation takes place by licensing or writing-off.

The damage is seen as not worth bothering about, either because each incident is trivial (although the cumulative cost may be high) or because enforcement and preventive measures are impossible to apply or cost more than the actual damage. Under certain conditions the damage itself may be looked upon with tolerance or amusement; 'they were just having fun', 'it's youthful exuberance', 'we also used to do it when we were young'. On the whole, though, defeatism does not imply any approval or condonation of the behaviour. It is rather an attitude of resignation to its existence: 'It's bad, but what can you do?': 'we've just got to grin and bear it'. These attitudes derive not only from the practical difficulty of doing anything about the problem, but from rationalisations such as 'it used to be worse'.

Almost all victims of vandalism react to some damage in a defeatist fashion. Local authorities are particularly prone to this sort of reaction unless they are stirred by moral enterprise. The LGIO and CBCSM surveys

235

explicitly condemned the 'don't care attitude' among local authorities and many such victim organisations adopt specifically defeatist policies. For example, there are separate votes in annual budgets to cover expected damage to parks, bus shelters or street signs and the costs will be taken into account in levying the rates. Sometimes contractors when submitting tenders for house building will add £100 per dwelling to cover the costs of vandalism or else a percentage of the contract sum will be allowed to contractors to cover damage.

In some cases the licensing of vandalism is more explicit, as when organisations hiring dance halls or rooms in pubs have to pay danger money. In 1967 an agreement was reached between British Rail and the National Federation of Football Supporters Clubs whereby Clubs chartering special trains would be subject to a clause agreeing to responsibility for damages up to £900. Although this was suggested as a possible way of ending vandalism, there was a clear acceptance by both parties that a certain amount of damage was to be expected.

In some situations the defeat is more literal. After continued attacks on particular targets—for example, public conveniences, park benches or old buildings—the organisation concerned will simply give up any attempt at preventing or detecting the offence and not bother to repair the property. (Such property is then almost totally wrecked and eventually left alone). In other cases the facilities that are damaged—such as liquid soap containers or towels in public conveniences—are withdrawn. Damaged public telephones are often left unrepaired for long periods (or else repaired only so that emergency calls can be made) but this is as much due to shortage of labour and equipment, as to defeatism.

Deflection in the form of graffiti boards for adults and children

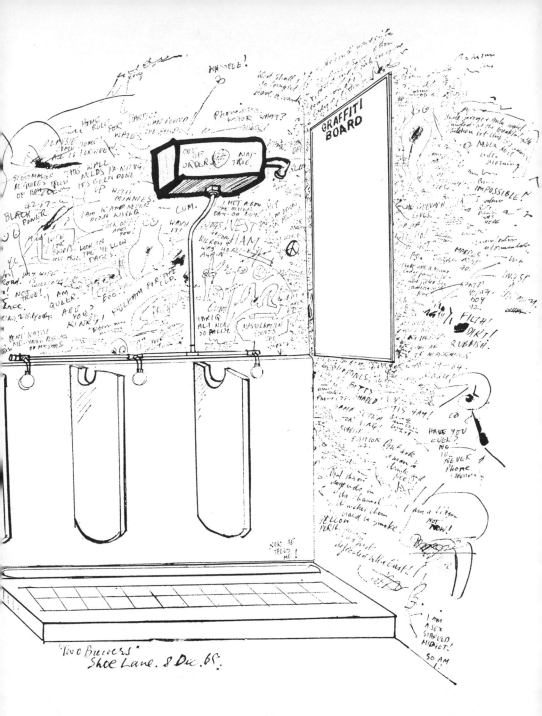

"Two Buzzers" Shoe Lane. 8 Dec. 65.

2. Deflection: understand and channelise

A more active and complicated response is not simply to accept the presence of vandalism, but to try to understand this presence and use this understanding to deflect or channelise the behaviour into what are perceived as safer, harmless or constructive alternatives. This understanding is usually based on the use of a psychological notion such as

237

the 'destructive impulse' or the 'urge to destroy' or else on more sociological concepts such as the need for 'outlets' for childhood or adolescent excitement, 'high spirits' or the 'need for adventure'.

Deflection may take the form of literally providing substitute targets for vandalism. It has long been a fairly orthodox practice among psychoanalytically orientated child psychotherapists, for example, to deal with a child who is doing damage by giving him materials which one does not mind him destroying. A more widely applicable derivation from this theme is the encouragement of destructive play in certain types of schools and playgrounds. One variation of this is the erection by some local authorities of 'scribbling walls' in playgrounds, prominent places on council estates and youth centres. These are large walls with various drawing materials provided. This method has also been used for adults, with an interesting combination of defeatism and deflection, in the form of graffiti boards. Blackboards or white formica boards (in some cases actually labelled 'Graffiti') have been installed in the toilets of pubs and hotels in order to divert writing from the walls on to something easier to clean. The messages are erased after closing time or a period of a few days.

A more broadly based method of preventing vandalism is the use of adventure playgrounds and similar schemes. These measures are again based on the notion of providing harmless outlets for needs that would be otherwise expressed in vandalism. There is no unambiguous evidence for the effectiveness of such measures in reducing vandalism although most sources indicate a correlation between inadequate play facilities and vandalism. One survey notes that a number of councils mention that while play facilities on estates tend to reduce vandalism among the resident children, this effect is neutralised by drawing in 'marauding youth' from other neighbourhoods. A G.L.C. report cites evidence from one estate of supervised adventure playgrounds reducing the extent of vandalism.

Another variation of the deflection approach is based more on the assumption that vandalism is partly attributable to lack of identification with the property that is destroyed. Recommendations following from this view include the use of children as 'tree wardens' on new estates, arranging for children to look after trees or beds of plants or (as is done in some New Towns) naming personal trees after children. This sort of approach has been suggested—together with forms of 'creative vandalism' such as clearing up rubbish heaps and breaking up dumped old cars—by libertarians as being the most useful non-punitive response to vandalism.

The simple provision of better facilities is a variant of the Understand and Channelise approach to the extent that dirty and badly kept property is seen as likely to encourage vandalism. The suggestion that maintaining property in a decent condition is one of the best ways of preventing much vandalism is agreed upon by most local authorities and other bodies responsible for maintaining public property. There is,

238

A libertarian form of deflection: helping to break up dumped old cars

though, a sort of 'coals in the bath tub' attitude among many local authorities which leads them to the belief that: 'if you give them new things, they just destroy them'. It is often true that new, attention-attracting and sometimes alien property, such as a water-feature or abstract statue on a council estate, is destroyed. But this initial effect eventually dies down. The more important effect is the tendency to regard badly maintained and dirty property as fair game for destruction, in the same way as streets already dirty attract the most litter.

3. Utilitarian prevention: protect and detect
One of the most widespread approaches to preventing vandalism is the use of utilitarian technical methods. The emphasis is on devising techniques—often highly original and ingenious—to protect property from vandalism, to warn off the prospective offenders or to increase the chances of his detection. These methods are less often conceived in terms of rooting out potential offenders and bringing them to justice than on more pragmatic grounds such as maintaining essential services such as telephones, saving the public from unsightly defacements or inconvenience and saving the taxpayer or ratepayer money. The overlapping aims of protection and detection are achieved through strengthening of equipment and the use of warning signs (for protection) giving rewards for information and 'bugging' property (for detection) and using guards, patrols, caretakers and other types of surveillance measures (for both protection and detection). These methods are used in various combinations by large organisations such as public bodies.

The most favoured approach—and the most expensive one—is to

ON THE TRAIL OF VANDALS

Mr Henry Oakes (standing) and Mr Frank Neve (in the van), two of Bromley Council's new park security force, about to set off on a tour of duty round the borough's parks and recreation grounds.

They are part of the nine-man team who will combat the growing problem of vandalism and wanton damage which is costing ratepayers upwards of £30,000 a year.

Already dubbed the "yellow perils" because of the bright yellow vans they use, the officers will work a shift system making random checks on open spaces.

They are to be issued with field glasses so that they can spot any signs of trouble..

They are also to have two-way radios to keep in contact with their office and to call help if necessary.

Because much of the trouble is caused by girls, some of whom are abusive to officers when they try to intervene, a vacancy in the team may be filled by a woman.

The scheme was devised and piloted through the Council by Councillor Kenneth Crask, chairman of the Recreation Committee. Bromley is thought to be the first borough to introduce such a scheme, although others are now making plans to do so.

Mobile patrols to keep property under more or less constant supervision

240

keep the property concerned under more or less constant guard or supervision by caretakers, estate officers, porters or special police patrols. Mobile patrols are used on parks, estates and areas surrounding schools. In Birmingham, park keepers (called park rangers) were employed for a time on motor bikes. In Sheffield a private security company was hired to carry out anti-hooliganism patrols. In Liverpool 8 men in the parks police force were given walkie-talkies: vandals were to be faced with helmeted police who would call up reinforcements with dogs. These police were given the same powers (for example, of arrest) as the city police. Dog patrols are another favoured technique, particularly by local authorities and building firms. Many councils use guard dogs—usually trained Alsatians—to patrol the parks at night. The Parks Association of New York once recommended the use of dogs 'to flush vandals from the city parks'. Some more bizarre forms of patrolling have been recorded: a zookeeper in Northants after fences were broken and birds injured, threatened to use patrols of lions, tigers and leopards.

A final technique of supervision is the use of volunteers. These are usually called 'vigilante squads' or 'local citizens foot patrols' and (in one case) 'spotters groups'. These groups are often very well organised, tend to rise in response to a specific incident or series of incidents of vandalism and are reported more often in rural than urban areas. In some cases members of the council take turns to patrol at certain times of the night. Sometimes vigilantes are organised to protect private property: in one case a vigilante squad patrolled a golf course with Alsatian dogs and were armed with No. 8 irons 'to smash any vandals attacking the course'.

Another protective method is to physically strengthen or protect the property itself. This method—as is the case with most other utilitarian approaches—is designed for theft as well as vandalism. Techniques include boarding up property under construction; the use of strong fittings; greasing main water pipes; installing unbreakable glass; designing buildings in such a way that there is the minimum amount of glass and other vandalisable property; building concealed drain pipes and using burglar proofing or barbed wire fencing. These techniques are often ingenious (for example, the Commonwealth War Graves Commission have in some cases substituted fibre glass for bronze swords and other objects on war memorials to prevent acquisitive vandalism) and involve complicated designs (the CBCSM for example have reported on examples of special vandalproof toilets).

At other times the measures are not so much carefully planned as desperately resorted to: the parks committee in a Kent town erected a fence and post around playground equipment but these were stolen or damaged after the first night. Then steel pins were driven in up to five feet depth and the equipment wired to them, but the pins and wire disappeared. Even after chains were welded, the property was broken or removed. In other more obvious cases the erection of certain protective devices seems to attract vandalism in the sense of offering a challenge. Sometimes the methods resorted to are so desperate that they may present new problems: one rural district council proposed to use 'vandal-proof paint'—paint that never dries—on signposts and walls in a National Park. This sort of dilemma is illustrated in other ways in the attempts to design vandal-proof public lavatories and telephones. Proposals to build lavatory doors low enough for the attendant to observe and prevent acts of vandalism, are countered by the fact that this would remove the user's privacy, while proposals to build telephone kiosks without any glass at all are countered by the risk (whether realistic or not) that 'sexual malpractices' would take place in the privacy of the kiosk.

Of all organisations using technical protective measures, the General Post Office has been the most enterprising. Various devices are experimented with to reduce each kind of damage and if effective in a trial area, they are made available for use in other areas where local managers anticipate a particular need. Methods used include steel stranded cords, other stronger materials, steel plates instead of glass at the bottom of the kiosk, burglar alarms and steel plating of the coin box. Strengthening of the coin box is a particularly significant measure in the light of the increase in acquisitive vandalism following the introduction of the STD systems: this measure more than any other was responsible for reducing this type of vandalism. A special 'anti-vandal phone box' was designed in 1968; this had a three-quarter length panel of toughened glass on three sides to give maximum visibility from the street. [31]

Many organisations use warning signs to protect their property from vandalism. These range from posters giving straightforward information about the legal penalties for anyone convicted of vandalism to more specific exhortations not to commit vandalism. Examples of the former type are to be found next to railway lines, outside buildings being constructed and on the walls of the London Underground. Examples of the latter type are notices affixed to telephone kiosks such as "In case of illness or accident, your family may need this telephone. Please don't damage it". The effectiveness of such signs is not altogether apparent: often the poster itself is damaged and in at least some areas there is evidence to suggest that a warning notice on a telephone box actually attracts attention and increases the amount of vandalism.

The aim of detecting the offender, as opposed to warning him off and cutting down the risk of damage by installing protective measures, is met by the same surveillance techniques used for protection. In addition use is made—invariably with very little success—of offers of rewards for information about acts of vandalism, or general appeals to the public to 'keep their eyes open' or to 'have a go' at the offender. A novel attempt at both protection and detection was the construction by an Ayrshire village council of public toilets and two telephone kiosks directly outside the local police station. The measure failed to reduce any vandalism.

Traditional damage and utilitarian prevention: an 'anti-vandal' telephone box designed to give maximum visibility from the street

Various alarm systems have also been introduced, again with most success by the GPO. Details of these systems are kept secret but consist of variations on the use of warning lights on top of the kiosk which flash when equipment is damaged or messages which are transmitted to the nearest police station. Experiments have also been conducted on the feasibility of using close-circuit television in telephone boxes.

Alarm systems have also been tried in bus shelters. One Urban Council Council has installed a special type of glass in some of its bus shelters: when the glass is broken a signal flashes to the police station alerting a special 'anti-vandal patrol'. Schools, particularly in America, have used various types of alarm or 'bugging' systems such as the installation of hidden microphones at crucial places in the building.

These various methods of protection and detection are usually used in combination with each other. Schools, for example, might have special security guards, an alarm system and hidden microphones or television cameras. In an anti-vandalism campaign run by British Railways use was made of reward posters, the concentration of railway police patrols on selected routes and the increase of dog patrols in local black spots. In regard to football vandalism, a wider range of utilitarian techniques have been used or advocated; these include setting up barriers or constructing moats between the spectators and the field; increase of police and stewards; the use of plain-clothes policemen mingling with the crowds; warning notices or appeals over the public address system; banning all beer, milk and other bottles from the grounds; banning flags and banners; the formation of vigilante squads; changing the design of the ground to give the spectators less access to the field and the police easier access to the spectators; stricter police control in dispersing the crowd and measures to increase public support of the police.

Obviously the type of technique arrived at depends on the demands of the situation and although measures such as increased supervision and alarm systems are fairly generally applicable, others are more specific: for example, the attempt, by some cinemas in 'tough districts', to prevent damage to the screen (particularly during club films) by commencing the seating several rows back from the screen. Vandalism evokes highly innovatory sorts of responses. One licensee in Rotherham decided to draw up a "Rogues Who's Who"— a blacklist of trouble-makers to be circulated among his fellow licensees. He urged them to keep a camera under the counter and to photograph troublemakers to be added to the rogues gallery. Similarly, the Vicar of a new church at Barrow-in-Furness decided to compile a "picture dossier of vandals in action". A teenager seen trespassing on the site of the church would be photographed by the Vicar and a warning was issued to parents "Keep your children off the site or my picture dossier will be handed to the police". (A local police comment was that "anything which prevents vandalism is to be commended").

The one general point that might be made about these measures is that they are often very expensive and although they are primarily conceived as a way of saving the victim money, the cost of vandalism is often less than the cost of the preventive and detective measures themselves.

4. Education and publicity: bring the lesson home

The basic philosophy behind one approach to prevention and control is that if only people were more aware of the seriousness of the vandalism problem—its financial cost to the community, the potential physical dangers it presented, its threats to cherished values—then they would do something about it. The responsibility for action lies with the community, particularly informal agents of social control such as teachers and parents. The role of the victim organisation, the government, the welfare agency, the mass media, is to educate children to realise that vandalism is their problem. It is their duty to refrain from acts of vandalism, to persuade others not to commit vandalism, to report acts of vandalism and to co-operate with the police. Through one or other means of education and publicity the lesson must be brought home.

This approach is basically the one used by organisations attempting to define vandalism as a social problem. These campaigns, usually run by individual local authorities, very rarely go beyond the stage of vague appeals for greater community responsibility and co-operation. In other cases more specific measures are recommended, some of them of the deflect and channelise type, others directed towards greater detection and others calling for the imposition of more severe legal penalties. The educational techniques used include posters drawing attention to the damage, talks in schools by council officials, policemen or social workers and various types of exhibitions to increase public awareness of the problem. I will describe three of the more original and best organised of these local authority campaigns during the Nineteen Sixties, paying most attention to the Birmingham Stop Vandalism Week.

A typical sort of educational campaign was that organised in Gateshead in 1966. The Council initially decided to approach prevention through the schools, and the Civic Pride Committee organised an essay competition among schoolchildren on the subject of how to prevent vandalism. The list of suggestions that emerged is of interest if only to indicate that the measures arrived at by schoolchildren are not particularly different from those advocated by adults—either members of the public or those with specialised knowledge, experience and responsibility:

Repair of damage to be carried out by offenders.
Cost of damage to be paid by offenders.
More youth clubs to be provided so that young people have more to occupy them.
Formation of a special Youth Corps to prevent vandalism.
Young Citizens' Courts to try offenders.
More clubs for young people mainly for voluntary service to the community.
Use of hidden cameras.
More plain clothes policemen.
More guard dogs.

*Education and publicity: a selection
of posters to bring the lesson home*

Adverse publicity for vandals in press and on television.

More co-operation from the public.

Concentration on educating the next generation against vandalism.

Emphasis on creative work and gardening so that young people become more interested in creation than destruction.

The reintroduction of stocks and the pillory as a good deterrent to vandals.

Devices on telephone box doors so that they cannot be entered freely.

Talks by pop stars against vandalism.

The essay competition was followed up a year later by an exhibition staged in co-operation with the G.P.O., British Railways and the local bus company. The exhibition, which ran for three weeks, consisted of items of equipment and fittings damaged by vandals and photographs and mock-ups of various sorts of damage. Emphasis was on the cost of vandalism to Gateshead (£12,000 per year) which was compared in the publicity handouts to the equivalent sum with which the Council ". . . could provide 4 to 5 families at present without any housing accommodation or living in very poor housing conditions with a new home". The fact that the 'ordinary man and woman' was paying for the damage in the ordinary rate levy was stressed, as well as the physical dangers of vandalism: "See evidence of the destruction of your emergency services which could cost a life—your life!!" (from a leaflet advertising the exhibition). Civic pride was also stressed in the slogan "Beat Vandalism and Take a Pride in Your Town". Although the exhibition was well attended and attracted favourable publicity, the Council has not been able to provide evidence of any long term preventive effect.

A similar approach was used in Chertsey in 1965. The Chairman of the UDC organised a tour of the town by a lorry "loaded with examples

A winning entry in the poster competition for school children organised by Salford police in the 1971 anti-vandalism campaign

of wanton damage such as coin boxes, basins and pans from public conveniences, broken gutters, a seat and a mock-up of a house with broken windows". The Chairman sat in the driver's cab with a microphone and asked the public to co-operate in stamping out vandalism. He told them of the extent of the damage and said that if they saw anyone carrying out these acts they should either try to stop them or call the police. Again, there was no clear evaluation of the success of the campaign; the Chairman of the Council wrote to me:

"As to whether the campaign has had any effect is difficult to say—but at least thanks to the Press and T.V. publicity local residents have been talking about the problem and saying how bad it is. That at least is some return for our efforts."

As is apparent from these and other attempts at evaluating similar projects, the educative aim of creating a greater problem awareness is often primary and the question of whether the amount of vandalism is in fact reduced is left unresolved.

Earlier, I discussed the organization of the Birmingham "Stop Vandalism Week". It was clear that this campaign was of the Bring-the-Lesson-Home type; in the words of the General Manager of the Parks Committee:

"The purpose of the campaign was to focus the attention of the whole city on the enormous cost of the damage done by vandals which in the case of Corporation property alone amounts to some £50,000 per year and to find ways and means of reducing this onerous burden on the community."

The stress on community awareness and responsibility was expressed in these words by the local newspaper: ". . . the general public will be asked to realise that the 'they' who are expected to deal with problems such as vandalism are really 'us' "[32] (*Birmingham Post* 6/1/67). Community organisations such as social and youth clubs, voluntary organisations, trade unions, various industrial, commercial and professional bodies and political parties were drawn into the campaign and more than 650 organisations filled in forms giving details of publicity outlets and facilities they could offer. The 600,000 publicity items it distributed included 395,000 leaflets, 15,000 hanging cards, 9,500 posters, 31,000 vehicle window stickers, 100,000 stamps for sticking on letters, 20,000 lapel badges, etc. The campaign's slogan was "If you lend a hand, We can stop vandalism" and the publicity items bore variations of this slogan and suggestions of how the community could help to stop vandalism: the need for parents to impress upon their children how futile it is to wreck other people's property, and responsibilities of youth workers and teachers, the need to co-operate with the police, etc.

The week was launched with an inaugural meeting opened by the Lord Mayor in the Council Chamber. A large "Stop Vandalism" exhibition was mounted in the Bull Ring; the exhibition consisted of pictures of broken windows, smashed lavatory seats and other results of vandalism. Letter writing and poster competitions were organised in local newspapers and the campaign received wide local and national publicity. The estimated cost of the campaign was approximately £5,000.

It is obvious from the statements of those who ran the campaign that its success was defined primarily in terms of increasing the awareness of the problem. I have detailed figures which show that there was very little long term effect in reducing the amount of vandalism in Birmingham.[33] In fact, vandalism in the year after the campaign cost the council £10,000 more than in the year before (this increase was largely accounted for by a rise of about £6,000 in damage on council estates and clearance areas). If one adds to this figure the £5,000 cost of the campaign and takes into account the possible preventive effects of other measures used extensively in Birmingham over the same period (partincularly various protection, detection and surveillance techniques in schools and parks) one can only conclude that the preventive effects of such education and publicity campaigns are negligible.

Of other victim organisations, British Rail are the most consistent advocates of the education and publicity approach. A major Anti-Vandalism Campaign was launched in February, 1964: security patrols were increased and rewards of £25 were offered for information leading to the conviction of vandals. Posters announcing this offer went up on stations and railway property throughout the country. Press announcements of the campaign emphasised the safety hazard in railway vandalism, the inconvenience and loss of public goodwill because of delayed trains and the costs—which would have to be borne by the public—of making good the damage.

Besides these publicity campaigns, British Rail also used less obtrusive and more educational techniques. These were considered by the Public Relations Officer to be of more value than "general exhortations". The techniques were directed at schoolchildren, particularly the age group most responsible for the core types of railway vandalism, the 10-14 year olds. The safety aspects of railway vandalism were stressed throughout rather than threatening punishment and retribution.

The following are some of the educative techniques used:

Issuing a 'teaching aid wallet' to schools every two years. The material does not constitute a direct appeal for railway safety but is designed to promote interest and pride in the railways, in the belief that one doesn't injure property one is proud of.

Giving lectures and showing films to schoolchildren which emphasise the dangerous consequences of vandalism.

Railway sidings: a natural playground with activity toys

A collection of items found on one short stretch of railway line in the south of England

Lectures on railway safety (similar to those on road safety) given in schools by clowns and other entertainers.

Lectures at Women's Associations and Mothers' Unions, again stressing the safety message: "Don't let your child play on the line, this is what might happen . . ."

School essay competitions (for premium bonds) in which the theme is railway safety.

Placing a strip cartoon "Nights of the Road" in children's newspapers and comics. In the cartoon one character gets electrocuted tampering with railway equipment.

In certain areas enlisting the help of children at Saturday morning cinema clubs by asking them to report signs of vandalism to the police. In these same areas engine drivers and railway police visited hundreds of schools to talk about railway safety.

Showing, over a period of six months at the height of the railway vandalism wave, a special film at all Saturday morning juvenile film shows of the Rank Organisation. This film with a railway safety theme featured a leading pop group and in conjunction with it the Board ran a national railway safety competition.

In carrying out these campaigns, British Rail were very much aware of the standard public relations problems involved, especially the possible competition from other publicity with a different message and the need to aim at a specific audience. These problems are illustrated in the following extracts from departmental documents:

"The Board's efforts at education have not been helped by certain types of commercial publicity . . . (for example) picture cards included in packets of bubble gum purchased by children, illustrating incidents of railway sabotage with headings such as "train wreck kills 125 soldiers" and describing how the deed was done. Similarly, the showing of two films "Lawrence of Arabia" and "The Train", both of which display graphic acts of railway vandalism, has undoubtedly done something to vitiate the railway safety campaign. It would be ideal if one could pinpoint any section of the community as being particularly responsible to direct the maximum effort at that section . . . but the small minority responsible for most of this particular type of hooliganism is the stoniest of stony ground."

The educational techniques used are directly influenced by the victim organisation's perception of the nature of the audience, their images of the typical vandal. This again might be illustrated by quoting from a British Rail memorandum which distinguishes three groups for aiming a poster campaign at: firstly, younger children who need to be encouraged to take pride in the railways; secondly, "the weaker element of hooligans who probably indulge in such reprehensible practices because of the gang instinct or fear of the gang leader". For this group the appeal could be aimed at either "persuading them to assert their

252

independence" or at "dissuading them from doing anything which might hurt their friends and relations, or their favourite pop stars"; thirdly, "the hard core of hooligans", the objective here is to "frighten them off by fear of punishment or injury".

It is difficult to assess the general effectiveness of education and publicity campaigns. In the case of railway vandalism there was a clear reduction in the years following the campaign. How much of this reduction was due to the campaign and not to the other measures used at the same time (increased surveillance, new protective and detective devices, deterrent sentences) is impossible to estimate. In general, one can say that general exhortations and direct publicity appeals such as those used by the local authorities, are of little use and are less valuable than the more unobtrusive techniques such as those used by British Rail.

Publicity almost invariably works in the opposite direction to that intended. Vandalism often occurs in waves, much like waves of fashion, and the initial reporting of an incident often has the effect of triggering off incidents of a similar kind. At football matches appeals over the public address system, not to let off firecrackers or throw bottles on to the field, are immediately followed by an explosion of firecrackers and a barrage of bottles. This, in microcosm, is what often occurs in group phenomena such as waves of vandalism.

The relationship between publicity and vandalism is nothing like a straight causal one. Vandalism occurs at times and in contexts where there is no publicity at all. Publicity is not the primary 'cause' of vandalism, any more than the cause of a man barricading himself and his family in a house with a shotgun is the fact that he had been informed of similar incidents by the mass media. It would be difficult, however, to say that the event and the information were unrelated.

5. Deterrence and retribution: clamp down hard

The most frequent public reaction to vandalism is 'Hit Them Hard': all that is needed is better detection by the police and stiffer sentences by the court. The belief that stronger and more effective methods of deterrence will solve the problem is very rarely questioned and is held by those who advocated other approaches as well, such as Education and Publicity or Detection and Protection. Only the more forceful adherents of the 'Understand and Channelise' approach find the 'Clamp Down Hard' position difficult to reconcile with their own. Specific deterrent measures are advocated for different types of vandalism, but the general tendency is to support heavier fines, custodial sentences such as detention centres, corporal punishment and various schemes for restitution or compensation. The pyramidal conception of the problem means shifting the main burden of responsibility elsewhere, particularly in the direction of the courts. The attitude of victim organizations is: 'We can do so much, but it's for the police and the courts to really solve the problem'.

An examination of the criminal statistics shows that the monetary fine is the most frequent single sentence (about 65%) imposed on vandalism offenders. There is nothing to suggest that cautions, fines, probation and the usual range of measures employed against the younger group of juvenile offenders are more or less effective for vandalism than they are for other offences.

One point specific to vandalism should, however, be made. This is overwhelmingly a group offence and an offence which is situational in character: it arises spontaneously out of group interaction and—except in specific forms such as 'tactical' and 'acquisitive' vandalism—it is not deliberately planned. Consequently, general deterrent measures, and the publicity given to them, are less likely to be effective. Among young children especially, who easily rationalise vandalism as play, warnings of punitive sentences will not be very successful.

Nevertheless, the clamp down hard theme is the dominant one in the control culture and at times of high public awareness of vandalism, police and courts cannot but be affected by the moral panic around them. Take the following cases:

At Inner London Sessions an appeal was considered from a 22 year old man with no previous convictions against a sentence (from the Thames Magistrates Court) of 3 months' imprisonment for attempting to steal money from a telephone kiosk. The man was drunk, had gambled away his wife's Christmas club money and wanted to replace it. The Chairman told him, "You are earning good money which you gamble away, and then you tackle telephone boxes, an offence which is absolutely rife. This has to be dealt with by condign punishment and we think the sentence is inadequate". The court doubled the original sentence.

In the Court of Criminal Appeal the Lord Chief Justice refused leave to appeal by a 19 year old legless boy against a Borstal sentence for stealing from a telephone kiosk. The court sympathised with the boy (who had lost both legs in an accident at the age of 8) but had to harden its heart and uphold the sentence. There was too much wrecking going on, and this had to be stamped out. Locking offenders up was necessary. "This court will uphold any substantial sentences given for these offences."

The Chairman of the Inner London Sessions, imposing sentences of 18 months' imprisonment and borstal training on a 22 year old and 18 year old who had attempted to steal money from a kiosk, told them, "These offences are absolutely rife. At a time emergency calls are

required to be made, due to people like you, the telephone kiosks are out of action. The law therefore takes a grave view and sentences must be severe."

One example that is often quoted to show the effectiveness of harsher sentences (and the publicity given to them) in preventing vandalism was the apparently successful campaign against telephone vandalism in

Birmingham in 1965-1966. The Recorder of Birmingham was hailed as "the iron man in Britain's fight against crime" when it was announced that telephone vandalism in the city had been drastically reduced because of his policy of handing out sentences of up to three years' imprisonment for the offence.

There are two points to be made about this claim. A major proportion of the reduction was due to preventive measures introduced by the GPO in Birmingham. The newer STD coin boxes (which were almost the sole target for the damage) were strengthened and in some cases completely replaced. Other items of equipment were strengthened and in some telephones burglar alarms were introduced.

The other point is that, even if the deterrent effect is provable (which it is not), this is a very specific offence. Theft from coin boxes was committed mostly by adults who in some cases had been involved in anything up to 40 similar offences. Any deterrent for such an offence and such an offender cannot be generalised—as it widely was—to cover all types of vandalism.

In cases such as football hooliganism, each season shows a similar sequence: it opens with appeals from those concerned with the game for better behaviour, disturbances taking place, punishment given out, more appeals and more disturbances. As each season begins, statements and headings such as the following appear: ". . . another season opens with depressingly familiar outbreaks of crowd violence . . ." and "Violence is all part of the game now". Vandalism associated with soccer—in the streets after a match, on trains or buses—shows no sign of diminishing.

The mainstream only of clamp down hard measures have been mentioned. Vandalism, along with various crimes of violence and sexual offences, also evokes more innovatory and melodramatic retributive responses among a minority. The use of public ridicule and punishments such as the stocks is, for example, often suggested. A town councillor in Somerset, who suggested that the stocks should be brought back for teenage vandalism, was quoted as saying:

"I said this with my tongue in my cheek, but I had dozens of calls from local residents who congratulated me on the idea and who even offered to help put some stocks up."[34]

The Sheriff of Norwich[35] in a personal letter defended the use of stocks in the following terms:

". . . the type of individual who commits motiveless acts of wanton aggression or damage will tolerate (with little deterrent effect) supervision by probation, monetary penalty or even a short term of imprisonment, but in common with most of our compatriots abhors ridicule or to be held in contempt by his fellows."[36]

A more frequent variation of the punitive response to vandalism is in the direction of *restitution* rather than *retribution*. Various schemes are put forward to compensate the victim for the cost of damage. Many local authorities suggest that parents should be made liable for damage carried out by their under 14 year old children. Local authorities have also suggested that such sanctions be used outside the legal system, for example in obtaining compensation from parents in council housing.

Other extra-legal sanctions used include banning offenders from swimming baths, sports fields, youth clubs or play centres. Some local authorities have suggested the evicting of tenants whose children are responsible for vandalism: a GLC report considers that there is no more effective sanction than transfer or eviction and that this "valuable disciplinary measure" which is only used as a last resort, could be used more frequently.

For all types of vandalism the control agents and mass media are caught up in the dilemma I've already mentioned: the continual oscillation between claims that the recommended control measures have worked and, on the other hand, that the problem still exists and demands continual vigilance.

6. Primary prevention: strike at the roots

Deriving from the pyramidal conception of the social problem and a causative theory which posits a deeply rooted social malaise at the base, one approach to prevention and control stresses the futility of any measures which do not 'Strike at the Roots' of vandalism. The vandal is seen as operating in a society which does not set any limits to his behaviour. Even if we fully utilise technical measures of prevention—which we are obliged to do to protect the community—or develop more effective methods of deterrence—which again we are obliged to do for self-protection and to see that justice is done—these attempts will only touch the surface of the problem.

The actual implications for prevention and control that stem from this approach are not altogether clear. On the whole they consist of vague recommendations to stem the tides of permissiveness, to counter-act the breakdown in family life, to instil in parents and teachers a greater sense of responsibility and to generally strike at the roots of the malaise: the home, the school and the permissive society. In fact, the approach to the prevention of vandalism (and other social problems) envisaged in such public conceptions leads on to few, if any, policy implications.

Some versions of the strike at the roots theme call for psychiatric prevention and treatment programmes. These are more often suggested for vandalism than for delinquency as a whole, because the equation is made between 'senseless' action and psychological disturbance: 'nobody in their right mind would do something like vandalism.'

To the extent that this equation is fundamentally wrong, psychiatric approaches to vandalism do not offer much. A very small proportion of vandalism is associated with psychological disturbance and there is no evidence that vandalism in childhood is correlated with later disturbance. (On the contrary, a recent 30 year follow-up study of children referred to a child guidance clinic showed that vandalism was one of the few offences initially recorded at referral which had no relation at all to later 'sociopathic personality traits'). More often, the simple—and often quite justified—assumption is made that much vandalism among younger children arises out of a combination of the desire for adventure and excitement, and the opportunity presented in certain neighbourhoods by the presence of property (such as derelict houses, old bomb sites, large panes of glass in council flats, street lamps) which is regarded as fair game. If one further assumes that such damage cannot be tolerated but that the need for excitement is an acceptable motive and is blocked by the absence of adequate facilities, schemes such as the building of an adventure playground suggest themselves to prevent vandalism, and are certainly desirable in themselves—whether or not they 'work' in preventing vandalism.

Among the older age group responsible for vandalism, the element of hostility and malice cannot be neutralised simply by the provision of recreational facilities. The sort of trajectory to fringe delinquency which I suggested in the first chapter of this book, stresses the deficiencies of the educational and employment situations for the working class adolescent. The tension resulting from these deficiencies may occur in the realm of leisure, where vandalism, and delinquency in general, might provide the satisfaction and excitement that a dead-end education and an ever deader job-market patently do not offer. But the drift to delinquency cannot be counteracted simply by laying on more leisure facilities.

David Cooper has referred in the context of mental hospitals to "the ancient myth that tells us that Satan makes work (destructiveness, masturbation, promiscuity) for idle hands". One can free oneself from this myth by trying to understand what sort of realistic alternative to delinquency is possible.

Vandalism is a solution—albeit an ugly and incoherent one which the good citizens find difficult to explain—and it will continue to be used until society gets the message. By then, who knows what sort of property will exist to smash up?

Typical walk-up tenements

12 Community involvement

David Pullen

In 1969, the Policy and Finance Committee of Liverpool Corporation were asked by the City's Housing Department for additional finance of £16,000 to cover the cost of damage caused by 'vandals' in an empty block of flats awaiting modernisation. This event triggered off two responses which two years later, resulted in two separate (and in many ways contradictory) policies being adopted in Liverpool.

The reaction of the Policy and Finance Committee at the time was to order a rough estimate to be made of the cost of vandalism in the Corporation's budget for the previous year (1968/9). A figure of £870,000 was reached which was quickly rounded up by the press to "This £1,000,000 Problem." Immediately motions were placed in the city council calling for heavier sentences, special police powers, etc. However, discussions with the police revealed a strong feeling in the constabulary that any dramatic gestures would be counter-productive; and that, as a crime, vandalism was a low priority. Firstly, to be an indictable offence, vandalism has to be defined as either wilful damage or malicious damage, neither of which was regarded as being as serious as theft. Secondly, the age range of those involved, and the fact that few cases of 'vandalism' were reported to the police made it unlikely that successful convictions would touch more than a handful of those involved. (It was pointed out by the police, in support of this view, that no Corporation department had reported the acts of vandalism which were now blamed for the one-million-a-year-problem).

The reluctance of the police force at this time to take responsibility for the problem disarmed the 'law and order' group sufficiently for a less dramatic approach to be made which would seek alternatives to the traditional repressive tactics. It was suggested by the police that the way to do this was to invite the public to put forward ideas that might help solve the problem.

The limitations set on this 'community involvement' programme were that ideas of poster campaigns, vigilante groups (as tried out in Manchester) were to be put on one side. Presumably the theory was that problems that had unknown causes must also have unknown solutions. City-wide piano-smashing competitions, or promotional rhubarb growing would probably have stood a good chance of consideration at this time. In fact little response was to be seen and an inducement in the form of £25,000 was voted through to enable ideas to be tested.

Demolition—the Corporation's incitement to vandalism?

A high-powered Steering Group was set up to co-ordinate this operation. It included the Lord Mayor for that year, the leaders of both major parties, the Chief Constable, the Town Clerk and the Chairman of the Neighbourhood Organisations Committee. This last body was entirely independent of Corporation control, being a standing committee of the Liverpool Council of Social Service. It had developed over the previous three years as a co-ordinating body for the various community groups springing up at the time throughout Liverpool; and it was through its channels of communication that it was hoped ideas would come forward.

Unfortunately, though the money did indeed encourage ideas to come forward, the request that they should cost in the region of £500 meant that few saw vandalism as more than a passport to grant aid for existing play schemes, youth clubs, football teams, etc. The reluctance of the police to be associated with the 'problem' was not shared by most community councils who duly applied for their £500 slice of the cake.

Significantly, it was those groups dominated by a youth or community worker who saw the need to try and get away from traditional youth provision; and in three such cases the £500 applied for was to finance a Community Service Volunteer to work with young people and involve them in the 'improvement of their environment'.

The result of this in terms of amenity provision was in fact in all three cases a concentration on play (as opposed to club) provision for the under 14s. In other words, they emphasised the need for the youth service to reach down to the age range responsible for much of the delinquency if it was to be a successful diversion, and agency of change. However, it was not this element of these three schemes that helped to

260

produce a more comprehensive approach to vandalism. What they revealed was an ambiguity in speaking of 'community involvement' as integral to the proposals for dealing with vandalism. Not simply the gleaning of ideas, but the actual process of putting them into action could be a 'community involvement process', since the Community Service Volunteers were to work with the children and adults in the area, not the professional workers.

Looked at from a youth work angle, this could be described as Youth and Community Work in a much fuller sense than simply turning Youth Clubs into Community Centres or Youth Leaders into Community Workers. The hope was that they would be the catalysts in a process whereby 'the community' organised facilities for its own 'youth'. The management and running of activities was to be the responsibility of residents; even if they did decide to employ professionals to work for them.

However, it is important to remember that just as vandalism is a symptom of other more concrete problems, so community involvement is a method of applying solutions to these problems rather than a solution in itself. If it was felt (by the agencies concerned) that vandalism in an area could only be reduced by providing play facilities, then it was necessary to link this to the aspirations of local residents for safe (and educational?) amenities to be provided for their children. Out of this might arise an agreement for the authorities to release resources in terms of buildings and money in exchange for the local people taking the responsibility for the operating of activities, etc.

But just as it is often argued that the formation of a local Community Relations Council 'creates' race relations problems, by bringing the problems into the open, so it was clear that 'anti-vandalism' schemes, however subtle, could only promote 'the Vandal' as a symbol of the disenchanted, and alienate local parents whose good-will and active involvement were essential to success.

That this has not happened in Liverpool reflects firstly the low key at which schemes have operated (as far as the press is concerned the vandals are winning hands down); and the general indifference to the issue shown by nearly all the residents spoken to over the last year. Unlike racial tension, vandalism is not a prime issue of concern in those areas where it is most prevalent, and consequently 'bringing the issue into the open' does nothing to broaden people's attitudes.

Yet it clearly describes problems confronting such agencies as the housing department, environmental health, police and probation. That the project over the last year has united these (and other) professional bodies with local community groups is due to the nature of the solutions to the problems, rather than to the analysis of the problem itself. In this respect vandalism is the complete inverse of unemployment, which is seen by nearly all as an issue of primary concern, but for which no consensus solution is liable to be arrived at. In contrast to this many of the projects which the vandalism fund has promoted were supported by police, probation officers, housing management, local youth and community workers, shopkeepers, cleansing managers, teachers and all section of local resident population. Yet their motives were probably very different and a simplified analysis of their respective primary aims in helping with such projects could be given in something like the following terms:

Residents—provision of facilities for children.
(i) parents—know where they are, safety, etc.
(ii) children—gives them somewhere to go and something to do.
(iii) other residents—distracts children from playing outside their homes or annoying them in more direct ways.
Police—gets children off the streets and into a structured, disciplined situation.
Probation, Social Services—provides a learning situation where anti-social behaviour traditions can be broken down and more acceptable values substituted. Also preventative.
Youth Workers—provides a way of operating with the under 14 age range.
Community Workers—opportunity to involve residents in organising facilities, developing their expertise in operating premises, working with professionals, etc.
Housing—development of local community spirit will create 'happier and more involved tenants who will see their dwellings as *their homes* with all the consequent advantages both to tenant and landlord' (a housing manager).
i.e. houses and flats will be easier to let, provision by tenants of facilities for youngsters will deter them from playing (vandalising) on housing property (e.g. lifts and refuse chutes).
Environmental Health and Protection—community involvement is needed to improve 'environmental standards' by encouraging 'home pride' to extend beyond the front door and to include staircases, back alleys, etc.

Thus while a project may be deemed successful by all those people, quite probably none of them will see its reduction of 'vandalism' primarily in financial terms. What is called community involvement by one may be seen as promotion of parental responsibility, preventative work reducing the number of children coming before the courts, or a way of reducing boredom, by others. Even the housing management, who stand to lose the most financially, would probably emphasise above all the long-term value of promoting local involvement as the only way of guaranteeing that money spent by them will improve an area as intended and will not be nullified by vandalism. Open sites, play areas, buildings, etc., which are the responsibility of their department will often be restored by them only if local people are prepared to take on responsibility for them. I shall return to this theme later.

Homes for the people of Liverpool

The shops are open

Communal facilities—communally abused and neglected

Corporation play area

However, it is worth emphasising at this point that it was the housing department, which was losing the bulk of the £870,000 a year, that first cast doubt on the idea of vandalism being seen as a 'cost through replacing damage' problem. To quote the housing manager more fully:

"In areas where we are the principal landlord, of which there are many, the benefits of community development and involvement should accrue to us more to any other single Corporation Department. I recognise that many of these benefits might not show for a number of years, as how one can measure objectively in the short term the contribution of the communities themselves to the decrease in the number of bad parents, the increase in the number of better controlled and happier children, the more pleasant and stimulating environment that trees and grass give in contrast to black tarmac and grey paving, the decrease, or decline in the increase, of vandalism and delinquency through decent and non-vandalised play and leisure facilities and opportunities; all of which should create happier and more involved Housing Department tenants who will see their dwellings as *their homes* with all the consequent advantages both to tenant and landlord."

Looking at this problem of amenity provision from another angle, it could be argued that the objects of vandalism are generally examples of social 'progress' e.g. new housing, schools, public parks, street lighting, public toilets, etc. The only quick way of reducing vandalism in financial terms, would therefore be either to remove the amenities because they are unappreciated (the coal-in-the-bath argument), or to protect them with guards, police patrols, threats of heavy sentences or building high walls, etc. Both moves would not only negate the whole social improvement programme they are meant to be protecting, but would show a lack of understanding of the inevitable teething troubles inherent in radical social change. The value of projects in many situations is simply to speed up the natural processes which will result in the development of a stable community.

What has taken 30 years in traditional new housing estates might take 15 years if resources and workers were injected early enough. Comparison of Kirkby, after twenty years a byword for new town social malaise, and Runcorn, where communal resources and neighbourhood workers have been liberally supplied by the Development Corporation in the initial stages, will provide us with dearly bought guide-lines for future New Town developments.

But while the values and social structures of the suburbs might be applicable to many new (or renewed) housing areas, they will not adequately answer the needs of those living in either high- or low-rise flats. Many such areas are already fairly well serviced in the way of communal facilities, yet social malaise continues to be serious. In such situations, even more than in traditional housing areas, new ways of organising amenities need to be devised. For whereas the growth of

A laundry built because of pressure from local residents, has remained unvandalised for three years

traditional family/community structures in housing areas will limit the demand for communal facilities, no such self-reliance can be hoped for in blocks of flats.

Such housing provision presents two essentially insoluble problems, as far as providing a stable, self-regulating community where such anti-social acts of vandalism do not go un-noticed, is concerned.

(i) The actual design, by stacking homes on top of one another, reduces adult (and in particular, parental) responsibility for the children of the area. The children are obliged to play at ground level where they can only be under the effective surveillance of those living on the ground floor.

(ii) The property is seen as second class. Everyone would prefer to live in a house. At best the attraction of flats is their geographical position and usually it is either their low rents or the fact that they are offered to those well down on the waiting list. The other consequence of the property being seen as second class is that the bureaucracy is liable to treat the tenants as just that. The temptation to use already down-graded areas as dumping grounds for bad risk tenants must be considerable. Even if the bureaucracy takes care not to treat them in this way, tenants and prospective tenants, by their attitudes, will still produce polarisation.

The school in the distance was handed over to local residents when closed, to be used as a neighbourhood centre. The nearer one was not
Part of a block of flats that won a national design prize seventeen years earlier. Many of the flats are now unlettable

Coffee bar project. The other shops are open too

A vandalised play shed restored for use by residents. The school beside it has since been burnt to the ground

That many of the older walk-up flats have not deteriorated more than they have, in the face of such handicaps, is often attributable to the resolve of long-standing residents. Building on such local pride and welding it into a more self-supporting group with finance and buildings being supplied by the authorities has done much in these individual blocks to reverse the downward spiral in which so many areas find themselves caught.

However, the temporary improvement that such community development engenders can easily evaporate or turn sour if increasing resources are not released in those neighbourhoods. For, as mentioned above, the inherent characteristics of such neighbourhoods make it almost impossible to turn them into adequate homes without seeing adjacent communal space as a growth area for such things as laid-out open space, play facilities, neighbourhood centres, shops, and so on.

Bearing in mind the different criteria applied by the various relevant bodies outlined above, it can be fairly claimed that a large number of the schemes financed in the year 1970-71 have been successful; and in some cases they can be shown to have had a direct effect on the financial cost of vandalism expressed in terms of windows broken, fires started, etc.

1. *Soho Street*   The most successful project, promoted by residents, local community worker, probation, police and housing.

By being situated in an area of considerable friction and delinquency, the coffee bar has attracted children of all ages who would normally be hanging around the squares. Beyond this it has provided a fresh start for many unemployed lads who have had criminal records—they have virtually run the shop—as well as giving a new point of contact between the other shopkeepers (local shops are uninsurable due to petty crime) and local residents. It has also acted as an invaluable run-up to the responsibility of operating the projected community centre to be financed by Urban Aid.

2. *Pavilion, ancillary rooms and play area—Crosbie Heights*

To quote the housing manager, "I think we can claim that this is so far one of the successes of community involvement. Twelve months ago the pavilion and ancillary rooms under Crosbie Heights were vandalised and gutted and the play area was a tip. Now we have reinstated the premises to somewhere near the original condition (no vandalism has taken place for twelve months on these premises) and Eddie Cartwright and the tenants of Haigh, Canterbury and Crosbie Heights have formed a committee to run the scheme. The IVS ran a play scheme there in the summer and the residents' committee which was formed to oversee the scheme, is discussing the provision of a pre-school playgroup, social events and information service."

3 and 4.   *Fixed play facilities in Sidney Gardens and Speke Road Gardens*

Owned and built by the respective residents' associations, these show clear signs of far greater care and respect being given by the children

Summer play scheme
Play scheme run by residents

than is usually true on comparable corporation facilities. This is best shown photographically.

5. *Dove Street Adventure Playground*

This temporary structure was operated as a play scheme in the summer by residents, and although it is made of wood, it has remained intact since the end of the holidays. As far as the playscheme itself is concerned, a local school caretaker said that for the first time in several years, he had not had vandalism problems during the summer of 1971.

6. *Abercromby Playscheme*

Another temporary scheme, operated by local residents with professional leadership. In this area people's comments differed. For example, the caretaker of the school adjacent to the playground was hostile, as the amount of vandalism had increased; although it could be argued that his hostility invited the vandalism, rather than resulted from it. The caretaker of the school opposite admitted that vandalism had decreased, and another school caretaker nearby also said this. The University authorities were also pleased with the scheme, along with the shopkeepers of the area, who felt that the drop in the number of children hanging around had been reflected in less petty theft.

Residents felt that accidents had decreased in the area (this had been a recurring problem) and there was also general agreement that the various blocks were quieter, with none of the usual stone-throwing battles.

7. *Kirkdale—Compulsory Purchase Order Area*

Although the playscheme was rather unsatisfactory and thin in local involvement, we did manage to make positive use of an empty cinema in Walton Road for the children, and to guarantee that they would not vandalise it while it operated as a play centre. The damage that was caused after the scheme had finished did not fundamentally alter the claim that without the project something like £2,000 worth of damage might have been caused, to judge by past experience. (The last tenant told us that his first six months of rent had been waived to offset the cost of damage caused by vandalism when the property stood empty).

8. *Salisbury Street, Everton*

While the Handicraft Centre, when closed by the Education Authority, was taken over by local residents and is now used for a pre-school playgroup, youth club, football training centre, discotheque and children's cinema, Salisbury School, 100 yards away, was immediately wrecked and set alight recently when it was closed without any firm offer for the use of the building being made to groups in the area. A similar contrast would be drawn from experience with other schools.

In attempting to cost vandalism, one's own point of view is of primary importance. Take, for example, a lift in a walk-up block of flats. As it is not an essential amenity, it is possible to leave it inoperative without undue hardship. Thus the 'cost' of vandalism in such a case can be seen either from the housing department's point of view (the cost of repairing the damage) or from the residents' point of view (loss of amenity).

That these viewpoints are in opposition can be seen by considering the logical result of applying either without consideration of the other. For the housing department, the cheapest way of solving the problem is simply not to repair the lift (which happens), while for the residents the most satisfactory 'solution' is for the department to repair the lift as an emergency every time it is damaged. Compromise is necessary so

A clearance area . . .

that the amenity is provided by the department and looked after by the residents. The actual bill to the Corporation may in fact go up—but the amenity thereby provided would be, in the opinion of both sides, worth the extra expense. In particular, bearing in mind the capital cost of providing such an amenity, the effective *saving* in fully utilising it is considerable.

To take another example, there are dozens of recently completed blocks of garages which are unused (and because of vandalism, often unusable) and are liable to be demolished (at further expense). At a rough estimate on the basis of £300 capital cost per unit, the average loss in capital investment and interest charges will be in excess of £5,000. The conversion of some such blocks of garages into a local centre at well below this cost could not only provide a future source of income, but would also provide a useful amenity in the area for meetings, playgroups, youth clubs, film shows, etc. Pressure by the residents for such an amenity would normally mean investment of some thousands of pounds in a new building. Converting the property already owned by the Corporation which is at present unused (and therefore more liable to be vandalised) would provide a useful amenity, promote community involvement and reduce the chance of damage, not only to the property in question, but to other facilities in the area.

In order to arrive at such a sharing of responsibility it is probably

. . . and its uses

necessary to do a 'deal' on a number of issues. This might involve other environmental improvements, or action on outstanding repairs by the Housing Department in exchange for local running of 'diversions' by parents for their children. On this wider plane, the relevance of the objectives of probation officers, youth workers, community workers, environmental health, etc., becomes clearer and eventually a situation arises where the effective running of the lifts, or use of the vandalised garages, becomes secondary to other long-term objectives.

Such a many-sided operation requires considerable time and dexterity if anything practical and on-going is to emerge from it. The middleman job, performed for instance, by Eddie Cartwright in Soho Street and Crosbie Heights, or by Teddy Gold in the Bronte area, is essential for results in such neighbourhoods, involving a mixture of talk and action which is attempting not only to develop facilities, but also to broaden attitudes and objectives.

Experience shows clearly that such a 'project organiser' must unquestionably identify with the area if he is to rally and coordinate local voluntary effort. The floating worker, whether a city-wide projects officer or a community warden, cannot give the time or total backing to one particular group, when he has so many others to deal with. As Projects Officer, my one big advantage was that the actual financial help could often be used to 'persuade' groups into action. In many cases it has been wisest to release money in small amounts as successive stages of the project are completed by local residents. For instance, in Grafton Street, Toxteth, a local group of residents cleared, levelled, and then fenced off a site as a play area/football pitch for their children at a cost of £150 to the Vandalism Steering Group.

Also the swing from building structures to organising activities has meant that projects have become increasingly labour-intensive. The need to sustain local voluntary involvement, particularly when things go wrong, means again that it is necessary to employ a local projects organiser whose job it is to deal with just these problems.

Vandalism has to do with amenities and social control. It reflects, on the one hand, the damage done to amenities already provided, and on the other, the lack of amenities appropriate to the needs of the area. It illustrates the breakdown of discipline between adults and children, and the need to restore this in a new form relevant to the prevailing attitudes of children and adults to each other, the organisational problems imposed by rehousing and modern architectural design, and the growing aspirations of residents for amenities in their neighbourhood, and a greater say in the control of those amenities.

Concentration on certain areas enables us to arrange for the immediate use, by local groups, of buildings when they become empty. Not only does this enable them to operate activities for different groups in the neighbourhood but it also ensures that the building or site remains an asset and does not become a liability.

It is significant that it was only possible to operate projects in areas identified by corporation departments as areas of high vandalism when a local leader existed who had the time, and who also had the confidence of residents, to link up the bureaucratic concern with the aspirations of local people. It is also worthwhile to note that it was in precisely these areas (Speke Road Gardens, Abercromby, Englefield Green, Soho Street, Crosbie Heights, Kirkdale) that our greatest successes have occurred. The playgrounds in Speke Road Gardens and Sidney Gardens (Abercromby), the summer playscheme in Abercromby, the football league, netball and summer holiday, equipped and run by the residents of Englefield Green, the coffee bar in Soho Street, the pavilion under Crosbie Heights, and the empty shop in Kirkdale CPO Area have all represented a partnership between Corporation and residents as well as being signs of concern in areas which seemed to be slipping away into 'twilight area' status.

It is to these neighbourhoods that we should look for results, and ideas for the future.

They are areas of high social malaise—as defined by police, the probation service, and the Housing and Environmental Health departments, etc.

They are areas which are severely lacking in communal facilities.

They are areas which still have stable communities which are at present dispirited by the deterioration of the neighbourhood over the last few years.

They are areas containing a local leader who could devote himself full-time to the organisation of projects.

It is possible to claim that in such areas:

(i) Local residents and Corporation departments have all been actively involved in a co-ordinated attempt to improve the neighbour-hood.

(ii) The continuity of one project, or the inter-linking of successive projects, has begun to turn the despair both of the residents and the professionals into an attitude of hope for the future.

These dual elements of partnership and the provision of an aim for the future are essential if we are to solve the problem where it exists, rather than disperse it by rehousing, or attempt to suppress it by intensive policing measures. Vandalism has been shown to be a clearer symptom of other, often more serious, *social* problems, than a symptom of more serious *crime*. Areas identified as problem areas from the point of view of the Housing and Environmental Health departments, and as providing, heavy case loads for the probation and social services, are often *not* areas of concern seen from a strictly police point of view.

13 Notes on the future of vandalism

Colin Ward

Our conventional and all too plausible picture of the immediate future is that it will be like today only more so: a mobile urban mass society, heavily dependent on the motor car in whose interests vast areas of the inner city are cut up by motorways with acres of sterilised no-man's land taken up by traffic intersections crossed by rat-runs for the remaining pedestrians. The affluent meritocracy commutes to the business district or lives in the expensively renovated inner suburbs, the skilled and semi-skilled workers employed by huge international combines live in vast estates on the outskirts or in the tower blocks left over from the nineteen-sixties, while the permanently unemployed and the fringe of drop-outs for whom idleness is less degrading than work, inhabit the transitional districts of run-down municipal or privately rented housing. There is no need to go on, you know it all backwards.

Can we seriously imagine that such an environment will be less prone to vandalism than the one we inhabit today? Or that some combination of education, exhortation and more efficient policing will reduce its extent? What is more likely is that the litter-strewn, windswept public spaces of the future metropolis will be more unkempt, battered and bedraggled because of the high cost and low prestige of maintenance work (in spite of unemployment), and that the spin-off of consumer technology (as Ian Taylor and Paul Walton indicate in Chapter 5) will provide facilities for more sophisticated forms of vandalism. It seems likely too, that the distinction between the vandalism of delinquent sub-cultures and that of disaffected ideologies will merge and blur. Michael Young in his prophetic satire *The Rise of the Meritocracy* foresaw an ultimate alliance between the lumpen-proletariat with their fully-certified low IQ, and the drop-out intelligentsia.

On June 22, 1971 eight young mechanics and sheet metal workers were each fined £150 and ordered to pay £100 compensation at Southend magistrates' court, after admitting 47 charges of causing wilful damage to clothing and vehicles and causing actual bodily harm. They were alleged to be members of a 'greaser' gang which set out to 'rough up' skinheads, but ended by attacking anyone or any vehicle in sight, on a round trip variously estimated by the press as 60 or 100 miles. They loaded a 15cwt van with two Redex oil spray guns from a garage, and cans of green and white paint, as well as washing-up liquid bottles and lemon juice, which, according to the prosecution, "a technical member of the gang said was good for staining Crombie coats and mohair suits."[1] The case is interesting in foreshadowing one kind of development we can expect in the future: a move from unpremeditated acts, using the materials and opportunities that come to hand, to mobile, planned and relatively sophisticated sub-cult games with an unpleasant spill-over into society as a whole.

Alvin Toffler declares that we can even see on the horizon:

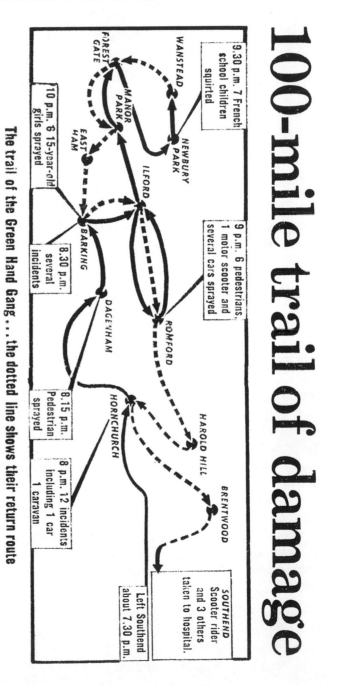

100-mile trail of damage

9.30 p.m. 7 French school children squirted

9 p.m. 6 pedestrians, 1 motor scooter and several cars sprayed

10 p.m. 6 15-year-old girls sprayed

8.30 p.m. several incidents

8.15 p.m. Pedestrian sprayed

8 p.m. 12 incidents including 1 car 1 caravan

SOUTHEND Scooter rider and 3 others taken to hospital.

Left Southend about 7.30 p.m.

The trail of the Green Hand Gang . . . the dotted line shows their return route

. . . mobile, planned and relatively sophisticated sub-cult games . . .

277

". . . the creation of certain anti-social leisure cults—tightly organised groups of people who will disrupt the workings of society not for material gain, but for the sheer sport of 'beating the system' . . . Such groups may attempt to tamper with governmental or corporate computer programmes, re-route mail, intercept and alter radio and television broadcasts, perform elaborately theatrical hoaxes, tinker with the stock market, corrupt the random samples upon which polemical or other polls are based, and even, perhaps, commit complexly plotted robberies and assassinations . . . ."[2]

Notice how Mr. Toffler resolutely declines to see anything beyond "sheer sport" in these possibilities, as though such games were not being played on ideological grounds between black militants and the police in his own country while he was writing, or between various ideologists, the police and the army in Ulster while I am writing, and as though the kind of disruption of telephone and communications systems were not continuously advocated on ideological grounds in the underground press and in publications like *Fuck the System*.

"Since machines run the society we live in, it's only fair that an equal degree of destructive creativity be levelled against them. Computers, because of their very nature, are extremely easy to render inoperative. When paying bills by computer, always remember that you have the ultimate advantage of an open mind and the ability to rationalise whereas the machine is programmed to do one thing. A good method of sabotage is simply to punch a few extra holes in the IBM card. Most of the time the card will be rejected, and it will cost the company a few dollars to rectify the mistake . . . . When I was working for a large New York corporation, I had to deal with a bank every day. I realised, after a period of time, that the people who were working at the bank had lost their identities, and were nothing more than machines themselves. Well, this sort of psychological surrealistic science fiction really got me interested. I viewed myself as a saver of identities, as the Messiah of the Spirit of Individualism. I was brought to earth quickly. These people didn't want to be saved. I was going to turn them on to acid, but then I decided that a better tactic would be to screw up the object of their emulation. On my daily deposit I placed a large quantity of Scotch tape. This resulted in the deposit slips themselves getting stuck in the bowels of the computer. It took the bank three or four hours to take the machine apart, and unjam the mechanism. In unjamming the machine, they somehow altered the program, and it didn't work right for weeks . . . ."[3]

But quite apart from the vulnerability of electronic computers, control and communications systems, the sheer scale of operations in modern transportation and supply systems magnifies the effect of quite 'ordinary' acts of vandalism, or of mere carelessness:

"Sabotage or vandalism may have caused a massive leak in explosive

278

naphtha which threatened thousands of people in Liverpool yesterday. Leakage of the liquid explosive caused the river Mersey to be closed to shipping, and a whole area of the city to be sealed off." [4]

"There have been about a dozen cases of deliberate damage to the £130 millions Wylpha nuclear power station over the past two or three years . . ." [5]

"Three boys brought near disaster to 6,000 homes in the Watford area of Hertfordshire by altering the setting of a gas pressure regulator." [6]

"Vandals were blamed last night for bringing the menace of a massive oil slick to the water supplies of two cities. The vandals opened the taps of an oil tank outside a Worcester printing works—and 900 gallons of heavy industrial oil spilled into the river alongside. By yesterday afternoon, a 12 mile oil slick stretched from Worcester to Upton-on-Severn, threatening Gloucester and Coventry water intake." [7]

"Vandals are believed to have sunk the Clyde Venture, a 475-ton bunkering vessel in a Clyde dock yesterday. About a hundred tons of oil escaped from the ship." [8]

"Children on a housing estate in Manchester are making an urban motorway one of the most difficult roads in the country to build. They have stoned workmen and loosened scaffolding and now the contractors say the children will be a danger to motorists when the road is finished." [9]

Adolescents as scapegoats and shocktroops

Vandalism is usually seen as an attribute of adolescence, and is 'explained' by psychiatrists in terms of the strains of the transitional period in life from childhood to adulthood—the adolescent, it is suggested, is 'full of undirected exuberant energy' and is 'careless of his own and other people's property because his interests are centred on people rather than on things.' In the strains to which the adolescent subjects the artefacts of the environment, there is an element of "testing to destruction"; he is putting to test his own strength as well as discovering the ultimate limitations of the material. He also, it is suggested, 'doesn't know his own strength', and the authors of Chapter 7 of this book are careful to distinguish between vandalism and the awkwardness of the secondary school age group which "tends to be naturally clumsy because of growing strength and growing limbs".

The future of vandalism is linked with the future of adolescence as a social phenomenon, but the moment you start to enquire into the nature of adolescence, you find conflict between what 'everybody knows' about adolescence and what turns out to be simply the fulfilment of social expectations. For example, everybody knows that a boy's voice 'breaks' during puberty and becomes cracked, unco-ordinated and uncontrollable before assuming its adult timbre. But changes in musical fashion—the abandonment of the 'cathedral hoot' and the cultivation of the 'natural' voice in boys' choirs, have revealed that the boy's voice does not 'naturally' break, but deepens and is capable of producing a musical and manageable sound throughout adolescence. Is there an analogy with the other attributes of this stage in life?

"In child development circles there has been much argument as to whether development is continuous or whether it occurs in 'stages', that is, in jumps separated by plateaux when little happens. Again, supposing stages to exist, there is an argument as to whether any *general* ones occur characterizing a simultaneous achievement of a number of anatomical, physiological, and psychological developments. Physical growth, as we have repeatedly stressed, does *not* occur in a series of jumps, but continuously (except for the minor seasonal variations seen in some children). Thus in physical growth it is clear that no 'stages' in the sense used above, exist, except in so far as one might consider the rapid change at adolescence as the achievement of a new, and mature, state."[10]

Ronald Brookes produced this 'Agro-Board,' a panel of variable density foam. "Aggressive instincts," he explained, "are harmlessly worked out of the system by punching a chosen portion with fists, head or feet . . . The cover should be made removable to provide for decorative change and to suit whatever new target the current situation demands."

Frank Musgrove argues that adolescence is a social invention. In an arresting passage he declares that "The adolescent was invented at the same time as the steam engine. The principal architect of the latter was Watt in 1765, of the former Rousseau in 1762. Having invented the adolescent, society has been faced with two major problems: how and where to accommodate him in the social structure, and how to make his behaviour accord with the specifications".[5]

Distinctive social institutions had to be fashioned to accommodate the newly invented adolescent, and "psychologically he has been made more or less to fit them, moulded by appropriate rewards and penalties". In Dr. Musgrove's view,

"The hatred with which the mature in Western society regard the young is a testimony to the latter's importance, to their power, potential and actual . . . Their seniors protect their own position with a variety of strategems, planned ostensibly in the best interests of the young: prolonged tutelage and dependence, exclusion from adult pursuits, interests and responsibilities, in order to 'protect them from themselves'; extended training schemes of negligible educational content which effectively delay the open competition of the young worker with his seniors."[11]

Here is an instantly recognisable description of the stereotype of adolescent behaviour, quoted by Tony Gibson over twenty years ago in his pamphlet *Youth for Freedom:*

"A gangling youth came strolling down the street, his strident voice now high, now low, hitting the air with unremittant persistence. Attached to him, writhing and twisting, her giggles interrupted by shrill admonitions, was a girl of about his own age. They cavorted all over the pavement, oblivious of all but themselves. In appearance the youth was tall and gawky, his coat ill-fitting, his trousers unpressed. The girl was more presentable . . . Not far behind them rollicked a group of about eight or more of the same age . . . boisterous and ill-mannered, the boys shouting and roaring in coarse, irregular voices, the girls shrieking and giggling."[12]

To Dr. Gibson there is nothing 'natural' about this kind of behaviour—he sees it as the result of the repression of sexuality in the young. "The adolescent boy or girl who are not suffering from sexual privation are not awkward, uncouth, and given to silly hooliganism. They appear to slip very gracefully from childhood to adulthood. The gracelessness of the average hobbledehoy and hoyden is not due to their ignorance of civilised behaviour; it is due to the fact that their inner conflicts make it impossible for them to act with natural poise."[13] This view is upheld by the evidence of anthropological writers like Malinowski, Verrier Elwin and Margaret Mead.

Shocktroops?

Alex Comfort, for his part, sees the "overt anti-sexual bias" of centralised urban societies as producing a "heightened emotional tension that leads to a state of persistent, because often unsatisfied, sexual excitement."

"The irritant is sometimes said to be 'lack of social purpose'—but the classical symptom of exasperation, namely explosive and undirected violence by relatively well-off youngsters who are not certain what it is they want to smash, is found both in Bingo-land and in the Marxist states, where 'social purpose' is as present as in wartime democracy, and probably as facile . . . . Aggression with sexual overtones is equally present in such apparently pointless activities as slashing seat cushions in trains." [14]

Superficially the sexual climate has changed. But today's 'permissiveness' that so worries the moralists, *is* superficial—ask any working-class girl who finds herself pregnant. We may *talk* a great deal more about sex, but we still make it difficult, as Comfort says, for youngsters to "outgrow the attitude which sees the opposite sex simply as a quarry upon which one chalks up points."

The 'edge of desperation' in the situation of the working-class male adolescent is described in the closing pages of Dr. Cohen's opening chapter in this book. Paul Goodman, the most perceptive observer of

282

the dilemma of the young, had a prescription. "The cure," he said, "for their violent sexuality is to allow them guiltless sex. The cure for their deviance is to teach them their real enemies to fight. The cure for their foolish activism is to provide them a world which has worthwhile tasks."[15] But the fact, as we all know, is that we *prefer* our social problems to the consequences of changing our society to solve them.

There is a well-known psycho-analytical theory that we "seduce" our young delinquents into acting out our own deviant fantasies. David Riesman remarks that "many adult males over-react to adolescent boys and young men, sometimes treating them as vicarious bearers of their own suppressed energies and aims." It might help us understand the social function of vandalism if we extended this notion to the point where we see the young not merely as the *scapegoats*, but as the *shock troops* of their elders. We are familiar with this idea in war, where the young men kill each other and the old men dish out the medals, from the poems of Wilfred Owen, but it is exhibited with equal clarity in the experience of the uprisings in Hungary or Czechoslovakia, or in Ulster, or in 'race riots' in the United States and elsewhere. The resigned and the old are sitting at home hating, while the young, who have not yet learnt resignation or prudence, or 'responsibility', or acquired responsibilities, are out there fighting. The point is spelt out in an official report on the appalling condition of many municipal housing estates in Scotland: "The years of deprivation have produced widespread apathy in the majority of tenants and violent protest among the minority of the young people".[16]

Vandalism as moral health

We can hardly expect the victims of vandalism, who not only have to put up with the inconvenience and sometimes the hazards that it brings, but must also pay the bill for it, to take a sympathetic view of the idea that vandalism can be an indication not of social malaise but of moral health. But if you believe that the future is bound to bring conflict and confrontation between the controlled and regimented mass society and those who for one reason or another reject its values, vandalism *can* be seen as a healthy affirmation rather than a pathological act.

Some observers, like Terence Morris, feel able to distinguish between 'revolutionaries' and 'vandals':

"Some of the revolutionary socialists at the London School of Economics were highly intelligent, responsible people who had already made a useful contribution to the Academic Board, a lecturer who has been on the LSE staff for 17 years said yesterday. On the other hand, Dr. Terence Morris, a penologist, said some of the students were emotionally disturbed people who in other circumstances might be in hospitals or approved schools. MPs from the Select Committee on Education, continuing their public hearings at the school, heard Dr. Morris draw a sharp distinction between a rational, radical revolutionary leadership, and "vandals" whose regressive behaviour was 'extraordinarily sick'. The latter had 'very serious problems about authority,' and had found in the university a totally permissive society which did not restrain them. Mr. Trevor Park, Lab. MP for Derbyshire SE, asked Mr. Morris how it was that such disturbed young people had gained admission to the school, or whether it was their experience at the school that had disorientated them." [17]

Others put more faith in the 'vandals' than in the 'revolutionaries': "Spray paint gang slogans ruining shop fronts (especially new ones), wrecked ripped buses, the enormous volume of pilfering that goes on in shops and works . . . . These are the only things that give me hope in these times when 'revolutionaries' offer nothing but obscure contorted obsessional dogmas which spring from this society as much as capitalism or fascism . . . Hope? You might say that the things I mentioned are pure vandalism and an intolerable imposition of your views on other people, or that they will achieve nothing because they are done un-thinkingly, blindly, like a pack of animals.

"Anything you do, conforming or not, is an imposition on other people—do nothing and you condemn the people around you to be imposed on by whatever happens to be the norm. You are being imposed on all the time. When an architect puts up a building its presence and form impose themselves on people's consciousness far more drastically than a spray paint slogan which can only enliven a dead unnatural inhuman *stone* thing. All this 'senseless' vandalism illustrates that people are aware of the real evils of this society—straight lines, boredom, grey walls, uniforms, more boredom, glossy uselessness—and not 'capitalism', the 'economy', 'social structures', the 'government', 'industry' . . . . The Revolution always has failed and always will . . . who can say a *person* has failed?" [18]

Perhaps the most persuasive case for seeing an outbreak of property destruction and 'non-utilitarian' looting as a factor in moral growth and the assertion of human dignity, was made by Guy Debord in his prophetic pamphlet *The Decline and Fall of the Spectacular Commodity Economy* after the riots in Watts, Los Angeles, in August 1965. "Before, people were ashamed to say they came from Watts. They'd mumble it. Now they say it with pride," declared a young black girl, and Debord remarks, "Let us leave the economists to grieve over the 27 milllion dollars lost, and the town planners over one of their most beautiful supermarkets gone up in smoke, and McIntyre over his slain deputy sheriff; let the sociologists weep over the absurdity and in-toxication of this rebellion."

Just as the brothers Paul and Percival Goodman in 'The City of Efficient Consumption', one of the three 'community paradigms' in their book *Communitas*, saw the need for a carnival of destruction in an economy of overproduction, so Debord saw ultimate truths about the affluent society revealed by the flames of Watts.

284

". . . But the fact that the vaunting of abundance is taken at its face value and discovered *in the immediate* instead of being eternally pursued in the course of alienated labour and in the face of increasing but unmet social needs—this fact means that real needs are expressed in carnival, playful affirmation and the potlatch of destruction. The man who destroys commodities shows his human superiority over commodities. He frees himself from the arbitrary forms which cloak his real needs. The flames of Watts consumed the system of consumption! The theft of large refrigerators by people with no electricity, or with their electricity cut off, gives the best possible metaphor for the lie of affluence transformed into a truth by play . . . Pillage is the *natural* response to the affluent society: the affluence, however, is by no means natural or human—it is simply abundance of goods . . . ."[19]

Debord sees these events as the beginning of what he calls a new proletarian consciousness, "the consciousness of not being the master of one's activities, of one's life, in the slightest degree." In a similar vein, a friend writes to me from Notting Hill:

"I fully support any act of vandalism, etc., without qualification, and without providing excuses for the people who do it. We do a disservice by turning 'hooligans' into a pure reflex of capitalism, their degree of viciousness depending upon current wage restrictions and the level of unemployment. I see the difficulty . . . that the sociologist, dealing with individual cases quite often can't say to the kids that what they did, acting from *free will* (even if that will had little perspective on which to act) was the best thing they, as individuals, could do in *their* position. The middle class kid who drops out and becomes so damned transcendent that when you say hello to him on the stairs he doesn't see you— he's the one with perspective, he is defeated, he knows the uselessness of a solitary act of tyre slashing, but the nice bright-eyed working class kid in acting out his frustration is affirming life, affirming the possibility of influencing his environment, in no matter what blind way . . . there is some hope here. I love his confidence even if in the cold light of middle class wisdom, which of course *understands* why he did it, it appears absurd."

Vandalism as a bargaining counter

The reader of the opening chapter of this book will readily see that what we call vandalism can relate to a variety of different acts with different motivations which have in common only the fact that they involve 'wanton' damage to property. But if we look at property destruction in the light of the witnesses for the defence whom I have quoted above, it is possible to see some vandals as urban guerrillas involved in a struggle for the control of the environment.

This was exemplified in the experience of American cities in the long hot summers of the late 1960s:

"Civil disturbances such as American communities have witnessed are situations of *temporary and localised redefinitions of property rights*. The urban disorders represent conflict on community goals and differences of opinion about economically valued objects. What was previously taken for granted now becomes a matter of open dispute."[20]

The authors of this comment suggest that American society, "if it wishes to ensure domestic tranquillity, should move to institutionalise non-violent means for redistributing certain property rights" and that if it does not "looting may establish itself as a major structural device for change in the American social system".

Other contributors to this book draw attention to a similar interpretation of Luddite machine-breaking as a means of negotiation with employers, this mechanism being, as Hobsbawm says, "perfectly understood by both sides".

Everyone who has argued before a housing committee the case for adequate and appropriate play space has used the argument that without such provision wilful damage would increase. Today, the kids themselves are aware enough to use such arguments. The Groves Estate at Penge in South East London has fifteen hundred children and two small playgrounds in one of which ball games are prohibited. Residents, particularly the elderly, suffer from such 'meaningless' acts as the immobilisation of lifts, menacing banging on doors, and burning paper thrust through letter boxes. Talking to the Chairman of the Housing Committee after interviewing children on the estate, the BBC interviewer remarked, "The kids say they are forcing your hand. In other words, violence pays off".[21]

There is in fact a land-use conflict in the residential environment, a conflict in which the young have no weapons to fight with except their nuisance-potential. It arises in its most irreconcilable form in the redeveloped areas of big cities. And unless he exploits the situation the child is invariably the loser. Pearl Jephcott illustrates this with five factors:

(*a*) Today's children are taller, heavier and more robust than those of earlier generations, which may well mean they are harder in terms of wear and tear on the environment and the amount of noise they are liable to make.

(*b*) Now that families are smaller they have fewer domestic jobs in the home . . .

(*c*) Urbanisation is continually restricting the areas available for their play and limiting what they may legitimately do. In multi-storey housing their play is hedged in by negatives—you mustn't play in the hall, chalk on the pavement, make a see-saw on that wall, cycle on this path. Moreover, the places where the child plays are becoming more exposed to public view. Parents contrast the relative privacy of their old back courts and 'our street' with the openness of the estate which has few defined spots to which their child has his own right.

287

(*d*) The multi-storey estate demands a setting that is spick-and-span and this is what the adult longs to maintain since he has so often come from a down-at-heel area. The children are unconcerned with such niceties. What they need is a place and things they can *use*.

(*e*) The open, tidy estate makes a most inferior setting for play compared with the variety of the street, its passages, old walls, derelict buildings, culs-de-sac, stairways, unexpected corners. Children are natural foragers but where, on a multi-storey estate, is the flotsam and jetsam which is treasure-trove to the child—an old door, a cardboard carton, a plank, a bucket, a length of rope?[22]

High flats are just an extreme case of environmental deprivation so far as children are concerned. Is it surprising that the bolder spirits fight back?

But the needs of the young are systematically ignored in the environment as a whole. The national average proportion of the population aged under 21 is 31%. In any new housing area, because of the predominance of young families, the proportion is very much greater— nearly 50% at Easterhouse in the period described in Chapter 3, 47.5% at Partington outside Manchester, and similar proportions in many other places with a high incidence of vandalism. "No self-respecting child" says the report of the Scottish Housing Advisory Committee, "will confine his activities to a recognised playground, and the whole housing environment should be designed to cope with the activities of children. This also means that the environment should be designed to discourage or prevent children's play where this would result in inconvenience to residents or danger to the children themselves.'[23] (see Chapter 8).

The urban environment is not geared to the needs of children, and the premium on urban land and the surrender of even the back-streets, the traditional playground of the town child, to the motor car, makes it less so every day. It is no new thing for the young to point this out:

"If people don't want gangs they will have to give us something else and make it very attractive too, for the gangs have a good time. I don't see why the city can't make a place for baseball and that sort of thing."[24]

In the municipal ghetto

The only contact most architects have with their ultimate clients in local authority housing is at the maintenance inspection after the job is handed over and occupied. Many must come away aware, not only of their own professional shortcomings, but also of the mixture of dependence and resentment which is part of the council tenant syndrome. Stuck there in the vandalised brutalism of Harold Wilson Court, the tenants reveal little pride and pleasure in the load of architecture which provides a roof over their heads. On the other side of town the mortgagees of Ted Heath Close (unblessed by architectural hands) lovingly

288

tend its privet and parquet, even though its quality and space standards may very well be lower, for, as Allen Cunningham remarked, "be it never so humble, there's no place like sub-Parker Morris ticky-tacky, where the improving hum and hammer of do-it-yourself echoes from one privately overlooked space to another."

The reason for this paradox is obvious. People care about what is *theirs*, what they can modify, alter, improve and take pride in. They must have a hand in their environment to make it truly their own. They must have a direct responsibility for it. The rigid paternalism of most local authority housing departments breeds more resentment than exploitation by private landlords. We all loathe being manipulated for our own good, and this natural and healthy resentment has been fanned into bitterness during the last decade by very steep rent rises and especially by differential rent schemes, with a means test, so that the Council is not only Big Daddy and general provider but also the arbiter of how much pocket money shall be left in the tenant's hands at the end of the week. Current legislation on 'fair rents' is going to push these built-in antagonisms to fever pitch as it pushes out better-off families into the house-purchase scramble and turns the municipal estate into a repository for the 'deserving poor'.

In these circumstances there is not the slightest reason to suppose that 'vandalism' will diminish in the future. A Croydon councillor, speaking of one of the country's largest housing estates, known to some inhabitants as Little Siberia, declared, "New Addington is a prison; as youngsters take hold up here there will be a revolt."[25]

N. J. Habraken, in his brilliant and sustained attack on the idea of mass housing, notes that it is sometimes said that the inhabitants 'are not yet ready for what is offered them' and that they 'have to grow into it', and he replies

"The question is not whether we have to adjust with difficulty to what has been produced with even more difficulty, but whether we make something which from the beginning is totally part of ourselves, for better or worse. Therefore what happens today is nothing but the production of perfected barracks. The tenement concept has been dragged out of the slums, provided with sanitation, light and air, and placed in the open. Important though it is that sanitation, light and air be available to all, the fact is that we only provided them in a gigantic barracks situation. The only way in which the population can make its impression on the immense armada of housing blocks which have got stranded around our city centres is to wear them out. Destruction is the only way left."[26]

I would not quarrel with Habraken's last sentence, but there is another way, which is to *hand the estate over to the tenants*. I do not mean the divisive gesture adopted by some councils of selling off individual houses on selected estates to their tenants. Obviously very many tenants could never afford to become owner occupiers and many others, seeing house-ownership as an investment as well as a status symbol, would not see the point of owning an elderly council house. Nor do I mean the notion of a tenants' consultative committee, which like similar arrangements in other fields would simply be a safety-valve for grumble sessions. The tenants would not be fooled. They know that power and control lie elsewhere.

For the success of tenants' co-operatives we have the fully-documented case-history of Oslo as a guide. It began with the problems of one of their pre-war estates with low standards, an unpleasant appearance and great resistance to an increase in rents to cover the cost of proposed improvements. As an experiment, it was turned over to a tenant co-operative, and the estate was transformed. Now Oslo's whole housing policy is based on this principle.[27] We can also learn from the experience of Span housing, whose architect, Eric Lyons, remarked ". . . As far as I am concerned, it does not affect me whether it is leasehold or not. The important thing is that the Residents' Societies are in charge legally and formally. They have their own committees and take an active part. If someone's child starts digging up the lawn, someone will want to know why. Everyone has a stake in the issue . . . ."[28]

School for vandals
"Thousands of works of art are burnt, smashed, pulped and destroyed each year in England and Wales."[29] But the school vandals here are not pupils but examiners. The work submitted in the 'O' level examinations in art and craft subjects by 15 and 16-year olds is sent to the examiners "who look at them, award marks and then order their destruction". In Manchester, the Joint Matriculation Board selects pieces of pottery and sculpture to adorn its own office, then consigns the rest to the rubbish heap.

"A group of art teachers in Essex became so annoyed with the Associated Examining Board's policy of not returning children's work that they offered to collect it at their own expense to give it back to the pupils. They were told that this was not possible . . . Mr. Richards wrote to the examiners asking why children's work could not be returned. The reply was that the rules of the exams said so. After further letters and telephone calls he was told that the matter was at an end and no further correspondence would be entered into."[30]

However, this is not the kind of school vandalism that makes headlines in the local papers. Most school vandalism, as Dr. Cohen points out in Chapter 1, consists of the daily quota of destruction taken for granted by pupils and staff. The more spectacular outbreaks take a monotonously predictable form. The premises are broken into at the week-end, and apart from overturning cupboards and tables, scattering books and papers around, emptying inkpots and paintpots, the des-

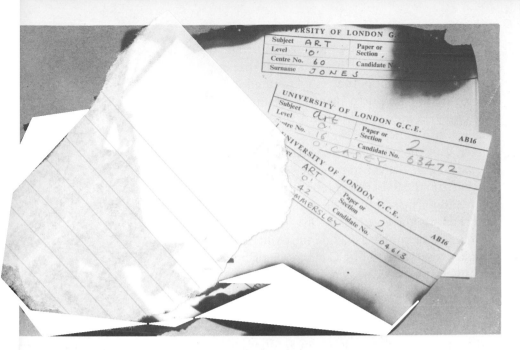

UNIVERSITY OF LONDON G...
Subject ART
Level 'O'
Centre No. 60   Paper or Section
Surname JONES   Candidate N...

UNIVERSITY OF LONDON G.C.E.
Subject Art
Level O
...tre No. 16   Paper or Section
O' CASEY   Candidate No. 2   AB16
63472

UNIVERSITY OF LONDON G.C.E.
ART
O'
42
...MERSLEY   Paper or Section   Candidate No. 2   AB16
0 4 6/3

Examiners who look at them, award marks and then order their destruction . . .

poilers write obscenities on the walls and blackboards, and someone shits on the teacher's desk. In Jean Vigo's celebrated film of a school revolt *Zero de Conduite*, the persecuted boy Tabard turns on his hated teacher in a desperate gesture of defiance and bursts out, *Monsieur le professeur, je vous dis merde*! You do not have to be a social psychologist to interpret the meaning of this kind of 'meaningless' vandalism, though it is interesting that Dr. Cohen concludes that "most research, in fact, indicates that there *is* something wrong with the school that is damaged. The highest rates of school vandalism tend to occur in schools with obsolete facilities and equipment, low staff morale and high dissatisfaction and boredom among the pupils."[31]

You have only to teach in a school or to visit one, to see that many current architectural approaches are out of touch with the actual treatment which the building gets:

"The space at the top of the teaching block staircase, where any number up to 120 children might be milling round trying to change rooms, was less than 150 square feet, and even a saintly child if there was one would find himself shoving there. There was no soundproofing in the building; you could hear even conversation with startling clarity through the walls.

On a windy day the clock above every door was almost bound to fall off when the door was slammed; if it didn't, it stopped. The glass panels were so large that if a window was broken twenty square feet of glass had to be replaced. (Nine tenths of the windows broken were broken out of school hours, sometimes by stones thrown by adults). The LCC refused to protect them with wire, and told Mr. Duane to restrict the children's playing space. He refused, saying they had too little as it was. The glass in the doors too, as he pointed out, should have been wired; the regulations required them to be, but in fact they were plain glass; eventually a child put his hand through one and had to have twelve stitches in it. The place was like an oven in summer, a refrigerator in winter. But the most appalling thing was that the windows were made to slide open, leaving an open space of twenty square feet at waist height from the floor. They terrified the staff and fascinated the children.

Mr. Duane asked for these windows to be altered in 1960, 1961, 1962 and 1963. By the autumn of 1961, he was asking the National Union of Teachers to help. He asked on the children's behalf and on the teachers' behalf. Eventually the LCC made a half-hearted and useless attempt to do something as cheap as possible. Then, in 1964, a child fell fifteen feet to the ground. Several children saw him fall, or heard him scream. His father came to the school. The LCC saw to the windows at last."[32]

The school architect is in an intolerable dilemma. He is asked to produce a building reflecting current educational theories—although these may change between the inception and completion of the structure, and although those who brief him may have quite different ideas from the people who actually teach in the school. He is expected to produce an atmosphere of sweetness and light, and at the same time he is blamed for the building's vulnerability. His budget does not allow him to produce a building solid enough to withstand the onslaught that it is certainly going to receive. Obviously old schools inherited from the school boards of the end of the last century or dating from the earlier decades of this one, with their glazed bricks, heavy joinery and solid ironmongery are inherently more resistant to damage than post-war schools, especially those built with the restricted circulation space imposed by economy regulations. Modern system-built schools with their lightweight partitions and poorly-anchored precast panels have revealed the flimsiness of their construction to their conscripted inhabitants.

Now of course everybody's memory of school includes reminiscences of school vandalism. Stanley Hall, the famous American psychologist (who was born in 1846) was the man who originated the theory that children's activities live out the past of the human race—an attractive hypothesis which would be useful in discussing vandalism if there were any evidence to support it. He wrote in his autobiography,

"In the treatment of the schoolhouse and its surroundings we were vandals. The first schoolhouse I attended is still standing as it was. The desks were carved by the jack-knives of generations of pupils, especially on the boys' side. There were rude initials deeply indented, and the walls had to be whitewashed often to obliterate pencil marks and drawings. At the end of the term the rounded ceiling of the room was

Cleaning names from the walls of Eton reveals earlier ones underneath
Since 1964 the number of fires in educational buildings has increased at
a much faster rate than the national average. The most significant cause
has been malicious ignition

building
bulletin

DEPARTMENT OF
EDUCATION AND SCIENCE

JANUARY, 1971

7

FIRE AND THE DESIGN
OF SCHOOLS
HMSO 35p NET
(FOURTH EDITION)

covered with chewed paper wads which it was a favorite diversion to throw and make stick there. We tore up the floor in the wood-house and raised havoc in the cellar, while the outhouses, both that of the girls and boys, were indescribable."[33]

But how innocent Professor Hall's vandalism was—or how easily it was *contained* by the structure of the little red schoolhouse! The writing on the walls was obliterated by whitewash, no doubt made on the spot by the school-keeper from lime and tallow rather than bought expensively from the paint industry. The carving of the desks was part of a routine which enhanced the sense of historical continuity—note now some English 'public' schools cherish the initials carved by Robert Clive or Winston Churchill.[34] The chewed paper wads on the ceiling were part of a yearly ritual—at the Fitzroy Tavern in London the customers attached their small change to the ceiling wrapped up in this way, and it was retrieved at Christmas and given to charity.

In the modern school (although in one London school teachers do a hasty annual round of 'reading the desks' before the maintenance men come to sand down the surfaces) such activities are considered as a threat to discipline, and to the spick and span image of an institution completely under the control of authority, and the very structure is often incapable of undergoing the treatment it is bound to get. 'Vandalism' consequently takes a less acceptable form.

The most expensive single cause of damage to school buildings is fire, and quite a large proportion of school fires are started deliberately. One South London school—with a high reputation—was set alight so frequently that the staff supported detectives who had been refused permission to fingerprint the 2,000 staff members and pupils.[35] The latest edition of the DES Building Bulletin on fire and school design reports an increase in fires in schools from 650 in 1958 to 1416 in 1968, and an increase in known cases of "malicious" fires from 53 in 1962 to 156 in 1968. The bulletin notes that "since 1964 the number of fires in educational buildings has increased at a much faster rate than the national average. The most significant cause has been malicious ignition."[36] The Fire Protection Association's *Journal* examined 29 large fires in schools (where the estimated damage in each case was valued at £40,000 or more) from January 1967 to June 1970 and reported that

"Of the 29 fires, 27 occurred outside normal schools hours between 6 pm and 8 am; seventeen of them occurred between midnight and 6 am. Thirteen of the fires in the survey were started deliberately, maliciously or in circumstances which led fire brigades to doubt whether the cause was accidental."[37]

Architects, teachers and the public are perplexed. What they perceive as an educational institution—inviting, creative, exciting, is seen as a prison by a proportion of its inhabitants, who react accordingly. One architect told me of his bewilderment in going to inspect some damage which actually threatened the stability of the structure. A square-section steel handrail, which had been anchored thoroughly to the spine wall of the staircase in anticipation of heavy and clumsy use, had actually been used to lever the brickwork, with the result that the wall had shifted along the line of the mortar joints. Yet in going to look at the damage he had had to thread his way through a display of marvellously inventive and colourful works of art produced in the school.

He told me of another instance in a heavily vandalised school, where the authority had produced at the last minute rows of pupils' lockers made of chipboard. The visit of the maintenance men to paint the lockers was delayed and the students themselves had painted a huge flowing design across the front of the lockers. But the painters' visit had been set in motion, and in spite of pleas that it was now unnecessary the design was painted out (and no doubt recorded as vandalism) and the lockers officially repainted a uniform grey. It brings to mind the obvious reflection that the last people to be consulted about the design and decoration of schools are the children. The only occasion I can think of when *their* opinions were solicited was the competition organised by *The Observer* in December 1967 for descriptions of 'The School that I'd Like'. Edward Blishen edited the results in the book of that name, and he sums up the competitors' opinions on school buildings thus:

"As they look in other areas of education for more excitement than they have now, so in this matter of building. The domes, the curiously much-favoured round schools were reactions against a quality in school buildings that many inveigh against; their *squareness*. I think I understand this. The children are saying what some of their elders say when they grumble about the box-like quality of so many houses. An assemblage of box shapes, and most schools of any period are that, rarely provides any sense of mystery, or has a romantic quality. Children, most to whom are quite naturally enormously romantic, would like their daily environment to have some devious and unobvious characteristics. Almost certainly, we fail to take even cautious note of this need in them when we build these usually very rational and four-square schools of ours. They cry out for colour, and are very conscious of the drab uniformity of many of the walls within which they sit. They would like to have some say at least in the ephemeral decoration of their schools. They long for attractive grounds, and especially for trees. "We do notice," says one girl; and one is reminded of the statement that sometimes the best of teachers makes, that the school building doesn't matter."[38]

The use of carpet as a classroom flooring material, an interesting experiment in 'civilising' the school, has been accepted by clients

Next door to Tollington Park School, Islington is an open space with a public lavatory. Architect David Lee invited the school to decorate its walls, which the pupils did with this mosaic of bottle-glass, plates, tea-pot lids, coloured stones and tiles. June Thornton of the art department called it "Four hundred square feet of naive and spontaneous creation."

Children's Rights Magazine
This letter is to be destroyed after use.

CHILDREN'S ANGRY BRIGADE COMMUNIQUE NO.1
WARNING BY CA BRIGADE
EDUCATION CAN DAMAGE YOUR MIND

WE ARE TIRED OF BEING A REPRESSED GENERATION.
OUR GENERATION IS REPRESSED BY CENSORSHIP LAWS,
AGE REGULATIONS, SCHOOL? (PRISONS), AND SADLY
OUR OWN PARENTS. NO LONGER SHALL WE ACCEPT
THIS REPRESSION. WE ARE ANGRY. THE ONLY HOPE
FOR A FUTURE SOCIETY LIES IN US. THE PRESENT
SYSTEM OF INDOCTRINATION WILL FAIL TO MAKE WAY
FOR THE NEW REAL EDUCATION. THE REPRINTING OF
AN UNCENSORED 'LITTLE RED SCHOOL BOOK' FOR
FREE DISTRIBUTION WAS OUR FIRST ACT. WE SHALL
NOT LIMIT OURSELVES TO NON-VIOLENT ACTS IF THE
SCHOOL SITUATION PERSISTS. ANGRY PEOPLE ARE VERY
DANGEROUS TO ANY SYSTEM. NO LONGER DO WE
ACCEPT BLIND ORDERS FROM OUR ADVERSARIES.
NEVER DO WE GROW UP LIKE THEM. ALL SABOTAGE IS
EFFECTIVE IN HIERARCHICAL SYSTEMS LIKE SCHOOLS
– UNSCREW LOCKS, SMASH TANNOYS, PAINT BLACK-
BOARDS RED, GRIND ALL THE CHALK TO DUST –
YOU'RE ANGRY – YOU KNOW WHAT TO DO.

VANDALISM

Vandalism is usually defined as wanton, po
destruction but 'political vandalism' is purpose
intelligent vandalism. In the USA at the mome
students are becoming political vandals by bur
destroying school files. This is purposeful vand
They don't want their futures decided by scra
insignificant paper – do you? This is just one
example.

Schools are ugly, depressing buildings. So w
take along some paint and paint the walls. Stic
and information on the walls. (Paint blackboar
white?). Leave boxes of magazines, old film re
stuffed animals in the corridors. Draw on the v
desks, film-screens; etc. Plant trees and flowe
earth. If there's only asphalt, dig for the earth.
big sign, with all the teachers' and students' na
it, next to the school name-sign. If it is your s
why not make it look nice? *'Creation is born
destruction'.*

If anyone is interested in (a) distributing *Child
Rights* in school, (b) participating in a nationw
schools movement, please contact Viv Berger a
24 Manor View, London N3.

At Victoria Primary School, Shoreham, the children painted this mural, in weatherproof paint provided by the parent-teacher association. On instructions from the Education Department it was obliterated by council workmen on the grounds that it was not only defacing council property but was causing offence to local people who thought it "lurid". Parents, teachers, managers and children were not consulted.

PLAY

IS A REVOLUTION-ARY ACTIVITY....

Vandalism as Children's Liberation:
left: from Children's Rights No. 1, 1971;
right: from the annual report of the
Great George's Project, Liverpool.

297

The unutterably dre

largely because it is cheaper to issue the schoolkeeper with a vacuum cleaner than to pay a large cleaning staff. An American report failed to uncover differences in observable behaviour (above the 6 to 8 age group). "But some teachers complained that by muting the sound of movement, children could leave the room undetected. Generally, however, teachers, parents and pupils were enthusiastic about carpeted classrooms if only because they were comfortable, quiet and convenient."[39]

Police patrol the corridors of a Pittsburg high school

th Camberwell Open Space

But a carpeted prison is still a prison, and those authorities which, using the argument of economies of scale, have embarked on a policy of huge uncontrollable schools are certainly going to regret the decision. Already educational thinkers are piling up the evidence in favour of smaller schools, sometimes on social and sometimes on educational grounds, sometimes simply because such a vast proportion of the energies and facilities of a large school are devoted to the maintenance of the institution itself.[40] The arguments of the 'de-schoolers'—people like Ivan Illich, Paul Goodman and Everett Reimer—for alternatives to school will grow as the pressure from below mounts.

The mass of recalcitrant and rebellious pupils, imprisoned in the system for another year by the raising of the minimum leaving age, will be the most powerful lever for change. There has always been a proportion of pupils who attend unwillingly, who resent the authority of the school and its arbitrary regulations, and who put a low value on the processes of education because their own experience tells them that it is an obstacle race in which they are so often the losers that they would be mugs to enter the competition. They learnt *this* lesson at school, which they couldn't wait to enter at five and can't wait to get out of at fifteen. What will happen when this army of also-rans, no longer cowed by threats, no longer amenable to cajolery, no longer to be bludgeoned by physical violence into sullen acquiescence, grows large enough to prevent the traditional school from functioning with even the semblance of efficiency? Sir Alec Clegg had held out this prospect before us for years as a warning that we should change our schools. The vandals are ramming home his arguments.

Vandals in the landscape
The threat to the landscape, both rural and urban, from the respectable citizens using their motorcars is so immeasurably greater—and presumably will continue to be—than the damage done by the people we label as vandals—that it is hypocritical to discuss the latter while taking

299

for granted the former. Happily there are two superlative books which tackle with insight and enthusiasm the problems of democratising the landscape in country and city respectively, and both of them consider the greater as well as the lesser vandal. I refer to Nan Fairbrother's *New Lives, New Landscapes* and to *Parks for People* by Ben Whitaker and Kenneth Browne.

Nan Fairbrother remarked that

"Our social democracy is much newer than our political, and from generations as the have-nots of society it is natural to inherit a Them-and-Us mentality: that the world belongs to Them, the hostile powers always ready to do Us down. Vandalism is Our defiance of Them (it is surely why it increases as dawning prosperity makes us bolder) and the only way of survival is in Our defended private corner of existence.

"Prosperity has improved this private territory, but it is only now bringing the realisation that the outside world belongs to Us as well as Them, and that our private fence now defines not the limits of our life's territory but only a changed degree of ownership in the whole environment. This is the liberating consciousness of true privilege, an extra dimension of living than those born privileged can ever know.

"But what we share we are also responsible for, and this is not yet accepted. At present the contrasting attitudes to private and public are everywhere marked—houses are spotless, public places squalid; private cars immaculate, buses and trains maltreated; and gardeners of pin-neat gardens dump their rubbish over the fence (even over open chestnut palings where it still remains part of the garden scene—vision, it seems, like behaviour, depending on public and private). In this version of Galbraith's private affluence and public squalor only our own is valued, and our landscapes therefore will only prosper when we feel they too are ours to cherish as we do our own gardens."[41]

The traditional behaviour of the townsman in the countryside represents not so much the Us-and-Them syndrome as that of a rampaging carnival like that of children released from the constraints of the classroom into the playground. Garth Christian quotes a parish magazine of the 1890s complaining of the marauding town-dwellers who "tear through the Derbyshire woods and fields like swarms of devastating locusts, and dragging the fern and hawthorn boughs they had torn down in the dust, end the lovely summer day drinking gin and tumbling into the night train, sodden, tipsy, yelling creatures . . ." His own picture of vandalistic excursions into the woods is one of a more purposive and more individually mobile destructive foray:

"Even as I write these words, the night sky to the north is aglow, with the reflection of fierce fires blazing down in Ashdown Forest, fires that are deliberately started by highly mobile young hooligans. Each evening this week the fires have raged, reducing the variety of plant and animal species and producing a surface slime that increases the run-off of surface water. Last night there were ten outbreaks at the same time, and as the fire engines of the district converged on the scene, all too meagre reserves of men and machines remained to deal with other emergency calls. Tomorrow night, unless the much needed rain descends, it may happen again; for the culprits, this annual exercise presents both opportunities to indulge in their anti-social flair for defying authority, and scope for those very qualities of enterprise, courage and the spirit of adventure that warrant general approval."[42]

In the context of the town park, Ben Whitaker writes, "We need opportunities for participation, from involvement in the planning of

Members of SOC 'EM—*Save Our City From Environmental Mess— putting crosses on trees in the Brandling Park area of Newcastle-upon-Tyne. More than 300 trees were due to be felled and were already marked with crosses. The new crosses were put on other trees to confuse officials. The area is to be the site of a three-deck motorway interchange*

parks to painting and graffiti and a Fun Palace from Joan Littlewood; we need toboggans and skis and bicycles for hire ..." The message that he and Kenneth Browne emphasise, apart from the absolute need to tame the motor car ("in Venice or Dubrovnik one hardly notices the absence of parks because one can walk at will") is that we must abandon the paternalistic Victorian park tradition, remove prohibitions, and give people a chance to do their own thing. Pull down the fences, take away the Keep Off signs—parks *are* for people:

"It is interesting how often the warning notices themselves, as well as fences, are targets for vandalism. Brighton, which has hardly any fences in its parks, suffers only about £150 worth of damage a year from vandalism. Mr. J. Evison, its park director, comments, 'Fences are an anachronism. They are also a challenge, and you can do much more damage hidden behind a fence. If a couple want to kiss and canoodle in the park at night, who am I to stop them?'"[43]

Popular use of parks is the best policeman, Jane Jacobs reminds us, and this is certainly the lesson of the recent history of Central Park, New York. It also is a reminder that the traditional roles of vandals and police have everywhere been reversed in the struggle for "People's Parks", whether in Berkeley, California, in the Pocket Park movement in New York, or in Powys Square, London. When the students sought to protect those famous trees in Stockholm, who were the vandals, the rioters or the police? In March 1972 a group of people were arrested for deliberately blocking the traffic in Oxford Street in a demonstration suggesting that it should be transformed into a pedestrian boulevard. How long will it be before the police are employed there in keeping out not the people but the vehicles?

The pitfalls of technology
Architects, when they make the decision to introduce mechanical equipment, tend to assume a *consensus:* a consensus of skill and care as well as sophistication in using it, and above all a consensus of goodwill and responsible behaviour. But there is ample evidence that this is an erroneous assumption, and one which may bring hardship and danger to the users of the building, as well as great expense to the client. The obvious example is that of lifts in high blocks of flats. The architect's experience of lifts, in offices and service flats, is probably of high speed installations often with an attendant, and he has no conception of the waiting times, or the misuse which the occupants of the municipal tower block has to endure. Pearl Jephcott's *Homes in High Flats* includes an appendix surveying waiting times and failures in Glasgow flats which the professionally involved reader should certainly consult. Her own recommendations are:

"1. The lift should be suited to the size and demographic character of the block and variations in lift type explored, e.g. high-speed lifts for upper floors, service lifts, etc.

2. A tougher and more child-proof version of the lift should be designed to meet the self-operated service of the multi-storey block.

3. Detailed records should be kept at every block of the times and length of breakdown and normal length of waiting time. To avoid the formation of stereotypes about the lift it might be as well to make these records easily available to those living in the block concerned.

4. When, as in two of the blocks at Red Road, the lifts still prove inadequate even after $3\frac{1}{2}$ years, special safeguards should be provided. This might mean an attendant and/or a resident technician on 24-hour call.

5. When planning the facilities for a multi-storey estate, account should be taken of the tenants' necessity to use a lift and the lift's unpredictability. The availability of facilities should be measured in terms of time as well as geographical distance."[44]

It was reported on March 18, 1972, that tenants of a multi-storey block in East London were frightened to use the lift because of boys riding on the roof of the lift car, having somehow gained admission to the shaft.

Needless to say, lifts are a constant source of trouble in schools. In an effort to avoid the need for them the architects of one large London school on a restricted site were obliged to plan very deep classrooms with narrow end walls which, as well as the sloping roofs, were heavily glazed. To avoid discomfort on sunny summer days, they installed air-conditioning throughout the south side of the building. But the air-conditioning was put out of action in the first fortnight after the school's opening and has not worked since.

Here is a salutary tale of a travelator:

"Uniformed guards went on patrol today to protect the £82,000 Shepherd's Bush Green travelators from children who are causing £200-worth of damage weekly. The guards will cost the Greater London Council £7,500 a year. The gently-sloping escalators without steps which carry pedestrians to or away from the footbridge over the busy road have been out of action for 80 per cent of the time since they were installed in September. Patrols will be on duty 16 hours a day."[45]

For the adult the travelator is a means of locomotion. For the child it is a fairground attraction, with the added advantage that you don't have to pay to get on. Unruly and abusive he may be, but when he is striding down the up escalator, or pushing all the buttons in the animated museum exhibit regardless of what is displayed in the glass case, or exploiting the play-cornucopia of the supermarket in the ways described by Ian Taylor and Paul Walton in Chapter 5, he is *using* the artefacts that the built environment provides in a way which, however selfish or inconsiderate, makes sense to him, even though it is the despair of his elders.

303

Since there is no sign that juvenile behaviour is going to change in the immediate future, and since there is no sign that we are going to pay any greater attention to the environmental needs of the child in the city, the prudent designer will either avoid the need for elaborate and vulnerable mechanical installations, or make them absolutely fool-proof—if that is possible. It is certainly worth while to go to great lengths to avoid them.

The writing on the wall

Many aesthetic enthusiasms begin as a joke and are subsequently cultivated in deadly earnest: the Gothic revival, or the cult of the paintings of the Douanier Rousseau are examples. Nobody took comic postcards seriously until George Orwell published his essay on the Art of Donald McGill, and nobody noticed the visual merits of coal-hole covers until somebody started taking rubbings of them or sticking them on the wall. Once our attention has been drawn to the aesthetic appeal or the sociological relevance of the unnoticed bric-a-brac of life, we look at it in a new way, and find it full of appeal, or at least interest, so that we regret the re-styling of old trade letterheadings, shopfronts or cigarette packets. I once disparaged the *News of the World* to Alex Comfort (who has also been fined for writing on walls). "Nonsense," he replied, "It tells you things about the English that you won't find spelt out anywhere else, except on lavatory walls." Mind you, it was a different paper in those days.

The graffiti-fancier responds to the message on the wall with interest rather than with outrage, because his receptivity has been enlarged so as to take it in as part of the urban scene. Since imitations of wall-writing entered the vocabulary of the professional artist—pioneered by Watney's Wall—graffiti have won acceptance as an art form. Dr. Cohen reminds us in Chapter 1 of Marshall Coleman's claim that it is the last folk art. Suppose it were generally accepted that walls were for writing on: would we be appalled or fascinated? Wouldn't the wall in the city become a palimpsest of the life of the street and the preoccupations of the citizens? The environmental correspondent of *The Times* is moving perceptibly round to this point of view. In his book *Battle for the Environment*, written in Summer 1971 he criticised the "squalid, ill-lit concrete rat-runs" known as pedestrian subways, pointing out that they could have "gay, vandal-beating mosaics and good lighting"[46] but by March 1972 he was commending underpasses which were "wide, well-lit, and with surfaces for graffiti rather than lavatory-like tiling inviting aerosol vandalism".[47]

The outbreak of felt-tip and paint-spray graffiti in the subway trains and stations of New York in the winter of 1971-2 led to a discussion of its significance in the columns of the *New York Times*, where one reader concluded that the graffiti were "stunningly beautiful and socially heartening: a kind of people's concrete poetry". They represented, he thought, "an encouraging humanisation of the brutally impersonal environment of trains and degrading ads." Philadelphia, where the police force has a 25-man graffiti squad, aided by handwriting experts, also has its champions of wall art. David Katzive of the Philadelphia Art Museum says, "We sense that there is a lot of creativity in these graffiti. Most interesting, the trend is away from profanity and toward simple signatures—a kind of identity thing." Together with the art department of the University of Pennsylvania, the Museum launched a Graffiti Alternative Workshop, which recruited some prolific wall-writers, caught in the act, to decorate a bus at $2 a hour. Another group was hired by the Penn Mutual Life Insurance Co. to decorate the fence around its office, while yet another graffitist was commissioned to paint a mural on the wall of an art patron's house. According to *Time* magazine one member of the City Council found the Graffiti Alternative Workshop "unbelievable" and proposed an ordinance to ban the sale of aerosol spray paints.[48]

The same demand was made by a speaker from the floor at the 1971 Conference of the Civic Trust in London. But any open-minded student of graffiti will agree that this particular medium has improved the form, if not yet the content, of graffiti, since it raises the standard of lettering simply because it imposes a bold, free-flowing line on the user, by comparison with the effect of dripping paint or hesitant chalk.

I would not like the reader to think I am being flippant. Let him

A street in Naples. "The massive basement walls at ground level below the piano nobile *are encrusted with slogans for the last election, with fading messages and peeling posters . . ."*

305

The Wall of Dignity, Detroit. "Wouldn't the wall in the city become

imagine some ancient palazzo in an Italian town. A dozen families live there, the washing is strung across the *cortile*, lean chickens and beautiful urchins scratch among the worn flagstones. The massive basement walls at ground level below the *piano nobile* are encrusted with slogans from the last election, with fading messages and peeling posters as well as new pronouncements from the *municipio*. Doesn't he, if he has any feeling for the drama and continuity of urban life, and the needs of the citizens, *prefer* that the building should be used and defaced rather than become a museum, expensively renovated (1955 style) for the benefit of the visiting tourist? The point I am making is that the environment has to be *used* by its inhabitants—all of them, including the vandals, and it must be strong enough, and flexible enough, to *contain* the vandalism it is certainly going to receive.

Towards a malleable environment
Look at the photograph on p.268. In that street, all the shops, though

impsest of the life of the street and the preoccupations of the citizens?"

open, are permanently shuttered, except for the cafe on the corner. One reaction to the picture would be "Have we really come to the stage where these hooligans assume that they have some kind of right to destroy everything except the place where they congregate in the evening?" Another would be to conclude that an increasing number of young people feel themselves to be at war with the environment, and have presumably felt this from infancy. An apprenticeship of guerrilla warfare, followed by a lifetime of resigned indifference—is this the pattern of the relationship between the ordinary citizen and his environment?

What is the missing element in this relationship? Prof. Habraken expresses it beautifully when he makes a distinction between possession and property:

"We may possess something which is not our property, and conversely something may be our property which we do not possess. Property is

307

FILM CO. require large bridge, viaduct or anything spectacular to blow up for filming purposes Tel.

Creative vandalism: corporate enter prise. *This bridge, which cos £1000,000 to build, was blown up with a real train on it in 'The Bridg on the River Kwai'. Although th author of the original book objected the film-makers argued that the audi ence 'would feel frustrated' afte watching for two hours if this sensa tional piece of action did not take place.*

Creative vandalism: individual spontaneity. *Without asking permission, four boys arrived and repainted in gold, black and white this dilapidated transformer chamber belonging to the London Electricity Board. The police took their names and addresses, but returned later to say that the LEB had given its consent.*

a legal term, but the idea of possession is deeply rooted in us. In the light of our subject, it is therefore important to realise that possession is inextricably connected with action. To possess something we have to *take* possession. We have to make it part of ourselves, and it is therefore necessary to reach out for it. To possess something we have to take it in our hand, touch it, test it, put our stamp on it. Something becomes our possession because we give it our name, or defile it, because it shows traces of our existence . . .

We have this need to concern ourselves with that which touches us daily. Through this concern it begins to belong to us, and become a part of our lives. There is therefore nothing worse than to have to live among what is indifferent to our actions. We simply cannot get used to what appears intangible, to what receives no imprint from our hand. Above all we want to comprehend our environment. It is known that if this urge for possession has no other means of expression it would rather become destructive than look on passively. A child will destroy a toy with which he can do nothing, and content himself with playing with the pieces. A good educator therefore does not tell a child not to touch anything, but teaches it activities such as constructing, building, or maintenance and care. He gives a box of building blocks rather than a finished doll's house." 49

This is one of the clues to our 'social problem' of vandalism. This is why the exhortations, or the calls for stiffer penalties (which we already have in the form of the Criminal Damage Act) are concerned with symptoms and not with causes. This is why the schemes for involvement, for better provision for the needs of the young, for getting the children to plant the trees, have at least grasped the real issue. This is why those architects who are looking for the lessons of South American shanty towns are right, and those who put their faith in advanced technology miss the point. The poorest inhabitant of the barriadas of Lima has, as John Turner insists, won for himself the freedom to shape his own environment and to invest in its future. The poor inhabitant of the affluent Western city lacks, as Habraken observes, an elementary freedom closely interwoven with human happiness and human dignity: "Man no longer houses himself: he is housed."

Another Dutch architect, Herman Hertzberger, in his address to the RIBA, "Looking for the beach under the pavement" underlined the implications of this approach.

"Everything that is organised for people, even with the best of intentions, will be experienced as imposed from above, and cannot therefore be annexed by them. The whole repressive system of the established order is an institution for the avoidance of conflict, protecting citizens from each other's singularities but acting over their heads. That is why there is a dominating fear of disorder, mess, and the unexpected, and why distance takes the upper hand over inter-action.

Everything has to be regimented and quantifiable for it to be constantly under control. This is the oppression exercised by the orderliness that makes us lessees instead of owners, subordinates instead of shareholders." 50

The missing political element is the politics of participation. The missing cultural element is the aesthetic of "loose parts". Simon Nicholson, who evolved the theory of loose parts, sets it out thus:

In any environment, both the degree of inventiveness and creativity, and the possibility of discovery, are directly proportional to the number and kind of variables in it

We are deprived of a variable, manipulable, malleable environment, Mr. Nicholson claims, because of cultural *elitism*:

"Creativity is for the gifted few: the rest of us are compelled to live in environments constructed by the gifted few, listen to the gifted few's music, use the gifted few's inventions and art, and read the poems, fantasies and plays of the gifted few. This is what our education and culture conditions us to believe, and this is a culturally induced and perpetuated lie.

"Building upon this lie, the dominant cultural *elite* tells us that the planning, design and building of *any part* of the environment is so difficult and so special that only the gifted few—those with degrees and certificates in planning, engineering, architecture, art education, behavioural psychology, and so on—can properly solve environmental problems.

"The result is that the vast majority of people are not allowed (and—worse—feel that they are incompetent) to experiment with the components of building and construction . . . Playing around with the variables of the world in order to make experiments and discover new things and form new concepts—has been explicitly stated as the domain of the creative few, and the rest of the community has been deprived of a crucial part of their lives and life-style. This is particularly true of young children who find the world incredibly restricted —a world where they cannot play with building and making things, or play with fluids, water, fire or living objects, and all the things that satisfy one's curiosity and give us the pleasure that results from discovery and invention . . .

"It does not require much imagination to realize that most environments that do not work (i.e. do not work in terms of human interaction and involvement in the sense described) such as schools, playgrounds, hospitals, day-care centres, international airports, art galleries and museums, do not do so because they do not meet the 'loose parts' requirement; instead they are clean, static and impossible to play around with. What has happened is that adults—in the form of pro-
310

fessional artists, architects, landscape architects and planners—have all the fun playing with their own materials, concepts and planning alternatives, and then builders have had all the fun and creativity has been stolen: children and adults and the community have been grossly cheated, and our educational-cultural system makes sure that they hold the belief that this is 'right'." [51]

His opinion dovetails perfectly with Habraken's view. Habraken reminds us that the urge to 'restore' old buildings increases in proportion to the decline of building as a social activity, a sign, he thinks, of the degeneration of building as a means of self-expression by the user. "We cannot, moreover, draw the conclusion that the initiative to construct, improve or change is to be found only among the more affluent members of society. One has only to look at the backs of the poorer housing districts of some 40 years ago. The quantity of extensions, balconies, pigeon lofts, sheds, conservatories and roof houses come, in their chaotic character, as a relief to the observer who would rather see people than stones. They are the expression, the primitive expressions of the energy I spoke of." Might we not conclude that the destructive fury of the vandal is a thwarted form of creativity, and that an environment with "unmake", loose ends, loose parts, alternative uses, and variables would be one in which the vandal in all of us would be transmuted into the creator in all of us and our children?

A society which offers to the descendants of those who built our cathedrals no other function than, at best, to be their caretakers, should not be surprised if some of them, for sheer distraction, end by smashing the windows.

CHARLES PEGUY

311

Notes and references

Introduction

1. Tony Aldous: *Battle for the Environment* (Fontana 1972)
2. *The Architectural Review* November 1967
3. Stanley Cohen (ed.): *Images of Deviance* (Penguin Books Ltd. 1971)
4. Guy Debord: *Society of the Spectacle* Paris 1967, Detroit 1970
5. Ralph Nader: 'The Professional responsibilities of a professional society' *American Institute of Planners Newsletter* November 1970
6. G. P. Hoefnagels: *Welzijnscriminaliteit* (Environmental Crime) (Amsterdam: Boom Meppel 1972). See also Colin Ward: 'The pollution of our land: an enemy of the people.' *Journal of the Royal Society of Health* August 1972
7. Stanley Cohen: *op cit.*

Chapter 1: Property destruction: motives and meanings

1. J. B. Mays: *Growing Up in the City* (Liverpool University Press 1954)
2. *Justice of the Peace and Local Government Review* 23 March 1966
3. M. Clinard and A. Wade: 'Towards the Delineation of Vandalism as a Sub-type of Juvenile Delinquency' *Journal of Criminal Law, Criminology and Police Science* 48 January-February 1958 pp 493-399.
4. Few serious studies of the subject exist. Richard Freeman has compiled an anthology of graffiti (mainly found in London) which he intersperses with some speculations about patterns behind the writing and the motives of the artists; Richard Freeman: *Graffiti* (Hutchinson 1966). For a scholarly study of the original graffiti at Pompeii see Jack Lindsay: *The Writing on the Wall* (London: Muller 1960). See also Violet Pritchard: *Medieval English Graffiti* (Cambridge University Press 1967)
5. Marshall Coleman: 'Graffiti: The Moving Finger Writes' *Unit* No 10 February 1968 pp 17-21
6. *News of the World* 24 October 1965
7. Laurie Taylor and Paul Walton: 'Industrial Sabotage: Motives and Meanings' in S. Cohen ed. *Images of Deviance* (Penguin Books Ltd. 1971)
8. R. A. Ramsay: *Managers and Men: Adventures in Industry* Sydney: Ure Smith 1966 p. 123. I am indebted to Peter Fricke, who is carrying out a study of the merchant navy, for drawing my attention to this source, and for giving me other material from his research and his own experience in the navy.
9. P. Docker-Drysdale: 'Some Aspects of Damage and Restitution' *British Journal of Delinquency* 4 July 1963 pp 4-13.
10. See, for example, Terence and Pauline Morris: *Pentonville: A Sociological Study of an English Prison* (London: Routledge 1963)
11. G. Rude: *The Crowd in History: A Study of Popular Disturbances in France and England* 1730-1848 (London: John Wiley 1964). See also E. J. Hobsbawm 'The Machine Breakers' *Past and Present* February 1952 pp. 57-70, reprinted in *Labouring Men* (London: Weidenfeld & Nicholson 1964)
12. Roger Moody in *Peace News* 16 July 1963
13. R. Prewer: 'Some Observations on Window Smashing' *British Journal of Delinquency* Vol 10 October 1959
14. *ibid.*
15. *The Sunday Telegraph* 4 June 1967
16. Walter B. Miller: 'Violent Crime in City Gangs' *Annals of the American Academy of Political & Social Science* 364 March 1966 pp 96-112
17. *ibid.*
18. Andrew Wade: 'Social Processes in the Act of Juvenile Vandalism' in Clinard and Quinney eds. *Criminal Behaviour Systems* (New York: Holt, Rinehart and Winston Inc., 1967)

19. Nathan Goldman: 'A Socio-Psychological Study of School Vandalism' Syracuse NY: Syracuse University Research Institute, *Final Report* 1959

20. David Downes: *The Delinquent Solution* (London: Routledge and Kegan Paul Ltd. 1966). See also Peter Willmott: *Adolescent Boys of East London* (London: Routledge and Kegan Paul Ltd. 1966) and David Hargreaves: *Social Relations in a Secondary School* (London: Routledge and Kegan Paul Ltd. 1967) and 'The Delinquent Subculture and the School' in Carson and Wiles eds. *Crime and Delinquency in Britain* (London: Martin Robertson 1971)

21. Paul Goodman: *Growing Up Absurd* (London: Gollancz 1960). Still the best account of the situation of young people in industrial societies.

Chapter 2: The meaning of the environment

1. See for example, P. Solomon et al. ed. *Sensory Deprivation* (Cambridge: Harvard University Press 1961); A. D. Biderman and H. Zimmer ed.: *The Manipulation of Human Behaviour* (New York: Wiley 1961). The best review article is: J. P. Zubek, 'The Effects of Prolonged Sensory and Perceptual Deprivation' *British Medical Bulletin* Vol 20 No 19 January 1964.

2. H. J. Eysenck: *The Dynamics of Anxiety and Hysteria* (London: Routlege and Kegan Paul Ltd. 1957). H. J. Eysenck: *Fact and Fiction in Psychology* (Penguin Books Ltd. 1965)

3. M. Orne: 'The Contribution of Nonprivation Factors in the Production of Sensory Deprivation Effects: The Psychology of the 'Panic Button' *Journal of Abnormal and Social Psychology* Vol 68 1964.

4. For an excellent introduction to this area see the first part of T. Morris: *The Criminal Area* (London: Routledge and Kegan Paul Ltd. 1957)

5. R. Park, E. Burgess, and R. D. McKenzie: *The City* (Chicago University Press 1967 p. 107

6. T. R. Fyvel: *The Insecure Offenders* (Penguin Books Ltd. 1961)

7. P. Leyhausen: 'The Sane Community: A Density Problem?' *Discovery* Vol 26 No 9 1965

8. S. Cohen and L. Taylor: 'The Closed Emotional World of the Security Prison' *New Edinburgh Review* Vol 15 November 1971
S. Cohen and L. Taylor: 'The Experience of Time in Long-Term Imprisonment *New Society* 31 December 1970
S. Cohen and L. Taylor: *Psychological Survival* (Penguin Books Ltd. 1972)

9. This distinction is derived from A. F. Westin: *Privacy and Freedom* (New York: Atheneum 1967)

10. R. L. Birdwhistell: *Kinesics and Context: Essays on Body-Motion Communication* (London: Allen Lane, The Penguin Press 1971)

11. See E. Goffman: *Relations in Public* (London: Allen Lane The Penguin Press 1971)

12. L. Taylor and P. Walton: 'Industrial Sabotage: Motives and Meanings' in S. Cohen ed. *Images of Deviance* (Penguin Books Ltd. 1971)

Chapter 3: Delinquency and some aspects of housing

1. Alan Lipman: 'The Architectural Belief System and Social Behaviour *British Journal of Sociology* Vol XX No 2 June 1969

2. See for example the 'Manplan' series which dominated the *Architectural Review* during 1969 and 1970. Also Anne Buttimer: 'Sociology and Planning' in *Town Planning Review* Vol 42 No 2 April 1971. The News column in the *Architects' Journal* 27 May 1970 reports that: "The RIBA will be not be publishing any more advertisements in its campaign to impress the profession's social conscience on readers of *The Times* . . ."

3. To quote directly from the syllabus (Subject E.1. Social and Planning Implications of Building 1970-71): (the student is expected to) "become aware of the

effects that building has on people and their environment and to appreciate the social forces which may be released by the work of the architect" (and) "to understand that within the architect's role of decision-maker lies the need to be able to translate into design conclusions evidence which indicates the human response to the built environment."

4. Chermayeff and Alexander: *Community and Privacy* (Penguin Books Ltd. 1963) p. 51.

5. *ibid.* p. 34.

6. *The Sunday Times Magazine* 7 February 1971

7. See for example the editorial comment in the *Architects' Journal* 27 May 1971.

8. Festinger, Schachter and Bach: *Social Pressures in Informal Groups* (New York: Harper 1950.)

9. See the reference to Young and Willmott's study of *Family and Kinship in East London* in Tom Burns: 'New Towns for Old'.

10. See for example the work of R. E. Pahl. A recent work is *Patterns of Urban Life* (Longmans 1970)

11. Clinard: *The Sociology of Deviant Behaviour* (Holt, Rinehart, Winston 1964) p. 112.

12. This school, originating in the early 20's with the work of Park and Burgess, studied the relationship between crime and aspects of urbanity in Chicago. For a careful critique of its work, see the early chapters of David Matza: *Becoming Deviant* (Prentice Hall, 1969).

13. Scott Greer: 'Problems of Housing and the Renewal of the City' in *Social Problems* ed. Howard Becker (John Wiley and Sons 1966).

14. For a review of these classical poverty surveys, see C. A. Moser: *Survey Methods in Social Investigation* (Heinemann 1958).

15. See H. Ashworth: *The Genesis of Modern British Town Planning* (Routledge and Kegan Paul Ltd. 1954)

16. See Matza: *op cit* for a brief history of the concept.

17. See Leslie Wilkins: *Social Deviance, Social Policy, Action and Research* (Tavistock 1964) pp 169-174 for a history and critique of ecological theory as applied to criminology.

18. For a clear account of such errors, see Stanley Cohen ed.: *Images of Deviance* (Penguin Books Ltd. 1971). See also the introductions in Howard Becker: *op cit* and Rubington and Weinberg: *Deviance: The Interactionist Perspective* (Macmillan Co. 1968.)

19. L. Yablonsky: *The Violent Gang* (Macmillan Co. 1962).

20. Aaron Cicourel: *The Social Organisation of Juvenile Justice* (John Wiley and Sons 1968).

21. See Irving Pilliavin and Scott Briar: 'Police Encounters with Juveniles' in Rubington and Weinberg eds. *op. cit.*

22. For a lively discussion of this process on the basis of evidence supplied by newspaper reports, see Dennis Chapman: *Sociology and the Stereotype of the Criminal* (Tavistock 1968).

23. Edwin H. Sutherland: *White Collar Crime* (New York: Holt, Rinehart and Winston Inc. reissue 1960).

24. Lipman: *op cit* pp 196-198.

25. For a discussion of this process in relation to subcultures, see Wilkins (*op cit*). Stanley Cohen has documented such a process in relation to the Mods and Rockers phenomenon: see his *Hooligans, Vandals and the Community: A Study of Social Reaction to Juvenile Delinquency* (Unpublished PhD thesis, University of London). See also Cicourel: *op cit.*

26. Part of a news report which appeared in the *Scottish Daily Express* 3 July 1968 covering Frankie Vaughan's proposals for an amnesty between Easterhouse gangs and the police, in return for an ambitious youth centre.

27. *Scottish Daily Express* 11 July 1968.

28. See Jock Young: 'Mass Media, Drugs and Deviancy', paper delivered ·to British Sociological Association, April 1971; also Halloran, Elliott and Murdoch: *Demonstrations and Communications: A Case Study* (Penguin Books Ltd. 1970) for media treatment of deviants.

29. This was the *Scottish Daily Express*. The paper claimed that other papers had given similar treatments of Easterhouse delinquencies.

30. Armstrong and Wilson: *History of a Delinquent Area*. (Paper delivered to the National Deviance Symposium, April 1970) enlarges on this theme.

31. Jock Young: 'The Police as Amplifiers of Deviance' in *Images of Deviance* ed. Stanley Cohen.

32. Armstrong and Wilson: a forthcoming book on this subject is to be published by Allen and Unwin.

33. Frankie Vaughan: quoted in the *Scottish Daily Express* 11 July 1968.

34. Traditional Glasgow one-roomed house, often with an outside communal lavatory.

35. See West: *The Young Offender* (Penguin Books Ltd. 1967). Chapter 2 lists studies which indicate the extent of actual law-breaking among juveniles.

36. We are indebted to Donald McKenzie of the Scottish Information Office, for giving us access to this paper written by W. M. Ballantyne, and for permission to quote from it.

37. This quotation and the one that follows are abbreviated tape recordings of conversations between local boys and one of the researchers.

38. We have gathered empirical material which indicates that during 1970 employers were more likely to offer interviews to job applicants from housing estates *other* than Easterhouse.

39. See I. Goffman: *Stigma: Notes on the Management of Spoiled Identity* (Penguin Books Ltd. 1968.)

40. See Matza: *op cit.*

41. *Scottish Daily Express* 25 March 1969.

42. David Matza: *Delinquency and Drift* (John Wiley 1964).

43. Yablonsky: *op cit.*

44. Stanley Cohen: 'The Politics of Vandalism' *New Society* 12 December 1968.

45. Ann Buttimer: 'Sociology and Planning' *Town Planning Review*, Vol 42 No 2, April 1971.

46. See letter: 'Architects Must Accept Changes' by T. R. Foster in *Architects' Journal* 13 May 1970, p. 1166.

47. From a letter from Wyndham Thomas, (now General Manager of Peterborough Development Corporation) when Director of the Town and Country Planning Association: *Architects' Journal* Vol 137 No 17, 24 April 1963.

Chapter 4: A field experiment in auto shaping

1. As reported in *Time* magazine 28 February 1969.

Chapter 5: Hey, Mister, this is what we really do

1. Albert K. Cohen: *Delinquent Boys* (New York: Free Press 1955).

2. Walter Miller: 'Lower Class Culture as a Generating Milieu of Gang Delinquency' *Journal of Social Issues* 14 1958 pp 5-19.

3. Stanley Cohen: 'The Politics of Vandalism' *New Society* 12 December 1968.

4. Brian Higgins: 'The North' Penguin Modern Poets.

5. *South London Press* 17 March 1972.

Chapter 6: Vandalism and the architect

1. Stephen Gardiner: 'Building for crime' *The Observer* 6 May 1971.

2. Vere Hole: *User needs and the design of houses* Building Research Station Current Paper 51/68.

Chapter 9: Planners as Vandals

1. C. A. Doxiadis: 'Confessions of a criminal' *Ekistics* (Athens) Vol 32, No 191, October 1971.
2. W. Mahoney: letter to *RIBA Journal* July 1972.
3. Nan Fairbrother: *New Lives, New Landscapes* (Architectural Press 1970).
4. Paul G. Hoffman: 'Is environmental quality a luxury?' *Bulletin of Environmental Education* July 1971.
5. Norman Dennis: *People and Planning. The Sociology of Housing in Sunderland* (Faber and Faber 1968).
6. See also Jon Gower Davies: *The Evangelistic Bureaucrat; A Study of a Planning Exercise in Newcastle-upon-Tyne* (Tavistock Publications 1972).
7. *Liverpool Challenge* Issue No. One, (Liverpool Corporation Planning Department, March 1971).
8. Chrissy Maher: 'Liverpool: the real priorities' *Community Action* February 1972.
9. Alan Stones: 'Stop Slum Clearance—Now' (*Official Architecture and Planning* February 1972) followed by a Reply by Francis J. C. Amos, Liverpool City Planning Officer, and in the March 1972 issue, a rejoinder by Alan Stones.
10. David Triesman in *Street Aid News* 1972. His evidence is given in full in *The Urban Crisis: Evidence at the Covent Garden Enquiry* (Street Aid and Covent Garden Community 1972).
11. Richard Sennett: *The Uses of Disorder* (Allen Lane, The Penguin Press 1970).
12. Guy Debord: *Society of the Spectacle* (Paris 1967, Detroit 1970).

Chapter 11: Campaigning against vandalism

1. J. D. Salinger: *The Catcher in the Rye* (Hamish Hamilton 1951).
2. William Burroughs: *The Naked Lunch* (Caldar and Boyars Ltd. 1964).
3. Local Government Information Office (L.G.I.O.) *Report on the Cost of Vandalism to Local Authorities.* (Local Government Information Office 1964). See also later reports from this organisation.
4. *ibid*
5. *The Guardian* 3 March 1966.
6. *The Birmingham Post* 19 November 1965.
7. *The News of the World* 8 May 1966.
8. *The Daily Mirror* 6 January 1966.
9. Nathan Goldman: 'A Socio-Psychological Study of School Vandalism.' *Crime and Delinquency* July 1961 pp 221-230
10. *The Sunday Mirror* 5 June 1965.
11. The term is used by Howard Becker in *Outsiders: Studies in the Sociology of Deviance* (New York: Free Press 1963). For a study of moral enterprise in connection with Mods and Rockers see S. Cohen: *Moral Panic and Folk Devils: The Creation of the Mods and Rockers* (London: MacGibbon and Kee 1962.)
12. *Survey of Washing Facilities in Public Conveniences in Great Britain and also of Vandalism in Public Conveniences* (Stoke-on-Trent: Council of British Ceramic Sanitaryware Manufacturers 1964).
13. *ibid* p. 26
14. *ibid* p. 32
15. Circular letter from the CBCSM March 1965.
16. Council of British Ceramic Sanitaryware Manufacturers: *op cit* pp. 17-18.
17. *The Birmingham Post* 22 February 1966.
18. *ibid*
19. *The Daily Telegraph* 8 December 1966.
20. For one interpretation of their reasons for this, see Ian Taylor: 'Soccer Consciousness and Soccer Hooliganism' in S. Cohen ed. *Images of Deviance* (London: Penguin Books Ltd. 1971).

21. *The Daily Telegraph* 11 October 1965.
22. *The Sunday Mirror* 10 October 1965.
23. *The Daily Sketch* 10 December 1966
24. *The Sun* 17 January 1966
25. Editorial: *The Sun* 21 April 1966.
26. *The Daily Sketch* 8 May 1967.
27. For an analysis of the views of these groups see John Harrington *et al*: *A Preliminary Report on Soccer Hooliganism* (Birmingham Research Group 1968).
28. Mr. A. Hardaker, Secretary of the Football League 17 January 1966.
29. Mr. H. Catterick, Manager of Everton Football Club 18 January 1966.
30. *The Daily Mirror* 2 February 1968.
31. During 'epidemics' of the telephone vandalism, the G.P.O. is inundated with suggestions from the public on how to deal with the problem. These include: using live electrified apparatus; charging a fee to get into the kiosk; an automatic device which would lock someone into the kiosk if anything was damaged; bombs which would blow the offender up and the use of tokens so that there would be no money in the coin box.
32. *The Birmingham Post* 6 January 1967.
33. One short-term event which embarrassed the organisers was the theft, an hour after the exhibition opened, of 800 campaign lapel badges bearing the slogan "I am lending a hand to stop vandalism."
34. *The Daily Mail* 7 December 1965.
35. *The Sunday Telegraph* 31 July 1966.
36. *The Sunday Telegraph* 7 September 1966.

Chapter 13: Notes on the future of vandalism
1. *Southend Standard* 24 June 1971.
2. Alvin Toffler: *Future Shock* (Bodley Head 1970).
3. William Powell, quoted in *Oz* No. 33, 1971.
4. *The Guardian* 14 June 1971.
5. *ibid* 11 May 1970.
6. *The Daily Telegraph* 20 June 1970.
7. *The Sun* 17 October 1969.
8. *The Times* 2 July 1971.
9. *The Guardian* 6 August 1971.
10. J. M. Tanner: *Education and Physical Growth* (University of London Press 1961)
11. Frank Musgrove: *Youth and the Social Order* (Routledge and Kegan Paul Ltd. 1964).
12. Thistle T. Harris: 'A plea for the adolescent' (*Journal of Sex Education*, Vol 2 No 1 1949, quoted in Tony Gibson: *Youth for Freedom* (Freedom Press 1951).
13. Gibson: *op cit.*
14. Alex Comfort: *Sex in Society* (Penguin Books Ltd. 1964).
15. Paul Goodman: 'Dead End' *Anarchy* 27 (Vol 3 No 5 May 1963).
16. *Council House Communities: A Policy for Progress*. Report by a Sub-Committee of the Scottish Housing Advisory Committee. (HMSO 1970).
17. *The Guardian* 2 May 1969.
18. *Skelf*, Glasgow January 1972.
19. Guy Debord: *The Decline and Fall of the Spectacular Commodity Economy* (Paris: Internationale Situationiste 1965; English translation New York: Situationist International 1967).
20. E. L. Quantelli and Russell R. Dynes: 'Looting: a social index' *New Society* 8 August 1968.
21. BBCtv programme *Nationwide* 6 January 1972 (Interviewer Michael Dorman).
22. Pearl Jephcott: *Homes in High Flats* (Oliver & Boyd 1971).
23. *Council House Communities op cit.*
24. 'The East Side Boy' *New York Tribune* 2 September 1900.

25. Councillor Page, quoted in *Suburban Press* No 4 March 1972.
26. N. J. Habraken: *Supports: an alternative to mass housing* (Architectural Press 1972).
27. See Andrew Gilmour: *The Sale of Council Housing in Oslo* (Architectural Research Unit, University of Edinburgh 1971). For a fuller presentation of the case for tenant control see Colin Ward: 'Tenants take over' (*Anarchy* 83. Vol 8 No 1 Jan 1968) and Harold Campbell *et al. Council Housing and Co-operative Ownership* (Co-operative Party 1970).
28. Eric Lyons: 'Domestic Building and Speculative Development' *RIBA Journal* May 1968.
29. *The Teacher* 10 December 1971.
30. *ibid*. 'The following boards have a policy of not returning works of art: Associated Examining Board; Joint Matriculation Board; London University; Oxford and Cambridge (joint); the Southern Universities Joint Board; and the Welsh Joint Education Committee.'
31. Stanley Cohen: 'The Politics of Vandalism' (*New Society* 12 December 1968).
32. Leila Berg: *Risinghill: Death of a Comprehensive School* (Penguin Books 1968).
33. G. Stanley Hall: *Life and Confessions of a Psychologist* (New York: D. Appleton & Co. 1927).
34. In the English 'public' schools, at least before the reforms of Dr. Arnold, pupils were taught by their social inferiors, who might well be resigned to the antics of the young gentlemen. In the typical school of today working-class pupils are taught by teachers with a predominantly lower middle-class background with a 'civilising' mission in the school.
35. *Daily Telegraph* 21 June 1971.
36. *Fire and the Design of Schools* Building Bulletin No 7, 4th edition. (Department of Education and Science, HMSO 1971).
37. 'The growing number and cost of fires in schools', reprinted from *FPA Journal* No 89 December 1970 (Fire Protection Association 1971).
38. *The School That I'd Like* ed. by Edward Blishen (Penguin Books Ltd. 1969).
39. *Architects' Journal* 23 February 1972, reporting *Carpeting and Learning* US Bureau of Educational Research and Service (Ohio State University, Columbus, Ohio 1971).
40. See report by Elizabeth Halsall in *Trends in Education* Summer 1971 (Department of Education and Science, HMSO 1971).
41. Nan Fairbrother: *New Lives, New Landscapes* (Architectural Press 1970).
42. Garth Christian: *Tomorrow's Countryside* (John Murray 1966).
43. Ben Whitaker and Kenneth Browne: *Parks for People* (Seeley Service 1971).
44. Pearl Jephcott: *op cit*.
45. *The Evening Standard* 24 January 1972.
46. Tony Aldous: *Battle for the Environment* (Fontana 1972).
47. Tony Aldous: *The Times* 24 March 1972.
48. *Time* magazine 13 March 1972.
49. Habraken: *op cit*.
50. Herman Hertzberger: 'Looking for the beach under the pavement' address given at the RIBA, 2 February 1971 *RIBA Journal* August 1971.
51. Simon Nicholson: 'The Theory of Loose Parts' (*Landscape Architecture* USA October 1971, and *Bulletin of Environmental Education* April 1972).

Bibliography

1. Sociology and Psychology

Bates, William: 'Caste, class and vandalism' *Social Problems* Vol 9 no 4 Spring 1962.

Cohen, Stanley: 'Vandalism' *New Education* October 1966.

Caplovitz, D. and Rogers, C.: *The epidemic of anti-semitic vandalism in America* New York: 1961.

Clinard, Marshall B. and Wade, Andrew L.: 'Towards the delineation of vandalism as a sub-type in juvenile delinquency' *Journal of Criminology, Criminal Law and Police Science* Vol 48 No 5 1958.

Ehrlick, Howard J. 'The swastika epidemic of 1959-60: anti-semitism and community characteristics' *Social Problems* Vol 9 No 3 Winter 1962.

Clark, W. H.: 'Sex differences and motivation in the urge to destroy' *Journal of Social Psychology* No 36 November 1952.

Goldman, Nathan: 'A socio-psychological study of school vandalism' *Crime and Delinquency* July 1961.

Gordon, Raymond: 'Vandalism' *Federal Probation* XVIII September 1954.

Martin, John M. 'Some characteristics of vandals' *American Catholic Sociological Review* Vol 20 No 4 1959.

Martin, J. M. *Juvenile Vandalism: A Study of Its Nature and Prevention* Springfield, Illinois 1961 C. G. Thomas.

Maslow, A. H.: 'A comparative approach to the problem of destructiveness' *Psychiatry* No 5, 1942.

Newman, C. K.: 'A comparative study of family characteristics of two groups of offenders, auto-thieves and vandals' *Current Projects*, New York: 1962, Project 125.

Note in *Federal Probation* XXVIII March 1964.

Prewer, R. R.: 'Some observations on window smashing' *British Journal of Delinquency* No 10 October 1959.

Pringle, M. L. Kellmer: *Violence and Vandalism* London: 1972 Association of Chief Police Officers.

Stein, Herman D. and Martin, John M.: 'Swastika Offenders: variations in etiology, behaviour and psycho-social characteristics' *Social Problems* Vol 10 No 1 1962.

Symposium on Vandalism: *Federal Probation* XCIII March 1954.

Wade, A. W.: 'Social processes in the act of juvenile vandalism' in M. Clinard and R. Quinney eds. *Criminal Behaviour Systems* New York: 1967 Holt, Rinehart and Winston Inc.

2. Architecture and landscape

Council House Communities: A Policy for Progress Report by a sub-committee of the Scottish Housing Advisory Committee Edinburgh: 1970 HMSO.

Design for Pleasure and Hard Wear in the Landscape (Report of Symposium) London: 1960 Institute of Landscape Architects.

Fairbrother, Nan: *New Lives, New Landscapes* London: 1970 Architectural Press, 1972 Penguin Books Ltd.

Habraken, N. J.: *Supports: An Alternative to Mass Housing* London: 1972 Architectural Press.

Hertzberger, Herman 'Looking for the beach under the pavement' *RIBA Journal* Vol 79 No 8 August 1971.

Jephcott, Pearl: *Homes in High Flats* Edinburgh 1971 Oliver and Boyd.

Kirby, David A.: 'The inter-war council dwelling: a study of residential obsolescence and decay' *Town Planning Review* Vol 42 No 3 July 1971.

Kirby, David A.: 'The maintenance of pre-war council dwellings' *Journal of the Institute of Municipal Engineers* May 1972.

Landscape Maintenance (Report of Symposium) London: 1963 Institute of Landscape Architects.

319

Newman, Oscar: *Defensible Space* New York 1972: The Macmillan Company, London: 1973 Architectural Press.

Ravetz, Alison: 'The uses and abuses of the planned environment' *RIBA Journal* Vol 80 No 4 April 1972.

Rudofsky, Bernard: *Streets for People* New York: Doubleday & Co 1969.

Security Building Research Station Digest 122 October 1970 HMSO

Shawlands Estate, Glasgow: Report on the use of Polycarbonate Fittings J. & G. Coughtrie Ltd. October 1971.

Sommer, Robert: *Design Awareness* San Francisco: Rinehart Press 1972.

Stone, P. A.: 'The conflict between capital cost and running costs' *The Chartered Surveyor* June 1961.

Street Furniture Catalogue London: 1972 Council of Industrial Design.

Tandy, Cliff (ed.): *Handbook of Urban Landscape* London: 1972 Architectural Press

Whitaker, Ben and Browne, Kennth: *Parks for People* London: 1971 Seeley Service & Co.

Wilful Damage on Housing Estates Building Research Station Digest 132 August 1971 HMSO

3. Graffiti

Coleman, Marshall: 'Graffiti: the moving finger writes' *Unit* No 10 February 1968.

Freeman, Richard: *Graffiti* London: 1966 Hutchinson.

Kohl, H. and Hinton, J.: *Golden Boy as Anthony Cool: a Photo-Essay on Naming and Graffiti* New York: 1972 Dial Press.

Lindsay, Jack: *The Writing on the Wall* London: 1960 Frederick Muller.

Pritchard, Violet: *Medieval English Graffiti* Cambridge: 1967 The University Press

Reisner, Robert: *Graffiti: Two Thousand Years of Wall Writing* Chicago: 1971 Henry Regnery Co.

Robinson, Jack: 'A man's ambition must be small' *Anarchy* 23 Vol 3 No 1 January 1963.

Strafford, Peter: 'Portrait of the Artist as a Young Vandal' *The Times* 14 December 1972

Vaccari, Franco: *Strip-Street* Paris: 1969 Editions Agentzia

4. Various

Against Vandalism National Association of Parish Councils National Circular No 184 n.d.

The Cost of Vandalism to Local Authorities London: 1964 Local Government Information Office

'Creative Vandalism' *Anarchy* 61, Vol 6 No 3 March 1966. Includes John Ellerby: 'Notes on vandalism', Lewis Woudhuysen: 'Creative vandalism—a case history', Martin Small: 'The principle of creative vandalism'.

Hooliganism on Housing Estates Report by the Director of Housing to the Housing Committee London: 1967 Greater London Council.

An Investigation into the extent of Juvenile Vandalism and its causes in Murton and Seaham, Co. Durham Easington Committee for Education 1971.

A Report on Vandalism including a Short Survey with an Adult and School Population. Willowtown County Secondary School / Ebbw Vale Urban District Council March 1971

Vandalism: A Study of Washington New Town Washington (England): 1972 The Development Corporation.

INDEX

Figures in bold refer to pages in which illustrations occur and to their captions.

Abandoned buildings 166, **167,** 174, **174,** 259, **260,** 271
Aberfan disaster, the 182, 230-231
Adolescence 279-283
— as a social invention 281
— manipulation of by adults **282,** 283
— sexual privation in 281-283
Adventure playgrounds 58, 238, 270
(See also Parks, Play areas, Play Power, Supermarkets)
Aerosol paint 99, 115, 138, 141, 304, 305
(See also Graffiti)
'Agro-Board', the **280**
(See also Vandalism—deflection of)
Air-guns **100,** 101
American Institute of Planners, the 18
'Architectural crimes' 173-176
Architectural determinism 14, 64-72, 96-97
Architectural restoration **195,** 195-197
— late 19th century optimism in 176
Architects
— as usurpers of mass creativity 310-311
— as victims of 'role-inflation' 14, 82-84
— lack of feedback between Maintenance Departments and 172
— new 'welfare' role of 64-66, 67, 68, 71-72
— reaction to vandalism of one firm of 112-116
— social distance from mass client of 83-84
Arson 38, **38,** 46, 61, 226, 271, **293**
Auto-Destructive Art 40

'Bad' areas 19, **20**
— use of as dumping ground for high-risk tenants 266
(see also Easterhouse, Glasgow)
Bakunin, 39-40
Ballad of an anti-war criminal, the **38**
Black Hand Gang, the 40
Blackhill Estate, Glasgow, the **65**
Brickwork 152-153
— as missiles on building and demolition sites **152,** 153
— clay air bricks 115
— progressive removal of courses of **103**
— raking out of soft mortar joints in **100,** 101, 153
— removal of copings from 103, **103, 106,** 107, 163-164, **162**
— rough-textured 99
British Poster Advertising Association, the 229
British public, the (See Vandal, the; Motor car, the and Rubbish dumping)
British Rail 40, 41, 42
— anti-vandalism campaigns by 244, 250-253
— damage to property of **49, 109, 251**
— handling of architectural heritage by 176
(See also Euston Arch, the)
— policy on vandalism 218, 236

(See also Victim organisations)
British Transport Commission, the 189, 190, 191
British Waterways Board, the 15
Building Research Station, the
— study of wilful damage on housing estates at 97
(See also Design Guides)
Burroughs, William 217
Bus shelters 148, 244
Butyrate sheet 101

Canada Estate, Southwark, the 16, **17**
Car parks 178
— as magnet for vandals 169
— as venue for children's play 94
— demolition of good architecture to provide space for 178, 197, 212, 214
Chicago School, the 55-56, 67, 91
Circulation areas
— internal 128-129
— lighting in 127
— pedestrian 121-123
— short-cuts between **104,** 105, 121, 129, **129**
— staircases as 130
— supervision of 130
— vehicular 123-124, 129
Clearance areas 178, **179,** 250, **272, 273**
Commonwealth War Graves Commission, the 241
Community involvement 22, 52
— lack of in new council estates 169-170
Conservationists
— three progressive categories of 176-178
Constructive Nihilists, the 40
Council housing 13, 16, **17, 75**
— as a 'new start' 76
— community involvement in providing play facilities near 260-261, 262, **268, 270,** 274
— encouragement of emotional involvement in 169-170, 262, 265, **266**
— eviction of tenants from for vandalism 256
— ghetto image of 288-290
— individual allocation of trees to tenants in 115, 238
— installation of tenants before completion of **13,** 14, 109
— lack of recreational facilities near 52-53 76, 274
— monotony of **12,** 74, 152
— nuisance of ball games in 76, 133, **133**
— private gardens in 16, **17,** 134, **135**
— relation between private and public spaces in 169-170, 171
— restrictions on pets in 76
— siting of sculpture near 15-16
— sale of to tenants 289-290
— tenants' co-operatives in 290

— vulnerability to vandalism of certain types of 50
(See also Flats and Lifts)
Council of British Ceramic Sanitaryware Manufacturers, the 241
— survey of washing facilities in public lavatories (1964) by 223-224, 235-236
'Correctional perspective', the 91

Dadaism 40
'Danger money' 33, 236
Debord, Guy 18, 284-285
Defence Regulations, the 27
Demolition
— use of building debris as missiles on sites of **152,** 153, **260**
— personal violence by contractors in the process of **177**
(See also Listed buildings)
Demonstrations 35, 302
Dereliction
— as magnet for vandalism 26, 50, 165-166, **165,** 181, 200, 259, 271
— psychological response to 14
(See also Vandalism—in response to 'releaser' stimuli)
Design guides 20, 97-172
Designer, the
— as usurper of mass creativity 310-311
— professional responsibilities of 13-16, 20, 96-172
Destruction
— as art 29, **39, 40,** 252, 304-305, **308**
— as escape 49
— as form of attention seeking 43
— as form of pleasurable activity 89-90
— as therapy 32
— fascination of **37, 308**
— of aesthetic objects 34 (See also Car parks, Euston Arch, the and Listed buildings)
— progressive pattern in 170-171
Deviancy 69-70, 72, 75
— as a political process 69-70
— as a threat to society 19
— biological theories of 59
— relation to substandard housing of 66
— 'sceptical' approach to 17-18
— 'treatment' approach to 67
Doors **98, 156,** 157
— furniture for 103, 105, 107, 157
(See also Garages)
Doxiadis, C. A. 173
Drug addiction 69, 70, 93
Drummy, the 76, 79
Durham, County
— Category D villages in 182

East End, London, the 191-199 (See also London—threatened buildings in)
Easterhouse, Glasgow 19, 64, 66-67, 72-81, 288
English Food Riots (1766), the 35
Environment, the 13, 14, 54-63
— alienation from 62-63, 170, 307-311
— artificial uniformity of 18, 62, 74
— contamination of 18, **21,** 175, 279

— dependence of psychic health on stability of 56
— emotional commitment to 169-170
— psychological need for old buildings in 184-185
— relationship between delinquency and 64-72, 165-170, 183
— user response to 14, 18, 58, 168
— varying individual sensitivity to 54
Environmental crime
— characteristics of 18-19
(See also 'Architectural crimes')
Environmental determinism 64-72
— theories of 19, 55-56, 96-97
'Environmental signalling' 14-16, 168
(See also Vandalism—in response to 'releaser' stimuli)
Euston Arch, the 173, 178, **188, 189,** 189-191
— proposed re-siting on Euston Road of 190
— protests against demolition of 191

Fairbrother, Nan 13, 176, 300
Fencing 74, 159-161
— as anachronism in park planning 302
— avoidance of normal nailing methods for 164
— ranch 105, 152, **160**
— siting at top of slopes of **111**
— vertical boarding for 108, **160**
Field enclosure 176
Flats 56, **98, 267,** 269
— care-takers for 108
— circulation zones in 168-169 (See also Lifts)
— lack of parental surveillance in 266
— loitering in entrance of 167
— locked external doors to 108
— play privation in 175, 287-288
— unpopularity of 266
Football hooliganism 42, 46, 76-77, 78, 232-234, **234,** 236, 255
— measures to counter 244
Fountains 166-167, **167**
'Fun morality', the 217

Gang, the 24, 48, 69, 276-277, **277,** 288
— recent American study of 46
— violence of in Glasgow 67, 72-74, 75, 76-81
Garages **102,** 272
— damage to inadequate doors for **104,** 105
— heavy timber doors for 107, 158
— lay-out of 107, 124, 129, 168-169
— timber or metal fascias for 105
— 'up-and-over' doors for 107, 157-158
Geddes, Patrick 178
Georgian Society, the 191
Ghetto, the **57,** 58, **286, 306-307**
Glass 147-149
— armourplate 101, 147
— bricks of 99, 101, 148
— georgian-wired 147-148, **147**
— glazed screens 159
— laminated 147

— plastic sheeting as replacement for **99, 100,** 148 (See also Translucent sheeting)
— polycarbonates as replacement for **77, 100,** 101, 148-149
— reduction of in buildings, 130, 148
— use of large panes to deter vandals 148
— vulnerability of large panes of 99, 101, 103
Graffiti 27-29, 31, 41, 63, 82, **98,** 167, **286, 293,** 304-306
— aerosol sprays as implement for 99, 115, 220-221, 229, 304, 305
— as urban folk art 29, 304-305
— deflection of to graffiti boards **236, 237,** 238
— felt pens as tool for 115, 220, 304
— historical examples of 29
— in ghettos **57, 286, 306-307**
— materials which discourage 101, 115, 141, 143, **144,** 150, 152, 164
— materials which encourage **109,** 138, 141, 152-153, 220
Graffiti Alternative Workshop, the 305
Green Hand Gang, the **277**
Gully gratings **102,** 103, 107
Gypsies 181

Habraken, N. J. 289, 307, 309, 311
Hard landscaping 132-134, **133**
— ball games on 133, **133**
— use of cobbles as missiles 105
— small units for 150-151, **150**
(See also Soft landscaping and Trees)
Hardwick, Philip **188,** 190
(See also Euston Arch, the)
Heating and ventilation systems 114, 116, 132, 303
Hertzberger, Herman 309
Hoefnagels, Peter 18
Housing (See Council housing)
Housing associations 68, 203, 204
Housing Cost Yardstick, the 176
Housing shortage 74, **174,** 260
Hunts 29

Ideological vandalism (See Vandalism)
Imperial War Museum, London, the **38**
Industrial sabotage 30, 33, 35, 44
— history of in England and France 35-39
— in factories 30, 61-63, 114
— in the merchant navy 30-31, 49-50
— to computers 278
— to power stations 279
Inner-urban areas
— characteristics of 55-56
International Situationists, the 40, 60-61

Job disillusionment 52, 257
Joint Matriculation Board, the 290
Junking **42,** 42-43
(See also Vandalism—acquisitive)

Kinesics 60-61

Lavatories 27, 154-155, 168
— as venue for group art **296**
— concealed or protected services in 108, 132, **133,** 159

— damage in schools to 116
— graffiti in 31, **237,** 238
— proposal for low doors in 242
— removal of fittings from 49, 114
— survey (1964) of 223-224
— withdrawal of services from 236
Law of Diminishing Vandalism, the 14, 115
Licensed Victuallers Association, the 229
Lifts 271-272, 302-303
— as venue for children's play 262
— coffin doors in 103
— damage to control buttons of 101, 108, 159
— damage to indicator lights of 101
— defecating in 49, 108, 159
— design recommendations for 302-303
— floorings in 101
— lighting in lobbies of 127
— wall linings for 101, 159
Lighting
— bad positioning of 105
— fittings for **104,** 155-157, **156**
— in pedestrian subways **100**
— of external spaces 108, 127-128
— use of polycarbonates in **77,** 101, 157
— vulnerability of 167
Listed buildings 190-191, 199, 205
— demolition of without consent **210,** 211-214
— legal provision for removing dangerous 203-204
— penalties for illegally demolishing 185, 199
— proportion of in London 186, 205
— test case on illegal demolition of 214
London—threatened buildings in:
— Albury Street 204-206, **205**
— Bedford Way **187,** 188
— Drapers Almshouses, Bow, the 206, **208**
— Elder Street **194, 195,** 195-197
— Folgate Street 195
— Gower Street 176
— Grace's Alley 197
— Great James Street 200, **204**
— Hanbury Street 208, **209**
— Marine Square (See Wellclose Square)
— Mayflower Street **196,** 197
— Millman Place 200-204, **201, 202**
— Millman Street 200-204, **201, 202, 204,** 205
— Myerson's Ironworks, Clerkenwell 212
— Raine Street 206, **207**
— Rotherhithe Street 197
— Sekforde Street **211**
— Spital Square **192**
— Stoke Newington High Street **198,** 199
— Swedenborg Square 191-194, **192**
— Wellclose Square **192, 193,** 191-195, **196**
— Wilkes Street **210,** 211
— Woburn Square **186, 187,** 186-188
(See also Euston Arch, the and Listed buildings)
London Transport 27, 41, 242, **243**
Liverpool 22, 120, 126, **179,** 241
— community involvement in anti-vandalism projects in 259-275

— Crosbie Heights 269
— disparity between rates of slum
    clearance and re-development in 180
— social illness problem in 181
— Sidney Gardens 269-270
— Soho Street 269
— Speke Road Gardens 269-270
Liverpool Council of Social Service, the
    260
Local Government Information Office,
    the 225
— anti-vandalism posters published by
    246, 247
— crusade against vandalism by 223,
    235-236
Looting 41, 42
— as a mean of wealth redistribution 287
— of external copper piping 101
— of motor cars 20, **21**, 85, 86-88, **86**, 90
— use of steel piping to prevent 159
Luddism 35-39, 40, 61 (See also
    Industrial sabotage)
Lyons, Eric 290

Machine-breaking 38-39
(See also Industrial sabotage)
Mailer, Norman 92-93
Maltglade Development Company, the
— illegal demolition by 212-214, **213**
Mass media, the
— amount of attention given to vandalism
    by 218, 221-222, 225-226, 229, 230-231,
    240, 249-250, 259, 261
— and football hooliganism 232-234
— and gang violence in Glasgow 72-74,
    79, 81
— role of in spreading behaviour patterns
    41
Materials
— self-finished 153, **153**
— to be avoided in high-risk projects 99,
    101, 115, 126, **127**
(See also Brickwork, Glass, Graffiti,
    Lavatories, Lifts, Rainwater goods,
    Roofs, Translucent sheeting, Wall
    finishes)
Maunsel Metropolitan Housing
    Association, the 203, 204
Mental hospitals
— damage by inmates to 31
'Mini-max' 178
Ministry of Defence, the 20
Mobile police squads 78-79
Moral entrepreneurs
— definition of 223
Morris, William 176
Motor car, the 18, 29, 46, 49, 53, 238,
    239, 299
— as environmental pollutant 18, 19, 20,
    21
— as loot objects 20, 85, 86-88, **86,** 90
— demonstration to ban in Oxford
    Street, London 302
— ritual destruction of in America 85-90,
    85-89
Motor Show (Earl's Court), the 29

Nader, Ralph 18

Nash, John 176
National Federation of Football
    Supporters Clubs 236
'Naturalistic perspective', the 91
New Brutalism, the 16
Newcastle-upon-Tyne
— demolition of Eldon Square 178
— destruction of Scotswood Road 180

Orne, Martin 55, 56
Oslo, Norway
— housing policy in 290
Overcrowding 58-59, 69, 96, 112, **113**
— relation between high-density living and
    juvenile delinquency 168
Owen, Robert 68

Pak, the 76, 79
Parks (public) 92-93, 167
— damage to playground hardware in
    241-242
— lack of playground hardware in 94-95
— need for participation in planning of
    301-302
— use of security patrols in 241
Pedestrian subways **100,** 109, 304
'Personal and inter-personal space' 60
Planning
— arrogance of 181-182
— as legitimized form of vandalism
    173-183
— exclusion of consumers from decisions
    in 178, 182
— ineptitude of in Sunderland 178
— 'virgin site' philosophy in 180
Play areas 108, 124, **264,** 260-261, 262,
    268, 270
— vandalism as bargaining counter for
    obtaining 287
Play Power 92, 95, **297**
Posters and hoardings 27, 30, 41, 166,
    220-221, 229, 242, **246, 247, 248**
Prisons 13
— damage caused by prisoners to 31, 32
— environmental deprivation of long-term
    prisoners in 59
— regular window-breakers in 44
Privacy 59, 91, 126, 167
Public Inquiries
— into demolition of Eldon Square,
    Newcastle-upon-Tyne 178
— into redevelopment of Covent Garden,
    London (1971) 181
Public property
— contemporary alienation from 300
— vulnerability of 50, 109

Rainwater goods **100,** 158, **158**
— concealed or internal for garages 107
— damage to **100,** 101
— use of cast iron for 101
— use of for gaining access 163
Rebels, the 76, 77
Rioting
— 'collective bargaining' by 35, 38-39, 61
— in Watts, Los Angeles (1965) 284-285
— to save trees in Stockholm 302
Rodmersham Mill, Kent **177**

'Role-inflation'
— architects and teachers as victims of 14
Ronan Point disaster, the 182
Roofs
— avoidance of access through 162
— avoidance of access to 103, 130
— vulnerability of materials in 101,
115-116, 130-131, **149,** 151, 162
Royal Fine Arts Commission, the 191
Royal Institute of British Architects
— introduction of sociology into
undergraduate syllabus of 65, 82
Rubbish dumping 20, **21, 85,** 86, **102,
122,** 181, 300
'Rule-breaking' 17-18, 23-33, 41, 53,
215, 222, 229

Safety regulations
— damage to emergency escape devices
114, 116
— disregard of in factories 62
Schools
— accidental damage to 112, 279
— architects' dilemma in the design of
114-115, 292
— characteristics of high-damage schools
50
— child participation in decoration and
design of 295, **296, 297**
— crawling in ceiling voids of 115
— damage by pupils to 31-32, 33, 45, 63,
82, 92, 112-116, 126, 226, 290-299, 303
— damage by teachers to 114
— damage to accoustic ceilings in 115
— damage to lavatories in 116
— danger of phased occupation in 116
— furniture and carpets in 116, 295-298
— increasing incidence of arson in **293,**
294
— inappropriate design in 291-292
— lack of working-class allegiance to
51-52
— play-schemes to counter vandalism to
270-271
— radical alternatives to 14, 299
— security hardware in 244
— security patrols near 241, 244, **298**
— 'strong-rooms' in 132
— theft from 132, 162
— tradition of vandalism in 292-294, **293**
Sculpture 15-16, **16, 36,** 40, **42,** 166, 239
Security patrols 114, 239-241, **240,** 244,
265, 303
'Sensory deprivation' studies 54-55, 56,
57
Shopping centres **102, 104,** 109, **110,**
131, **131**
(See also Supermarkets)
Signs and lettering **100,** 101, 154, **155**
Slums 66, 67-68, 69, 73, 96
Social anonymity 18-19, 20, 27, 89
Society for the Protection of Ancient
Buildings, the 176, 191
Soft landscaping 14, 134-136
— choice of plants for 107, 115, 134-136
— damage to for short cuts **104,** 105, 134
— raised beds with planting **106,** 107

(See also Hard landscaping and Trees)
Spaces
— as litter traps 122, **122,** 132, **133,** 159,
166
— supervision of 103, 126, 127, **131**
Speculators
— as environmental criminals 175
— illegal demolition of buildings by **177,**
211, 212-214, **213**
— schizophrenia of in London 211
Squatters
— Redbridge Council (London) policy
against **174**
Students 24-25, 33, 35, 42, 52, 73, 89,
116, 283-284
— militancy in relation to subjects read
by 112
Sunderland (See Planning)
Supermarkets **65**
— as a venue for children's play 93-95,
93, 94, 95
— shoplifting from 27
Surrealism 40, 60

Teddy boys 56-57
Telephones (public) 41, 42, 43, 92, 217,
221, 230-231, 242, 254
— 'anti-vandal phone box', (1968), the
242, **243**
— GPO anti-vandal alarm systems 243
— prevention of damage to by design 172
— unrepair of 236
— urinating in receivers of 49
— vandalism to in Birmingham 221, 255
Territorial aggression 58
— as pattern for youth associations 76,
77, 80, 81
Terrorist, the 35
Toi, the 76
Tomb-stones **28,** 165
'Totalitarian architecture' 93
Tourism 18
Town planning
— history of 68
Translucent sheeting 115-116, 151
— as replacement for glass **99,** 101,
148-149
— use over circulation areas of 131, **131**
Trees
— allocation to individual households
of 115, 134, **135**
— campaign in Newcastle-upon-Tyne to
save **301**
— campaign in Stockholm, Sweden to
save 302
— damage to **104**
— protection of by prickly shrubs 134
— use of children as 'tree wardens' 238,
309
Truman Hanbury Buxton and Company
Ltd.,
— demolition of 18th century terrace by
208, **209,** 209
Turnbull, William 40

Urban Aid 269
Urban guerilla, the 40
Unemployment 53

University of London 176, 186-188
Ulster 34, **282,** 283

Vandal, the
— anonymity of 18-19, 27
— architects and planners as 173-183, 214
— British public as 18, 19, 20, **21,** 300-301 (See also Rubbish dumping)
— developers as 184-214
— licensed protection of 18, 20, 23-33
— stereotype of **12,** 13, 18, 19, 23, 34, 41-42, 45, 50, **77,** 217-218, **243**
Vandalism
— acquisitive **42,** 42-43, 101, 159, 241, 242, 254
— and social class 24-25, 39, 51-53, 82, 91-95
— as art 29, **39,** 40, 252, 304-305, **308**
— as attention seeking 43-44
— as debased term for environmental change 176
— as environmental protest 171
— as manufactured excitement 51-53, 89-90, 92-95, 257
— as pleasure 89-90, **88, 89,** 97
— as revenge 44-46
— as ritualism 23-24, 85-90
— as symbolic violation **28,** 29-30, 165, 167, 215-217, 220, 222, 226
— as a family activity 86-87
— as a group offence 47-48, 49, 50, 82, 89-90, 92-95, 254
— at commercial exhibitions 29
— by adults 25, 30, 31, 33, 35-39, 42, 45, 61-63, 86-88, 114, 230, 238, 255
— by public schoolboys 24, 33, 45, **293**
— by sports teams 33, 230
— by students 24-25, 33, 42, 89-90, 116
— by the Armed Forces 25, 33, 44, 112
— campaigns against 22, 215-275
— defeatism engendered by 235-236
— definitions of 13, 18, 19, 23-53
— deflection of **236, 237,** 237-239, 260-261, 262, **268, 270,** 270-271, 274, **280**
— difficulty in detecting 18-19, 27, 44
— environmental factors conducive to 165-170
— fashions in 112, 253
— financial compensation for 114, 255-256
— historical meaning of 33-34
— ideological 30, 34-41, **36, 38,** 42, 222, 276, 283-285
— in Ayrshire 242
— in Birmingham 225-229, **228,** 249-250, 255
— in Bradford 92-95
— in Chertsey 248-249
— in children's homes 31
— in children's play 20, 25-27, 31, 47-48, **48,** 92-95, **93, 94, 95, 102,** 124, 257, 262, 303-304
— in Coventry 220
— in Gateshead 245-248
— in hotels 33
— in Kirkby 265
— in Manchester 279
— in mental hospitals 31
— in New York 85-88, 89, 241
— in Norwich 255
— in Palo Alto, California 86-90
— in prisons 31, 32
— in relation to adolescence 279-283
— in response to 'releaser' stimuli 86, 88-89, 110, 112, 140, 181, 200, 259, 271
— in Runcorn 265
— in Salford **248**
— in Sheffield 241
— in Wandsworth, Yorkshire 95
— increasingly sophisticated forms of 276-278, **277**
— involving animals 25, 31, 48, 241
— lack of professional literature on 121
— legitimized forms of 18, 20, 23-33, 39, 173-214, 230, 290, **291**
— malicious 48-51, 257
— possible progressive pattern of 170-171
— prevention of by design 13, 14, 97-172
— prevention of by time phasing 171-172
— psychological damage caused by 18, 217
— punitive attitudes to 40, 96, 253-256
— pyramidal perception of 231, 232-234, 253, 256
— reaction by local authorities to 218-219, 225-229, **228,** 235, 245-250, **246, 247**
— reduction of opportunities for 20, 97-172, 239-244
— relative lack of to floors and ceilings 138
— role of good maintenance in countering 110, 111, 112, 137, 166, 236, 238-239
— society's unwillingness to accredit motives to 19, 34, 42, 92, 217, 256
— tactical 43-44, 254
— to churches **28,** 46, 167, 244
— to cinemas 244
— to landscaping 14-15
— to motor cars 85-90
— to motorways 279
— to national monuments 29, **38,** 222, 241
— to railways 40, 42, 48, 49, **49,** 50, **109, 251,** 282
— 'walling-in' of 30-32
— written-off forms of 27-30, **28,** 32
(See also British Rail; Car parks; Demolition; Dereliction; Destruction; Easterhouse, Glasgow; Environment, the; Football hooliganism; Graffiti; Hard landscaping; Industrial sabotage; Law of Diminishing Vandalism, the; Listed buildings; Looting; Liverpool; Mass media, the; Motor car, the; Newcastle-upon-Tyne; Play areas; Schools; Soft landscaping; Telephones; Trees; Victim organisations)
'Vandal-proof' paint 242
Vaughan, Frankie 72, 81
Vendome Column, the **36**
Victim organisations 15, 27, 40, 41, 42, 48, 49, **49,** 115, 148, 218, 236, 244, 250-253, **251**

Victorian Society, the 191
Viet-cong, the 73
Vietnam War, the **38,** 41

Wall finishes **98,** 99, 137-146
— applied coatings 99, 105, **110,** 115,
  138, 145-146
— applied film 138-140
— applied sheet 99, 101, 115, 138,
  140-143, **142**
— applied units 98, **98,** 99, **102,** 103,
  143-145
— tile-hanging 151
— timber 115, 151-152
— vulnerability of colour contrast
  between substrate and 98, **98,** 137, 138,
  139, 141, 143
— which attract graffiti **109,** 138, 141,
  152-153

— which discourage graffiti 101, 115,
  141, 143, **144,** 150, 152, 164
Weathermen, the 40
Wheathampstead
— illegal demolition of Old Town Farm
  173, 212-214, **213**
White-collar' crime 19, 70
Window-breaking 32, 35, 45, 46, 47,
  82, 124, 130, 166, 181
— as attention seeking 43-44
Window sills **162,** 162-163
Wirth 69
Working class, the
— as victim of planning disasters 182-183
— exclusion from planning processes of
  178
— 'focal concerns' of 91-92

Yablonsky 69
Youth clubs 52, 80, 81